Open Wide a Wilderness

Open Wide a Wilderness
Canadian Nature Poems

Edited by NANCY HOLMES
Introduction by DON McKAY

Wilfrid Laurier University Press
[WLU]

Wilfrid Laurier University Press acknowledges the support of the Canada Council for the Arts for our publishing program. We acknowledge the financial support of the Government of Canada through its Book Publishing Industry Development Program for its publishing activities.

Library and Archives Canada Cataloguing in Publication

    Open wide a wilderness : Canadian nature poems / Nancy Homes, editor ; introduction by Don McKay.

(Environmental humanities series)
Includes bibliographical references and index.
ISBN 978-1-55458-033-0

    1. Canadian poetry (English). 2. Nature—Poetry. 3. Ecology—Poetry.
I. Holmes, Nancy, 1959–   II. Series.

PS8287.N38064 2009   C811'.008036   C2008-906515-8

Cover design by Blakeley Words+Pictures. Cover photo *Going to the Sun; Study #2* by Frank Grisdale, www.FrankGrisdale.com. Text design by Catharine Bonas-Taylor.

Every reasonable effort has been made to acquire permission for copyright material used in this text, and to acknowledge all such indebtedness accurately. Any errors and omissions called to the publisher's attention will be corrected in future printings.

This book is printed on Ancient Forest Friendly paper (100% post-consumer recycled).

Printed in Canada

MIX
Paper from
responsible sources
FSC® C021996

Contents

 *Preface*

Notes on Selection

In the introduction to *Northern Wild: Best Contemporary Canadian Nature Writing,* editor David Boyd explains why he included no nature poetry in his anthology: "The thought of tracking down and evaluating a decade of Canadian poetry was simply overwhelming." After reading over two hundred years of Canadian poetry, I think he was understating the case. Is there any Canadian poet who has not written a nature poem of some kind or other? Thus, one of the first tasks in creating this anthology was to come up with selection criteria. This preface attempts to explain the principles of selection that guided the choices in this anthology.

Certain parameters were set from the start. The included work needed to be "Canadian," in that it was written by someone who had lived or does live in Canada. Next, the poem needed to be written about Canadian nature, not about the flora, fauna, and landscapes of other parts of the globe. Further, because of my own second language deficiencies, the work chosen was written originally in English; without poems in First Nations languages, immigrant languages, or French, this anthology is admittedly incompletely Canadian. Next, all the poems in this anthology have been published previously in book form. As the project progressed and I needed to find ways to reduce the sheer volume of poems I'd collected, I began to select only poems written about "wild" nature rather than "domesticated" nature; this principle meant that several exceptionally interesting and beautiful poems about pets, gardens, and farm animals were excluded. Obviously, some of these categories are permeable and far from absolute. For example, it is difficult to determine what is wild and what is domesticated in Al Purdy's "The Winemaker's Beat-Étude" or Lorna Crozier's "Carrots."

After these criteria were fulfilled, the goal was to find diversity while trying to maintain a few topical themes throughout the collection; waterfalls, bears, and crows, for example, appear countless times in Canadian poetry. As Canada becomes more urban, fewer moose and cougar are the subjects of poems, and more raccoons and pigeons are. Just as the deer population of the wilderness and the rural-urban interface explodes, so do the number of deer in Canadian poetry. As far as possible, the selection of poems tries to reflect these erasures and successions. Also, the anthology strives for a range of approaches toward the natural world: love of nature, fear of nature, the violence of nature, violence against nature, natural history observation, work in the natural world (logging, fishing, hunting and gathering), ecological concerns, and new philosophical eco- and geo-poetics.

Several poems were included not only because they met all the selection criteria but also because I unscientifically polled people on their favorite nature poems: Earle Birney's "David," Gwendolyn MacEwan's "Dark Pines Under Water," and A. J. M. Smith's "The Lonely Land" were among the most popular. Along the same lines, the canonized authors of Canadian literature (Lampman, Pratt, Purdy, Atwood) are included, as are, obviously, the new eco-poets themselves (McKay, Bringhurst, Lilburn); but I also wanted to make room for some of the strange and lovely poems by Isabella Valancy Crawford, Joe Rosenblatt, Colleen Thibaudeau, Peter Van Toorn, and Brian Brett, to name just a few. These poets are not generally seen in university or high school textbooks and might not be as self-consciously eco-theoretical as others, but they have written wonderful nature poems nonetheless. Among the standard authors, the selection includes canonical poems (such as the Birney's "Bushed") as well as less anthologized poems (Atwood's "Sundew").

Lastly, the selections were also informed by my reading of Don McKay's essay which serves as the introduction to this volume. His essay made me search out and appreciate certain kinds of poems, poems that refer in some way to what is "inappellable." Ideally, McKay's historical overview will play with and against the chronological arrangement of the anthology. Although not every poem mentioned in McKay's essay is in the volume, many are.

The anthology's principle of organization is the date of birth of the author. The dates that follow the poems in round brackets are the dates of the poem's first book publication, wherever that could be determined. If there is a huge discrepancy between the date of first book publication and the date of composition, the date of composition, if known, is included in square brackets. A subject index makes possible thematic or topical readings and is meant to offer other ways of entering the anthology, an "alternate guide" that is by no means complete or absolute. Because this book is the first-ever survey of

Canadian nature poetry, the anthology attempts to provide a fair chronological balance. About 20 percent of the book is devoted to poets born before 1900, another 20 percent to poets born between 1900 and 1930, and the bulk of the book, about 50 percent, is devoted to poets born between 1930 and 1960. The remaining 10 percent is for newer voices. Clearly, young Canadian poets are writing material enough for some enterprising anthologist to create a volume of contemporary Canadian nature poems.

Finally, I must add my voice to the chronic lament of anthologists: "This anthology could easily have been twice as long without undermining its quality or interest." Any omissions or errors are my responsibility alone. I am bound to have overlooked or excluded many favourite or remarkable poems. In the end, this book is not only an anthology of Canadian nature poetry but also an anthology of Canadian poetry, for the two are inextricably linked. Based on the volume and the quality of poems about the natural world in Canadian literature, I believe that assumptions about Canadians' profound relationship to nature and wilderness are, in fact, true.

Acknowledgements

I would like to thank the University of British Columbia (UBC) Okanagan, particularly the Faculty of Creative and Critical Studies, for its support of this project in the form of research and publication grants, as well as UBC's Hampton Fund. I would also like to thank the Faculty of Creative and Critical Studies for its secretarial support, especially Barbra MacDonald for her typing. The librarians at both UBC Okanagan and the Rare Books and Special Collections library at UBC Vancouver were unfailingly helpful, especially the librarians at UBC Okanagan who handled hundreds of books for me.

I appreciate the assistance of four student research assistants: Brian Boyce, Robert Coslett, Jannik Eikenaar, and Sarah Owen. Without the advice and enthusiastic support of my colleague Sharon Thesen, my task would have been fraught with much more anxiety and self-doubt. Friends and poets from around the country who sent me their "favourites" helped me immensely. I must acknowledge the lively and generous contributors to the listserv of the Association for Literature, Environment, and Culture in Canada (ALECC), who inspired me to read better and more.

More than anyone else, Don McKay was instrumental in making this book a reality. From the beginning when he first heard a proposal for a book of Canadian nature poems and then agreed to write the introductory essay, he has been a wise and wonderful help in every way. One thing you notice when reading widely in Canadian poetry of the past twenty years is how often Don McKay is thanked in the acknowledgements pages. I must add yet one more expression of gratitude to this long and growing list.

I am particularly grateful to Canada's numerous small presses and the handful of larger presses that publish poetry in this country. In particular, I would like to thank Matt Williams of the House of Anansi Press, Kitty Lewis of Brick Books, Andrew Steeves of Gaspereau Press, and Morgan Grady-Smith of McClelland and Stewart, who went beyond the call of duty helping me gather permissions. I am also grateful to the poets who have allowed me to reprint their poems and whose work has kept me delighted and astonished for the past two years. Similarly, the heirs and executors of authors' estates have been a pleasure to work with and, without exception, have been helpful and generous. I thank Brian Henderson, Lisa Quinn, and Clare Hitchens of Wilfrid Laurier University Press, whose support and patience have been unflagging.

I would like to thank Douglas Lochhead for his permission to use the title of his poem for the title of this anthology.

Lastly, my thanks and love to Dave Murray, best companion on all my walks, hikes, and cross-country ski trips; partner in backyard bird watching; and labourer extraordinaire in our garden ecosystem. He has been tolerant to the point of saintliness about the piles of poetry books strewn about the house and about the lack of time I have had to do all the above. This book's for him, even if I did take out the capelin poem.

Nancy Holmes
University of British Columbia Okanagan
Kelowna, British Columbia

Great Flint Singing
DON MCKAY

I Inappellable

There are some images emerging out of the poetic tradition so powerful, so rich in representative or conflicting energy, that they become icons; that is, they are pictures in the process of becoming stylized mythic versions of themselves. Think of such images as Ezra Pound in his cage at Pisa, Wordsworth in the stolen boat on Windermere, Yeats in Thor Ballylee summoning nocturnal presences, or Sylvia Plath at full gallop on Ariel. In the course of Canadian nature poetry, there are quite a few candidates for iconic status. Among them: Archibald Lampman leaving Ottawa to paddle the Lièvre, Sir Charles G. D. Roberts browsing the Tantramar Marshes, John Steffler alone on the Grey Islands, Margaret Atwood beholding the relief map of Canada at the tourist centre in Boston, Al Purdy picking wild grapes, Dennis Lee meditating in Nathan Phillips Square, Daphne Marlatt in conversation with Steveston fishermen, Earle Birney on a summit in the Rockies. But, for me, one stands out, leaps instantly into prominence the way some dreams signal to the dreamer that she ought to pay attention, that some fresh wisdom or awareness—probably not entirely pleasant—wants conscious recognition.

I'm thinking of the image of Duncan Campbell Scott at a portage on the height of land between the Lake Superior and Hudson Bay watersheds, the very height of land which is the setting for the poem with that title. This icon also happens to exist as a photograph, and that lends it a sort of meta-emblematic power, since the icon's natural tendency toward stylization and away from merely representative or empirical values is countered by the photograph's capacity to root its image in the historical present. In the photograph, the bush around Scott and his companion (Samuel Stewart) is unbeautiful, a flat swampy area composed of bay alders punctuated here and there by scrawny muskeg spruce. The stream beside them is a flaccid meander. Had Lawren Harris painted here, instead of in the spectacular country around the mouth of this river system (the Pic) on Lake Superior, rendering the landforms as vivid mystical presences would have been a tough slog. The poet is wearing a bug hat, heavy gauntlets, and knee socks with a fancy border. Stan Dragland, to whom I owe my awareness of the photo (and whose remarkable book on Scott wears the photograph on its cover), notes that Scott "looks freshly out-fitted by some wilderness store in Ottawa."[1] Samuel Stewart, dapper, watch-chained, and moustached, looks like Wyatt Earp—in my mind's eye, TV-conditioned version, of course. Neither of them risks being mistaken for the coureur de bois made famous in social studies class. The blackflies and mosquitoes—which, for anyone who has ever made one of these purgatorial marshy portages, will be recognized as the invisible furies of the photo—are no respecters of poets, not even poets on the verge of writing an important epiphanic poem. Scott isn't wearing that bug hat for show; this is long before Deep Woods Off.

Nor have the bugs been known to suspend their predations for great bat-tles, coronations, or—as in this case—the signing of treaties which alter the course of a people's history. For in fact, as we regard this photograph, we are not really looking at a poet who has ventured into wilderness to seek an encounter with the sublime, but at a bureaucrat charged with inducing (a.k.a. bribing) native peoples—the Ojibway and the Cree of northern Ontario—to sign a treaty surrendering their land to the government and accepting reduced status as wards of the state. Duncan Campbell Scott worked all his life for the Department of Indian Affairs and regarded the assimilation of native peoples into white society as a sad inevitability. Colonial exploitation might be thought an element as invisible as the blackflies but—as Stan Dragland points out—one of those boxes awaiting portage may well be the treasure chest full of treaty money. And so to the iconic image, already rich in conflict and ambi-guity, we can add the element we might call, after Hannah Arendt, the banal-ity of evil.

■

The poem which emerged from this political canoe trip is no less emblematic than the photograph, whose setting precedes Scott's scene of writing—so it seems—by only a few hours. "The Height of Land" is one of those meditations in situ, like Keats's "Ode to a Nightingale" or Wordsworth's famous Intimations Ode. But, when reading with such predecessors in mind, it is evident that Scott's poem has a particularly modern cast (the trip was made in 1906) to accompany its Canadian setting. In the poem, the figure of the poet is up late at the dying campfire while everyone else at the campsite (including the Indian guides, who rate slight mention) is asleep. The poet watches "the flakes of ash that play / At being moths" and muses to himself. In the midst of this peacefulness, he senses something, some presence that "comes by flashes / Deeper than peace" and is ambiguously inside the poet and outside in the wilderness at once. As is frequently the case in the Romantic epiphany poem, the speaker is outside normal time and space. But, rather than the conventional tower or summit, Scott's height of land is a continental eminence, between "the enormous targe [viz. shield] of Hudson Bay," which draws all the waters to the north and "The crowded southern land / With all the welter of the lives of men."

But here is peace, and again

> That Something comes by flashes
> Deeper than peace,—a spell
> Golden and inappellable
> That gives the inarticulate part
> Of our strange being one moment of release
> That seems more native than the touch of time
> And we must answer in chime;
> Though yet no man may tell
> The secret of that spell
> Golden and inappellable.

It is one of the benefits of lyric poems that they preserve, in language, peak moments that pass all too quickly in experience. So we can perch here for a while and think about the features of Scott's inappellable Something. To call it that, even with a capital *S*, is to name it without pinning it down, a kind of naming without nomination that leaves this presence on its own watershed between language and silence. Where some might see Scott's term as a vague placeholder for the ineffable, I read it as a deliberate chastening of noetic hubris, that tendency of language to grow too big for its boots and consume what it signifies. "Inappellable" is a negative term that suggests both what cannot be spoken and (as in the term "appellate court") what cannot be called. It seems to me that Scott is, in this passage, making two modern modifications to the standard Romantic view of nature: he steps away from the practice of understanding nature through human categories (as, especially, in Wordsworth) while dramatizing instead an acceptance of linguistic limits; and he suggests that this Something comes on its own and is not to be "called" to human use, that mindset known (in Heidegger's term) as "standing reserve," ever available for exploitation.

Later in the poem, once the epiphany passes and "Thought reawakens and is linked again / With all the welter of the lives of men," the purity of this Something is compromised, its inappellability domesticated to more usual humanistic values. Scott asks whether it might become "A Something to be guided by ideals? / That in themselves are simple and serene," a process of visionary domestication that we might recognize from Wordsworth or Keats. But at the watershed moment, Scott registers the inappellable Something as a pristine other that addresses a companion "inarticulate part" in our species and affords our "strange being" (note the humility implicit in that epithet) "one moment of release" such as it will not find within the covenants of time and language. At the height of the vision, deep speaks unto deep, the outer inappellable to its inarticulate equivalent within.

It is worthwhile perching a bit longer on this passage in order to listen to its music and contemplate the response the poet has made, in language, to all this unsayability. A mystic who is not a poet can answer the inappellable with silence, but a poet is in the paradoxical, unenviable position of simultaneously recognizing that it can't be said and saying something. The inappellable, paradoxically, calls *us*, despite the fact that "no man may tell / The secret of that spell." I think Scott fingers a recognition at the heart of wilderness poetry: a recognition that language is not finally adequate to experience and yet is the medium which we—the linguistic animals—must use. What to do? The poem's own soundplay holds the clue: "we must answer *in chime*" (emphasis mine), a term suggesting both rhymed response and one that harmonizes compatibly with the appeal. It works like a true rhyming spell, or charm, a small musical device that engages the senses in an aural dance while it baffles the intellect. In the last five lines of the passage, "time" is answered, in rhyme, by "chime" and "tell" by "spell," a Herakleitean marrying of opposites, which are then gathered back into the root enigma of "inap*pell*able." Answering the inappellable, it seems, doesn't mean solving the mystery; it means setting it to music.

■

As I mentioned, the poem then proceeds to weave this vision into the realm of human moral concerns (ideals "Of noble deed to further noble thought, / And noble thought to image noble deed"), but then it takes a fascinating turn. Suddenly, Scott is reminded of the disturbing country they have just paddled through—and where the photograph was taken—which provokes images of two sorts of decay: a charred forest still smouldering and stagnant putrid waters:

The last weird lakelet foul with reedy growths
And slimy viscid things the spirit loathes.
Skin of vile water over viler mud
Where the paddle stirred unutterable stenches

Yuck. Scott is not exaggerating here. Without much flow to carry off decaying vegetation, streams such as this one are really slow-moving swamps, pools of liquid compost farting at each stroke of the paddle. It's as though the height of land held both sorts of vision in suspension, the inappellable spell and the unutterable stench, spiritual exaltation and visceral horror.

■

Why did Scott include both visions in the poem? It would be neat, but inaccurate, to claim on his behalf a kind of yin-yang balance of uplift and mortality. In fact, Scott seems to treat the putrid lakelet memory as an unwanted distraction, something the poem overcomes rather than assimilates. At the poem's conclusion, as dawn arrives, he returns to the theme of noble thought and noble deed "immingled," asking whether even this ideal, given this progress of the human mind, may come to seem as uncouth as cave drawings. In the final lines he returns to the inappellable spell, quite unaltered by the memory of those "slimy viscid things the spirit loathes." It makes for a buoyant ending, but not an integrated one.

One answer to this puzzle, or one way to grope toward an answer, lies with a strange presence who (or which) appears twice, in both instances acting as a shifter of scenes. The "ancient disturber of solitude" first intrudes to negotiate the switch from epiphany to the mode of thought among the welter of men, then to inflict the memory of the putrid lake and the burnt forest. This figure has, understandably, puzzled Scott's critics. Is it simply a literary device, a semi-mythological imp whose function is to move the plot along? Is the ancient disturber the same persona as the "region spirit" that "murmurs in meditation"? I am struck by the entry of this alien element, itself—apparently—only appellable by what seems a nickname or epithet, who prods the poet out of conventional Romantic epiphany and sticks his nose into the fact of putrefaction. It's as though a trickster figure, or its undercover operative, had smuggled itself into Scott's poem—and experience—without a passport. Stan Dragland points out that the Indian presence, so firmly set aside in the opening passage (the guides are "dead asleep") may have found its way back in this disguise, flying under the radar of Scott's intention, to stir its "ancestral potion in the gloom." It is, at the very least, intriguing that one of the Ojibway names Scott uses as a kind of decor to set the scene, Chees-que-ne-ne, actually means "tent-shaker"—in fact, a shaman, rather than someone who "makes a mournful sound / Of acquiescence."[2] By committing this small act of cultural appropriation, Scott may have been welcoming into his epiphanic poem the very element that would disrupt its basic assumptions, disturbing the aesthetic solitude of its protagonist. As the poet stands by the portage in the photograph, or sits by the campfire in the poem, he embodies a contradiction pervasive in colonial experience—spiritual acuity and sensitivity to the landscape, coupled with a deafness to the voices already there. He is not really alone. The Indians are not really asleep.

II The Deepest Note of Nature's Lyre

One of the things likely to strike someone who reads through early Canadian poetry is the difficulty of addressing the wilderness of the new world using traditional conventions and forms. Neither the Enlightenment values of rational order nor the Romantic ideal of a humane and humanizing nature easily applies to the country which greeted—if that's the word—the pioneers. Some have construed the poetic responses as irredeemably colonial and derivative, but my experience is closer to Susan Glickman's when she contends that our poets "have consistently transformed their English (and broadly European) literary inheritance to make it speak to their confrontation with the land."[3] At the same time, I sense the burden on the medium as it takes the strain, trying to make its old forms work in the face of landscape and climate so radically other and so frequently hostile. Of course those forms are inadequate to the wilderness, but so are our contemporary responses. It's not as though poetry, passing through modernism and shedding Victorian conventions, had suddenly become congruent with the landscape; in large measure it turned away from the natural world to cultivate urban concerns, replacing Romantic sentiment with urbane irony. The root of the inadequacy lies not with stanzas and regular metre, but with language itself and the ontological assumptions embedded invisibly within it.

One of the most widespread of those assumptions, stemming from the pastoral and the Romantic traditions, is the moral differentiation of natural phenomena into good and bad. Howling blizzards, or, for that matter, fetid lakelets, are unlikely to be valued for their *thisness* or viewed as crucial components of an ecosystem. (And it's useful to remind ourselves that, if stuck in the middle of either, we will also find ourselves without easy access to such concepts!) Wilderness comes to us morally undifferentiated, truly ruthless in the sense that it is without ruth—compassion—as we are informed, often in a

Parks Canada pamphlet, every time we contemplate stepping a few kilometres away from the Trans-Canada Highway. Seen through the humanistic lens that pioneers brought with them, "wilderness" might indeed seem sinister and morally nihilistic; this is the view of Canadian poetry promoted by Northrop Frye and Margaret Atwood during the great surge of CanLit in the late sixties. What strikes me, however, is how resourceful poets have often been in struggling to meet the challenge posed by the landscape and its ruthless forces. It's helpful—at least to me—to bring in a totally different tradition here, not as a stick with which to beat our own tradition, but as evidence that, within the experience of our species, other attitudes to primordial energies are possible, that the Canadian experience is controlled by historical circumstances, not fate or the human condition. It may also serve to underscore the difficulties faced by our early poets.

In ancient Chinese poetry and culture, the wilderness, or rivers-and-mountains (*shan-shui*) tradition lies at the root of the cosmology, the very expression of the Tao. As such, it includes, like a giant respiratory system, non-being and being in constant alteration. Not having to cope with Western subject-object dichotomies, it simply gathers human being into the process by which all being emerges out of nothingness and returns thereto. As you may imagine, the kind of thinking we now call "ecological," based on the idea of the complex interdependence of life forms, comes to river-and-mountains poets such as T'ao Ch'ien or Wang Wei as an inherited belief rather than a late, difficult set of ideas growing out of advanced biological science and phenomenology. David Hinton, an eminent translator and interpreter of Chinese poetry, uses the term "ecology" explicitly and urges its importance as "an alternative vision in which humanity belongs wholly to the physical realm of natural process."[4]

But our poets do not have T'ao Ch'ien or Wang Wei in their luggage and must somehow cope with a set of forces challenging to their Judeo-Christian dualities. There is a fascinating passage in William Kirby's long narrative poem *The U.E.* in which his protagonists confront Niagara Falls. Kirby, with some ingenuity, adopts the Judeo-Christian cosmology to account for the violent energies he beholds.

Niagara's twin-born cataracts descend,
And eye and ear with their contention rend.
A spot of chaos, from Creation's day
Left unsubdued, to show the world alway
What was the earth ere God's commandment ran
That light should be, and order first began.

Having, in Alexander Pope's own preferred metre, postulated an energy that precedes creation and the institution of order, Kirby goes on (after several stanzas placing the cataract in its geographical context) to evoke this fury concretely.

> That dread abyss! What mortal tongue may tell
> The seething horrors of its watery hell!
> Where, pent in craggy walls that gird the deep,
> Imprisoned tempests howl, and madly sweep
> The tortured floods, drifting from side to side
> In furious vortices, that circling ride
> Around the deep arena; or, set free
> From depths unfathomed, bursts a boiling sea
> In showers of mist and spray, that leap and bound
> Against the dripping rocks; while loud resound
> Ten thousand thunders, that as one conspire
> To strike the deepest note of Nature's lyre.

On the one hand, Kirby creates a wonderful sense of Niagara's excess, all that pent energy straining against the couplet's containment and frequently enjambing, flowing through the line break and ignoring the invitation to closure offered by the rhyme. On the other hand, he renders an evocative description of the plunge pool at Niagara, with its furious vortices, which are themselves swept in circles, its boiling swirls rising from below, its showers of mist. Often the sublime is associated with summits, but here it is provoked by chthonic force rising from the depths, a "dread abyss" which, although it might normally be shunned, here strikes "the deepest note of Nature's lyre." English does not really give a name to energy that pre-exists moral division, but we are familiar with the idea through such borrowings as *mana, wakonda, tabu, phusis*, or *Tao*. (Honeymooners at Niagara Falls, one imagines, may sense some of that entering into their lives and develop their own coinages.) Dylan Thomas, in "Do Not Go Gentle Into That Good Night," pleading for the transmission of such energy from his dying father, conveys the sense by invoking both sides of the dichotomy: "Curse, bless me now with your fierce tears, I pray." Would such an insight have served to connect the disparate visions in "The Height of Land"? A worthwhile speculation.

Charles G. D. Roberts seems to be gesturing in this direction in "Autochthon," a poem written in the first person as the spirit of nature which echoes an ancient Celtic poem called "Song of Amergin."

I am the life that thrills
  In branch and bloom;
I am the patience of abiding hills,
  The promise masked in doom.

And later

I am the strife that shapes
  The stature of man,
The pang no hero escapes,
  The blessing, the ban.

The anaphora sets up a chant that—as in the psalms, or Ginsberg, or Whitman—gestures to the primitive roots of poetry in simple rhythmic repetition. The stanza form lends shape and the compulsion of musical cadence, alternating three and two stress lines until the seventh one, where a pentameter sets up—much in the manner of a leading note in music—the concluding trimeter. The effect, at least to me, is of a primal power lent shapeliness by the craft of the poet without suffering the usual sorting into good and bad versions of itself. As often with Roberts, there is a suggestion of Kiplingesque patriotic sentiment in the concluding stanza ("The omen of God in our blood that a people beholds"), but what interests me is the appeal to a spirit springing from the native and natural energies rather than, say, to the virtues of imperial fidelity and hard work as the forger of natural identity. The autochthon—one who springs from the ground he inhabits—may refer to a spirit of the place that has always been here, in which case the exclusion of the autochthonic native peoples is an eloquent omission, to say the least. But it may also refer to future post-colonial Canadians who finally become the land's creatures as opposed to its colonizers. It seems to me that Roberts is attempting to summon for white Canadians a culture-and-nature spirit who would be, for us, the equivalent of Nanahozho for the Ojibway or Glooscap for the Mi'kmaq or Raven for the Haida. And crucial to the composition of this hypothetical (and, given our collective disengagement from the land and cultural diversity, unattainable) figure is the combination of creative and destructive elements.

■

Since Canadian nature poets have from the beginning been unfavourably compared to their European—largely English—models, it is interesting to ask how well the Romantic poets cope with raw wilderness—as opposed to nature in a supportive or pictorial role. One of the more intriguing passages in

Wordsworth's *The Prelude* is the stolen boat episode (one of the icons I mentioned at the outset) in which wilderness as other suddenly surfaces into his account of a childhood in which nature generally functioned as the soul's benign guide and educator. Although Wordsworth sets up the experience as one of Nature's sterner ministrations within her balanced regime of child-raising (he is "led by her" into the episode), it's clear that it left him shaken and unable to integrate the shock into *The Prelude*'s web of lessons and delights. As he recalls it, Wordsworth "borrows" the boat ("an act of stealth / And troubled pleasure") and rows out onto Windermere, getting out far enough that his perspective alters and a distant peak, not visible when close to shore, suddenly looms. Here's the passage:

> I dipp'd my oars into the silent Lake,
> And, as I rose upon the stroke, my Boat
> Went heaving through the water, like a Swan;
> When from behind that craggy Steep, till then
> The bound of the horizon, a huge Cliff,
> As if with voluntary power instinct,
> Uprear'd its head. I struck, and struck again,
> And, growing still in stature, the huge Cliff
> Rose up between me and the stars, and still,
> With measur'd motion, like a living thing,
> Strode after me. With trembling hands I turn'd,
> And through the silent water stole my way
> Back to the Cavern of the Willow tree.
> There, in her mooring-place, I left my Bark,
> And, through the meadows homeward went, with grave
> And serious thoughts; and after I had seen
> That spectacle, for many days, my brain
> Work'd with a dim and undetermin'd sense
> Of unknown modes of being; in my thoughts
> There was a darkness, call it solitude,
> Or blank desertion, no familiar shapes
> Of hourly objects, images of trees,
> Of sea or sky, no colours of green fields;
> But huge and mighty Forms that do not live
> Like living men mov'd slowly through my mind
> By day and were the trouble of my dreams.[5]

The sudden experience of wilderness-as-other, especially if it has previously been experienced as an adjunct to human values or—as is often the case—as a commodity, can be terrifying. It's as though the thread of terror that lends to the sublime its tremolo and edge were jacked to full volume. As in the stolen boat episode, the wilderness suddenly reveals itself as an agent with its own intent, a "living thing" that seems to hold us in its sights or to pursue us as it strides after the boat. "Do you see nothing / watching you from under the water?" asks Margaret Atwood of the lady beholding the innocent tourist relief map of Canada. In such cases, which might be characterized as the substitution of infinity for eternity, the scene refuses to resolve into the foreknown and is felt as an assault on the very domesticating function of the mind. No familiar shapes remain, nor pleasant images of trees; it troubles our dreams; it turns us toward a blank desertion, not—as with the usual aesthetic experience— toward a broader sense of our humanity. In the 1850 version (I've quoted the 1805 version above), Wordsworth includes a phrase that—brilliantly, I think— throws his inventive powers into reverse to demonstrate how the power of the vision exceeds language. Wordsworth says it was "a huge peak, black and huge," dramatically humbling his own finely cadenced medium to the status of a kid saying "it was big, really really big." But notice also the sly craft within that gesture, creating the sharply consonantal "black peak" between the open assonance of the "huges."

Wordsworth's experience on Windermere, this notable exception in his experience of the natural world, is what our poets faced continually: wilderness without ruth. *The Prelude* generally segues gracefully from episode to episode, but here—after a stanza break—the next section opens with an invocation, "Wisdom and Spirit of the universe!", which not only changes the topic abruptly but, re-invoking the presiding genius of his youth, works to exorcise that "blank desertion" and that "undetermin'd sense / Of unknown modes of being." Enough of this dangerous stuff; we're on our way (fourteen lines later) to recognize "A grandeur in the beating of the heart," and have human values reassuringly endorsed by nature once again.

But of course there is a wisdom to Wordsworth's handling of raw wilderness. In carefully controlled doses it produces the experience of the sublime, with its delicious call note of terror. Beyond that the possibility of mental derangement is imminent, as the conventions of thought and language are simply swept away. In our literature and culture, the phenomenon is known as being "bushed," overwhelmed by wilderness energy and made strange to human society. The figure at the heart of Patrick Lane's evocative *Winter*, fleeing human contact, walking into the blizzard with snowshoes reversed, is one vivid version of this recurring persona, and the theme is directly addressed by Margaret Atwood in "Progressive Insanities of a Pioneer" and *The Journals of Susanna Moodie*. I think the prospect of that apotheosis, that crossing over, exists as an undercurrent throughout our poetry, and that, while it was experienced as new by the colonists, they had in fact imported it, or its embryo, in the form of the sublime. The soupçon of terror that was the magical ingredient in the experience of the sublime becomes, in the presence of unmitigated wilderness, an overdose. What might have happened to the young Wordsworth had he been unable to escape that "huge peak, black and huge" or shake off its troubling after-effects? Perhaps no poem puts this question more cogently than Earle Birney's "Bushed."

■

Possibly it impresses me more than it should when a poet writes out of experience, does fieldwork, and becomes intimate with her subject, so that these make substantial claims on the writing rather than simply serving the writer's aesthetic ends. The fact that Earle Birney worked in the bush (partly making cutlines, the forerunner of tree planting as the young person's summer job) and explored the mountains first-hand contributes to the effectiveness of a poem such as "Bushed," which brings personal experience to bear on a paradigmatic encounter. One of the exquisite things about this poem is its poise on the hinge of ambiguity: is the protagonist a victim of wilderness-induced madness, or is he a seeker who, pursuing his own quest, graduates from conventional notions of beauty to the visionary experience of wilderness as undomesticated presence? On the one hand, "Bushed" can be read as a sort of cautionary tale for those who would live alone in wilderness armed with inadequate notions of the sublime. Lightning strikes the protagonist's "invented rainbow," and the mountain, "clearly alive" (recall Wordworth's "living thing"), issues its own messages. At night the moon carves "unknown totems" out of the lakeshore—as opposed, perhaps, to the expected order of the picturesque—and the owls in the "beardusky woods" deride him. All these diminishments culminate in the remarkable image of the mountain itself:

> then he knew   though the mountain slept   the winds
> were shaping its peak to an arrowhead
> poised

> And now he could only
> bar himself in and wait
> for the great flint to come singing into his heart

Barred in, he waits for the bush's *coup de grâce*, which—since it is an arrowhead (visually enacted by the shape of that penultimate stanza)—can also be seen as a vengeance meted out on behalf of native peoples. But, leaning the other way on that delicate hinge, we can equally say that the speaker is at the point of apotheosis, when the old order breaks down, and he receives the presence into himself. Like Scott in "The Height of Land," Birney handles this breakdown/ epiphany with a lyric charm, using an intense interlinear music reminiscent of Welsh *cynghanedd*. Acoustically, the line sharpens itself with part-rhymes, moving consonantally from "great" to "flint," then assonantally from "flint" to "singing into," with the final "heart" reaching back again to "great." Rhythmically, it uses accelerating anapests to set up the central spondee (gréat flínt), the surprise term "singing," with its suggestion of ecstasy, and the terminal "heart." These slant rhymes and emphatic rhythms seem to be enacting linguistically the kind of whetting that the winds perform on the mountain.

Well, psychotic or shamanistic? Are we, in fact, obliged to choose between these versions? Birney has, to my mind, managed with great finesse to reach back past that bifurcation to evoke the power of a wilderness that excludes— in fact, attacks—such efforts of mind to sort its power according to its own categories.

So, here's a proposal for a thought experiment, or maybe a writing assignment, or maybe a mission to be undertaken by our dream lives. What happens after that moment of the great flint? Where is the protagonist today? (Consider this: at the end of *The Journals of Susanna Moodie*, Margaret Atwood brings her protagonist into the present as a bag lady on Toronto transit.) If we were to write the sequel, what special tasks would we be asking language to perform?

III A Tangle of Small Bells Afloat

> Again I heard the song
> Of the glad bobolink, whose lyric throat
> Pealed like a tangle of small bells afloat.
> —Charles G. D. Roberts, "Ave!"

When there are large conceptual or aesthetic flourishes in the air and poets, as Shelleyan "unacknowledged legislators of the world," are tasked with the spirit's enlightenment, some of poetry's small perceptual triumphs risk going undetected. Since there is considerable abstract rumble in Victorian verse (and not just in its Canadian subspecies), these moments may be subordinated— even by the poets themselves—to Grand Schemes and Designs. In "Ave!", Charles G. D. Roberts celebrates Shelley's centenary in a traditional ode, which he sets in his beloved Tantramar. For eight and a half very Wordsworthian stanzas he depicts his own soul's seedtime in that remarkable marshland. As in *The Prelude*, nature is presented as the spirit's guide and educator, combining a host of vivid perceptions (bobolinks, marsh hawks, field mice, the orange mud-saturated tides of the Tantramar River) with meditative moments when "my spirit grew more still and wise." Then, turning on the potent and "impetuous stress" of the river and its urgent tides, Roberts, in a set of capacious similes, applies them to Shelley. There follow another twenty-one and a half well-wrought stanzas celebrating the great Romantic's life, work, and spirit, after which Roberts returns us to the Tantramar, which is now transformed—thanks to the inspirational call of Shelley's example—to an emblem of visionary potential. The poem closes with a portentous epic simile comparing the roar of the ebb tide to a "lord of men" ascending his solitary tower to read the stars' conflicting messages until "the day he leads his legions forth to war." I think it safe to say that few of us, contemplating the ebbing tide in the Tantramar without the intercession of Roberts high on Shelley, are likely to conjure this warrior poet; he is the product of the epic simile's muscular ambition, not the phenomenological imagination tuned to the actual object.

It is important to credit Roberts' achievement, as well as to acknowledge the politics of the gesture, in grounding his ode in the closely observed Canadian setting. But part of what interests me in this poem is the rift between those closely perceived details of the marshland and the heroic figure at its finale. It illustrates a tendency in all Romantic writing to convert natural observations into rocket fuel for the spirit and lose·a sense of their inherent value in idealism's uplifting anthems. By contrast, Roberts' image of the bobolink's song, "a tangle of small bells afloat," is embedded in the scene, humble and testable by the ear. David Sibley's description, in his fine field guide (a "cheerful bubbling jangling warble") is certainly accurate, especially since it includes that element, in "jangling," of a slightly demented banjo. But Roberts' "tangle" catches this more elegantly and memorably. I will always be grateful for this, as I am for the metaphorical depiction of the rose-breasted grosbeak's song (this from Roger Tory Peterson) as resembling the song of a robin who has taken voice lessons.

Such precise images testify to Roberts' keenness as a fine natural historian, evident in many of his poems, including the pastoral sonnets. Among these, "The Clearing" is notable as a poem which considers altered wilderness rather than farmland, as well as for a close rendering of a slash-and-burn clear-cut. Here again, Roberts' account of the devastation (in the octave) and the process of regeneration (in the sestet) shows the precision of his observations. He notes that "the waste is touched with cheer" by the appearance of fireweed and "venture plumes of goldenrod," something that can be seen everywhere in boreal forest clear-cuts. Roberts reserves the last lines for our most ethereal birdsong: "across the solitude / The hermit's holy transport peals serene." He might stand to be accused of a Romantic inflation in this equation of the holy transport of the hermit with that of the Hermit thrush, but not by me. One utterance of that delicate four-stage set of musical wisps could, at a stroke, turn an entire taxi full of hyperskeptical young urban poets into momentary mystics. They might survive the moment with a shrug or an ironic aside, but I'm betting they'd Google the song in private.

Among our early poets, Archibald Lampman is often cited as the most Keatsean and sensuous; as Margaret Atwood says, he is absorbed in details with Zen-like intensity. But perhaps his acuity is rivalled by such poets as Ethelwyn Wetherald, who devotes whole poems to such species as golden-crowned kinglets and horned larks. "The Hornèd Larks in Winter" presents a detailed portrait of both birds and their behaviours.

> Lovers of the plowed field
> And the open sun,
> Pacing thoughtfully the ruts
> One by one.
> On each delicate small head
> Black and white are closely wed,
> And the horn-like tufts are lowered
> When they run.

Although we may be moved by the sublime to revere spectacular elements in the natural world, one reasonably suspects that we are in part revering our own emotion. It is acts of close attention, such as noticing how the horned larks lower their "horns" when they run (they *never* hop like robins or crows) that foster intimacy. (Notice how Wetherald mutes the rhyme from full to slant with "lowered," as though imitating the effect of the tufts.) This is nature poetry in the spirit of John Clare rather than Wordsworth or Keats, enabling us to know its subjects the way we come to know people, in terms of individuating expressions or quirks. The aim and end of poems such as Wetherald's, or Marjorie Pickthall's "When Winter Comes," or Seranus' [Susan Frances Harrison's] elaborate garland of specific Canadian flowers with its ingenious macaronic rhyme, is not an epiphanic vision but—as we might say today—of ecosystem, a slow-growing wonder wrought of many parts rather than peak moments and grand unifying themes such as one finds in English Romantic vision poems and American transcendentalism.

For the phenomenological poet, it is important to know the species in detail, to tell the horned larks from the meadowlarks, and the western meadowlarks with their musical gargling from the eastern species, whose song is the wistfulness of a world-weary aunt. This spirit persists in such recent poets as John Steffler, Daphne Marlatt, Sue Sinclair, and Stephanie Bolster. Some—I'm thinking of poets such as Brian Bartlett, Elizabeth Philips, and Maureen Scott Harris—have made a study of one or another branch of natural history a part of their poetic practice. Others—such as Tim Bowling with his fisherman's poems, Sid Marty with his poems derived from mountaineering jobs, and Peter Trower with his vivid glimpses of a logger's life—have made their working contacts with the natural world especially eloquent. And in the work of Jan Conn, we are privileged to observe a passionate engagement with nature (often in the tropics) interacting with the keenness of her biologist's eye. A wonderfully egregious counter-example occurs very early (1861) in Alexander McLachlan's "The Emigrant," in which he records how the settlers missed the birdsong of the old country and found the birds of the new world, although beautiful, songless. Besides this deafness, one has to wonder what perceptual anomaly led them, according to McLachlan, to see species with amber wings and golden rings around their necks. Possibly this was a side effect of excessive nostalgia, or the projection of an understandable desire, once the emigrants set foot here, to inhabit the tropics instead.

It will be obvious that I consider it fundamental to nature poetry that it be—whatever the thrust of its thought and language—grounded in empirical observation. This is not simply to lend the poem realistic detail: it is to approach the subject with respect, to acknowledge implicitly that it comprises beings as fully individuated as the poet. A fine prose poem by Robert Bly called "Looking at a Dead Wren in My Hand" illustrates my view. In it Bly riffs with his Deep Image catachrestic images on the "tiny ricelike legs that are bars of music played in an empty church," "the intense yellow chest that makes tears come," and (crucially) "the black spot on your head which is your own mourning cap." By these gestures of stretched metaphor Bly creates a sense of language reaching, reaching, demonstrating in the very extremity of the language act how vivid is the presence of the wren. Except that it isn't a wren but a warbler, a Wilson's warbler, as the yellow breast and black cap attest. So what? Well, would it matter if Bly had mistaken a dead Irishman for an Inuit? It's not the name that's important here, since that is simply a taxonomical label (and one that, in this case, illustrates some vintage human hubris), it's what that name gives entry to: the individuating, cherishable details of the small bird's being—its range, song, plumage, habits of eating and migration. For those stretched metaphors of Bly's to work they need to find purchase in the here and now, some anchor that poetry, in its efforts to celebrate or mourn, can pull against. It needs—as Ethelwyn Wetherald understood—a humble and enquiring eye to lend *gravitas* to those agile acts of language.

IV Thomson Is Done

It is usual to say that CanLit was born in the late sixties, but it would be more appropriate to say that Canadian literature, which had been quietly collecting for more than a century, was suddenly reborn with this nickname and a fresh, talkative, self-consciousness. This new, bumptious creature was as enthusiastic about exploring the patterns and configurations discernible in its own past as its predecessor had been reticent, preferring to defer to British or American paradigms. CanLit exhibited, it seems in retrospect, something of the buoyancy experienced by neurotic persons who, having suffered in depressed silence for generations, enter therapy and discover that their own histories, however grim and dusty with neglect, are actually mythic and interesting, shaped by patterns that help them identify themselves as characters in the stories of their lives.

The book which most vociferously announced the birth of CanLit was undoubtedly Margaret Atwood's *Survival*, a bold and brawny account of Canadian literature that identified survival as its central symbol (as opposed to "the Island" for England and "the Frontier" for America) and set forth the archetypal figures—all victims of different kinds—within it. *Survival* was a call to arms, a teaching manual, and a piece of inspirational writing urging that attention be paid to all Canadian subjects. As I mentioned, I find it hard to credit the view shared by Atwood with Northrop Frye (who is very much the intellectual uncle of the book) that poets saw the natural world primarily as sinister. But there is no disputing the muscularity and sweep of the project, nor the determination to make the colonial literary past useful and accessible, to insist that it behave as a coherent body, that it *take shape*.

But while the character of CanLit was seen to be shapely, it was also complex and coloured throughout by a fundamental paradox. We might state it like this: the key to overcoming the colonial condition and achieving identity lies in the recognition, acceptance, and exploration of that condition—one that had shifted, over time, from political subservience to Britain to cultural subservience to the United States. It became sort of a joke that a Canadian was someone obsessed by the Canadian identity she or he didn't possess: *sort* of a joke, I think, the way a koan is. Given a reflective turn, the joke suggests that identity may function like Buddhist enlightenment or Jungian individuation—that is, as a telos or goal to work toward and to experience in premonitory flashes, not as the genetic origin of a culture, like the myths of the American dream, or the chosen people, or the master race. If I'm right about this, then the idea of Canadian identity is missing—or is free from—the element of fatedness or "manifest destiny" which powers other culture myths. And, while we're still taking the joke seriously, it's worth reflecting that a dose of Canadian uncertainty about identity might not have hurt some of those fate-driven myths as they played—are playing—themselves out in the labyrinth of history.

■

The writer of the CanLit renaissance who has given the colonial paradox its most philosophical and lyric formulation is Dennis Lee. Two important works of the period, *Civil Elegies* (poems) and "Cadence, Country, Silence" (an essay), give it shape in a way that is personal, nuanced, and informed by a deep philosophical reflection. It might have seemed strange for me to cite, as one of Canadian nature poetry's iconic images, the figure of Dennis Lee sitting in Nathan Phillips Square, the "scene of writing" for *Civil Elegies*. One way to explain myself is to say that wilderness in that poem is an eloquent absence, or perhaps *the* eloquent absence, the poem's alter ego. Although the situation is civic, the deep focus of these lyric meditations is the idea of citizenship as being-in-the-world, and not simply as living as a political person.

But *Civil Elegies* and "Cadence, Country, Silence" also concern wilderness in the sense that they bring into Canadian writing a new ontological understanding of the natural world. Behind them lies the philosophy of George Grant, which had identified a strain of Canadian colonial aspiration (already, alas, lost) that differed from the American dream, with its implicit understanding that the material world is simply raw material available for our use. Grant had adapted Heidegger's concept of "standing reserve" for this exploitive attitude. Against this, the Canadian ethos included, as Lee puts it in "Cadence, Country, Silence,"

> a groping to reaffirm a classical European tradition, which taught that reverence is more fully human than conquest or mastery. That we are subject to sterner necessities than liberty and the pursuit of happiness....[6]

Well, what might that reverence toward the natural world involve? For Lee, the composition of poetry derives from the apprehension of what he calls "cadence," a "preverbal field of force," which the poet experiences as a "luminous tumble, a sort of taut cascade" going on continuously, even though the poet is able to tune it in only occasionally. "More and more I sense this energy as presence, both outside and inside myself, teeming toward words." It is quite fascinating to me, reading Lee's groundbreaking essay in this context, to realize that his cadence is another species of that undifferentiated energy toward which our early poets were groping, akin to *mana, phusis,* and *Tao.* When registered in the interior, as a response of the beholder, cadence provokes a sense of *mysterium tremendum*, a presentiment of earth-energy that is at once phenomenological and mystical. This thinking presents itself as a way of understanding and experiencing what *is*, the world itself, with fresh ontological and ethical intensity. Poetry, in Lee's poetics, is the leading edge of a potential change in individual and cultural consciousness. For me, and I suspect for many others, this was an extraordinary development: here was a poetics hewn out of the stuff of our own tradition, setting poetic attention vigorously at work in the world. It demonstrated that poetry might exceed the boundaries of craft, and even art, to become a practice.

To be colonized, as previously by the British and currently (at least in 1970) by the Americans, Lee claims, is to have cadence blocked, to be denied access to that energy and presence and rendered silent. In "Cadence, Country, Silence" the paradoxical turn—in itself a Heideggerean move—comes when the colonial disenfranchisement is used against itself, the way guerrillas make the very conditions of marginalization the source of their power.

> But perhaps—and here was the breakthrough—perhaps our job was not
> to fake a space of our own and write it up, but rather to speak the words
> of our spacelessness.[7]

That turn carries Lee into the silence of non-being which—although first experienced as deprivation—shifts into an ontological awareness, the astonishing realization that for any object or experience "this phrase, this event need not be" so that "it reveals its vivacious being as though it had just begun to exist." In other words, the route out of the colonial condition involves embracing the silence imposed upon us, which in turn leads to a radical re-seeing of the world from the vantage point of non-being, each of its beings precious, cherishable, vibrant with mortality, and shadowed by emptiness. As Lee acknowledges in his later essay "Poetry and Unknowing," this is a contemporary version of the *via negativa*, that European pilgrimage toward the insight which, I would say, underlies the Taoist cosmos.

The practice established by "Cadence, Country, Silence" and *Civil Elegies* differs greatly from the Romantic paradigm. In embracing colonial spacelessness, and—in the elegies—situating the narrator in the middle of "technopolis" in Nathan Phillips Square, Lee sets aside the attraction of epiphany, that "shiny ascent." The gesture by which he chooses the phenomenological *via negativa* over the conventional Romantic vision is made by invoking, then releasing, the potent image of Tom Thomson as a kind of shamanic conduit for wilderness.

> he paddled direct through
> the palpable dark, hearing only the push and

drip of the blade for hours and then very suddenly the radiance of the
renewed land broke over his canvas. So. It was his
job.

It's as though the very rhetoric used in the poem—the long line yearning, the
plosives invoking the soundscape of nocturnal paddling—had to be resisted
lest the old impulse catch hold and sweep the narrator out of Nathan Phillips
Square and off to Algonquin Park. So, he reminds us in curt deflating terms,
it was his job. Now, Thomson is done.

> and now the shiny ascent is not for us, Thomson is
> done and we cannot
> malinger among the bygone acts of grace.

Such enactive rhetoric has always been the hallmark of Lee's practice.
That determination, voiced in "Cadence, Country, Silence" and other essays
since, to write the voice of the ontological condition, carries forward into his
recent books, *Un* and *Yesno*. These are composed in the crunched and com-
pounded newspeak of techno-culture and address, in large measure, the con-
ditions of environmental devastation it has brought about: "I want verbs of a
slagscape thrombosis" he declares in *Un*, "syntax of chromosome pileups."
For Lee, as for Paul Celan (whose often violent neologisms in German have
influenced Lee's in English), the very structure of the real is under threat; it is
not so much that we have lived in contravention of natural process as that we
have managed to damage the processes themselves.

> Icecaps shrink in the brain-
> rays; noetic
> infarctions; clots in the tropic of hominid.
> Synapse events on the pampas, while
> consciousness voids itself in the bowl of sky.

■

Dennis Lee's work sets the stage for other writers who have used the medita-
tive essay as a vehicle for the investigation of poetic ontologies, dwelling specif-
ically on the problem of—to quote Tim Lilburn's title—*Living in the World as
if It Were Home*. For Lilburn, poetry is a practice and a way of knowing, an alter-
native to the appropriative and possessive epistemology left us by the Enlight-
enment and our colonial past. He has actively encouraged other poets to
engage in such reflections by conceiving and editing two collections of essays,
Poetry and Knowing and *Thinking and Singing*. In his poems, as in his essays,

he pursues a course of contemplative inquiry that seeks to renovate not only the way we see the world but the nature of that seeing. Books such as *Moose-wood Sandhills*, *To the River*, and *Kill-site* are (in different ways) meditations in situ, by which Lilburn affects an apprenticeship to particular landscapes of the prairies: the Moosewood hills, the land along the South Saskatchewan River, and the high plateau of grasslands close to the US border. He walks these forlorn places; he returns again on snowshoe; he digs a hole in the earth and sleeps there. The writing happens in long hyperextended linear throws like fly casts or impromptu prayers carried on their own ecstatic currents. The stacked hyphen-connected metaphors often draw on the traditions of the desert fathers and neoplatonism, although just as frequently they startle with surprising, stretched connections from other spheres: "Maybe the coyote's shady glide, bluff-lambada, is evangelical." In all his work, he presses his radical epistemology into practice: language, in presuming to name a thing (transgressing its inappellability) must at the same time cancel its own act, bring itself to the condition of mute astonishment at the thing's unknowable singularity or, as Lilburn often puts it, "oddness." Contemplation for Lilburn involves the opposite of the reduction of a thing to knowledge systems or taxonomy; it means beholding the thing intensely while knowing that it cannot be known.

Others, also crossing meaningfully between poetry and prose, have brought other issues to bear on the question of nature poetry and our being in the world. In Robert Bringhurst's work, which includes and integrates such diverse fields as poetry, typography, book design, linguistics, and translation, there is a consistent drive to find the material and concrete roots of the gesture: the movement of the hand within the typescript, the fit of the tool or weapon to the body, the live voice within and behind the poem or myth-tale. His groundbreaking work in translation turns an active ear to the wisdom of Native American traditions, giving in particular the Haida myth-tales a searching and attentive reading to accompany his translation, and urgently arguing that these should be treated, as we treat the epics of Homer or the Norse sagas, as treasures of world literature. Bringhurst's scholarly, linguistic, and poetic gestures can be seen as serious attempts to listen and learn reverently, and, since they are based on word for word transcriptions of myth-tales as spoken by Ghandl and Skaay to a meticulous transcriber—John Swanton—they begin much closer to the actual voice of these nineteenth century myth-tellers than is usual in reported anthropological records. Bringhurst insists on the artistic individuality of these myth-tellers, according them the equivalent status of poets in European cultures, and not (at the other extreme) simply mouthpieces for a culture. In taking such an approach he reverses the patronizing and assimilative attitudes of the past.

But after several centuries of abuse and neglect—including, as Bringhurst reiterates, a holocaust in the form of the smallpox epidemic and many egregious instances of appropriation—even such an informed and appreciative reading has been mistrusted by many Haida. It is a response that might lead us to reflect (outside the personal and political aspects of the dispute) on both what is lost as an orally rendered and remembered tale suffers translation into written literature and what is gained; and—this is crucial—by whom. At least we need to be alive to the ongoing paradox of translation in this context (one alters the medium in order to preserve it) and to bear with patience the mistrust we have earned. In the immediate future our tradition of nature poetry will benefit by listening hard, following Bringhurst's example, to its predecessors in North America. Duncan Campbell Scott needs to go back to the height of land and listen again to that "long Ojibway cadence" which was so much background music to his epiphany.

V Disturbed Ground

Place: our shibboleth, our darling obsession. Once, back in the seventies, I was teaching a class in children's literature, and I tried to demonstrate the centrality of place by pairing *Anne of Green Gables* with *Alice in Wonderland*, then by switching the prepositions and teaching the anti-books. *Anne in Green Gables* is a dark realistic novel about an orphan whose struggle to belong to a place simply increases her alienation from her humourless foster mother and the hidebound community; these stifle her lively artistic temperament, driving her to run away to Halifax where she dyes her hair green on purpose, starts experimenting with drugs...well, you get the idea. *Alice of Wonderland*, with "official" illustrations by Dali rather than Tenniel, is about the inner life of a prepubescent schizophrenic. (In case anyone connected with post-secondary education is reading this essay, please note that this is not a tactic I recommend, unless you are a collector of puzzled looks and very strange answers on the exam from the students who decided to skip reading the books and get the gist from the lecture.) Outside the academy, place and "where're you from" rivals weather as conversational material; inside the academy, the topic fuels innumerable exam questions and conferences. Often it is a problem, like identity, a struggle to be "of" and not simply "in." Often it's an unstable term, especially for persons interested in a post-colonial way of life and a rethinking of our attitudes to landscape. Place alters its sense according to the perspective of the viewer, who might be a recent immigrant, someone whose connections to an outport go back to the eighteenth century, or a native person who grew up on a reservation, a "place" imposed by an alien culture. One of those exam questions might focus on the Tantramar Marshes and ask for a comparison of the place as a setting for the poems of John Thompson and Charles G. D. Roberts. In another essay I attempted a thought experiment that turned the concept around to consider its otherwise place (that is, seeing place from the vantage point of the natural rather than the human world) as land to which we have occurred, or wilderness to which history has happened.

In many of our poetries, it seems to me, the process of engagement with place results, not in deeper roots (the happy ending in the mainstream version of Anne's story), but in a deeper, more complex sense of being here. Place persistently eludes our grasp, so long as a grasp is what it is. So long as we cling to the idea of place as something that belongs to us, removed from its mothering wilderness, we prevent ourselves from ever belonging to it. We remain colonizers and colonials.

One of the ways that grasp is loosened is by the introduction of time into what on the surface seems a purely spatial concept. Robert Kroetsch, whose approach to place makes brilliant use of demotic cultural forms such as the ledger and the seed catalogue, opens his "lifelong" poem, *Field Notes*, with a meditation on a native stone hammer found on one of his family's fields. Unlike the ledger and the seed catalogue, the stone hammer casts the poet's mind into the unknown prehistory of the fields over which ownership has been presumed, and effortlessly undoes that grasp.

> The stone maul
> was found.
>
> In the field
> my grandfather
> thought
> was his
>
> my father
> thought was his.

Let me add the image of Kroetsch sitting at his desk hefting that stone hammer to the list of nature poetry icons: it is potent as both a heavy fact and an emptiness, and because that emptiness opens a trap door into prehistory. Now "place" is like a receding horizon,

> old as the last
> Ice Age, the

retreating / the
recreating ice,
the retreating
buffalo, the
retreating Indians.

The stone hammer's gift to place is, ironically, to saturate it with losses and mysterious absence. And it is on this unstable foundation that Kroetsch erects his subsequent ledgering, cataloguing structures.

Christopher Dewdney's work manages a similarly unsettling effect, enlarging—even overwhelming—our sense of place by opening it up to deep time. A "known" locale such as London, Ontario, or a familiar object, such as a limestone cliff, becomes flooded with the infinite temporality that constantly attends it. In the preface to *Predators of the Adoration*, Dewdney gives an account of his introduction to geologic time.

> I have been fascinated by limestone ever since my father first pointed it out to me when I was 5 or 6 years old. On a summer evening as we drove down into the Grand River valley near Paris, Ontario, he explained that the limestone was almost entirely composed of the shells & skeletons of underwater creatures, millions of years old, compacted and turned to rock. His explanation transformed the rock into a miraculous substance, which, as I elaborated my passion over the next few years, became a slow oracular fountain of compressed millennia.[8]

The astonishment (that is, becoming "astonied") places Dewdney in the company of pioneering geologists such as James Hutton, who realized back in the eighteenth century, as he stared at the angular unconformity of Siccar Point in Scotland, that there was no way Earth could be only 6,000 years old—its age according to reckoning based on Genesis. The similar eureka experience of Dewdney in the Grand River Valley (another candidate for icon status? I guess so) may be a useful root context to return to when the reader becomes bewildered among the compressed pataphysical arcana of his imagery. If limestone—this grey, familiar, emblem of institutional stability—can become, with the simple addition of the deep temporal perspective, a "miraculous substance," what can't?

In fact, I think there are two defamiliarizing moves going on in Dewdney's work, often at the same time: the spatialization of time (the limestone is "compressed millennia") and the temporalization of space (all those crustaceans swimming in its "oracular foundation"). I'm guessing these are some of the "reciprocal inductions" mentioned on the cover of *The Paleozoic Geology of*

London Ontario (Dewdney's first full-length book, published in 1973), and that their reciprocity relates to a comparable linguistic phenomenon found throughout his work. When he declares, for example, "The fossil is pure memory," the statement is at once a propositional metaphor and a metaphorical proposition, flickering back and forth like the iridescence on a mallard's neck between a scientific declaration reaching across its frontier into poetry and a poetic expression insisting on materializing as a scientific fact. Metaphor has always occupied this subversive linguistic space (making it a problem for analytic philosophers), but it seems that Christopher Dewdney is the poet who exploits—or dramatizes—that vital strife most effectively, often managing to set both sides in motion at the same time. Consider, for example, how his work resonates with the following statement about global warming made by David Suzuki in 2006:

> The continued use of fossil fuels has released countless side-effects unknown to mankind. The highways are actually arteries carrying the lifeblood to an unarticulated primeval form using cities, oil refineries, jet and auto engines, factories, and any form of fossil fuel consumption to slowly replace the present composition of the atmosphere with the chemical composition of the atmosphere some 200 million years ago. After a certain critical point this atmosphere will become capable of generating the life-forms essential to this ancient form.

OK, you guessed it; that was actually Christopher Dewdney writing, prophetically, in 1973, and tricksterishly shifting the thrust of the greenhouse gas phenomenon from bad news for us in the Neogene to a sort of renaissance for the old form known as the Carboniferous, while treating the anthropogenic vectors (highways, cities, jet and auto engines) as though they were forces of nature. That kind of complex and radical defamiliarization in all his writings has made Dewdney one of the poets who most effectively evokes the mystery of planetary dwelling, effortlessly crossing—perhaps "dissolving" would be a better word—such usual boundaries as those between poetic and scientific thinking or material and psychic phenomena.

Given Dewdney's originality and virtuoso experimentation, one might well consider all his literary points of contact to be offshore, such as early twentieth-century pataphysicists and Dadaists. But I wonder if, at least in his use of deep time, he does not have an immediate ancestor in Al Purdy. It has often seemed to me that Purdy's large-muscled embrace of place and human endeavour, that ability to give voice to the ethos of the country north of Belleville or to render the Arctic from a non-resident's perspective, is informed by a reframing of the immediate and local in terms of the prehistoric or infinite. Typically, a confident narrator—or, more precisely, raconteur—large with his own energy, finds himself, over the course of the poem, chastened by the likes of a dwarfed alpine plant or a vanished race such as the Dorsets. It is interesting that Dennis Lee found Al Purdy, not simply a big homemade voice, but a writer who was able to transcend the colonial impasse by enacting the condition, recreating "the halt and stammer, the wry self-deprecation, the rush of celebratory élan and the vastness of the still unspoken surround in which a colonial writer comes to know his house, his father, her city and land...."[9] Among recently emerging poets, Adam Dickinson is notable for extending the tradition of deep temporality, as in *Kingdom, Phylum*, a book which especially interrogates the systems of taxonomy by which we have attempted to domesticate the natural world.

■

Place takes on a wholly intimate and immediate sense in Daphne Marlatt's writing, which combines a poetics of writing the body (carrying into feminist poetics the tradition emerging from the Black Mountain and Tish movements) and an intense concentration on the live moment. One way to think of Marlatt's extraordinary idiom is to imagine the repeal of the Wordsworthian principle of powerful emotions recollected in tranquility. It's as though Marlatt were rousing language, urging it out of that tranquil study and into the surge and flux of the moment, provoking it to feel and revel in its own physicality. Part of the excitement of such works as the classic *Steveston* is the sense of place being evoked through immediate perceptions rather than general notions or memories, with language tuning and retuning itself to meet the exigencies of the ongoing moments, and so extending its capacity to function as a truly phenomenological instrument. Its ear is out for each turn or eddy in the moment, as in the Fraser River flowing past the village. Part poem, part oral history, *Steveston* was originally a collaboration with a photographer, Robert Minden, which rendered the Fraser delta fishing village, with its Japanese-Canadian inhabitants and traditions, in vivid and immediate detail. It is part of Daphne Marlatt's eco-feminism that the language be made as flexible and receptive as possible, that it devote its orderly functions (syntax, grammar) to the service of the particular place and time, to render the pour of *phusis* linguistically.

■

One of our most comprehensive evocations of place, John Steffler's *The Grey Islands*, is set on the opposite coast from *Steveston*. Were the acute close-up poems which constitute part of this book its only element, *The Grey Islands* would be memorable enough. As it is, with its combination of poetry, prose fiction, travel writing, memoir, ghost story, cuffer (the Newfoundland oral tale similar to the tall tale), and pseudo-historical account, it works to create a multi-dimensional sense of the place. The Grey Islands are situated off Newfoundland's Great Northern Peninsula and are no longer inhabited, although they have long served as fishing depots. Steffler spent several summers there gathering material. In his fictive/poetic account, the narrator is a town planner who is also a restless seeker, craving some place where he can "corner himself": "some blunt place I can't go beyond." What he learns there is, in part, practical phenomenology, registering the experience of the glaciated, lichened rock, constantly changing sea and stark sky in vivid perceptions. And he also learns something of the spirit of people who have lived, and are living, in close contact with the elements. In the course of this transformation, the planner— passing through his own version of the "bushed" experience—becomes deplanned, relieved of the top-down analytic assumptions that tend to inhibit pure perceptivity. With its versatility of form, breadth, existential candour, and imaginative play, *The Grey Islands* evokes the power of place as a meditative focus better than any other book I know. For Canadians, with our vexed and complicated relations to wilderness, it might well serve environmentalists as *Walden* or *Sand County Almanac* serve them south of the border.

VI The Alternate Guide

The title of this last section is borrowed from a book of poems published by Monty Reid in 1985. *The Alternate Guide* makes reference to two "official" guides: *A Nature Guide to Alberta*, which Reid edited for Hurtig Publishers, and the index to topographical maps of Alberta, which divides the province into the usual rigorous grid, irrespective of watersheds or landforms, with maps identified taxonomically as 83E, 83F, 83G, and so on. Against these institutional orders, he wrote a poem "situated" in each map, a provisional, temporally located riff connected with each locale. For example, the poem entitled (labelled?) "84F 8 11 78" refers to the Bison Lake sheet in the northwest of the province, and the eighth of November 1978.

you were like none of these:

> the tongue of hound's tongue
> beard of goat's beard
> foot of goose foot

not the strife in loose strife
rue in meadow rue
or the wind in wind flower

the bed in bedstraw
foam in foam flower
either term in pussy toes

not prickly pear
touch me not
or skull cap

anything in blazing star
witch's butter
monkshood

unlike even the pale
death camas fringing
the sloughs

especially

That poem is notable for its economy of gesture, its Creeleyan quickness, and for its refusal of comparative linkage which would begin the process of domesticating the flora to human emotion, adapting Shakespeare's reverse simile in declaring his mistress' eyes to be nothing like the sun. As it names the plants it simultaneously probes the viability of the names already conferred upon them. And as these denials accumulate, there is a complementary evocation of wild extra-linguistic space associated with the mysterious "you," an empty receptacle for energy alive with pure potential. Simile and nomination join the official maps and guides as institutions to be queried and probed in order to uncover the vigour of the experience.

Well, having followed one wandering path among Canadian nature poetries, from one viewpoint or outlook to another, I'm aware that some gesture to alternate guides, some hedge against institution, is necessary. The list that follows derives from my sense that many other paths and viewpoints are possible, any of which, on other occasions, I might have fruitfully followed. The idea of a canon, which is what occurs when institution sets itself too firmly among literary phenomena, seems especially inappropriate as the principle of coherence for nature poetries. Whether derived from an academic genealogy passed down from Matthew Arnold and F. R. Lewis, or from snap judgments of Grub Street reviewing, the canon affords the poet with a working context that is hierarchical, exclusionary, and patriarchal. The system of coherence that has, over the last century, come to be recognized as the model which acknowledges the complex interrelationship of the natural world and the interdependence of species, is, of course, ecosystem. Sometimes the link is across a wide distance, as in, say, the connection between me exhaling just now and permafrost melting in the Arctic (another version of the famous butterfly effect); sometimes the link is intimate, as in the symbiotic alliance of a fungus and an alga collaborating in a lichen species. Again and again we have learned, through one natural disaster or another, that we ignore the complexity of these interrelations at our peril, and that we ought to remain humble and embrace our unknowing when we come to contemplate interventions. The old canon idea is a useful notion if you are interested in keeping the art world tidy, designing a manageable university course, or creating political affiliates and outcasts. But, like the technological mindset which misjudges the complexity of ecosystems, it tends, at best, to oversimplify the situation among the poetries actually practised and divide them into the equivalent of flowers and weeds. At worst, it renders the environment toxic.

At the end of a textbook there is often a list headed "For Further Study," which generally means further study for the reader. Here, it means further study for the writer, but I won't be upset if you find something stimulating in it as well.

For Further Study:
- the canoe: the borrowed, exquisite native technology that permitted explorers to cross the country and powered the fur trade. Read this in terms of Canadian communications theory, Harold Innis, Marshall McLuhan, Arthur Kroker. Notice how the canoe often shifts, in the works of confederation poets (Bliss Carman, Charles G. D. Roberts, Archibald Lampman) into a mystical instrument of drift and idleness. Also the erotic, rapids-shooting mode of Pauline Johnson's "Wave-won," and the strange male-and-female canoe reposing on furs to be worshipped in Isabella Valancy Crawford's "The Canoe." A Jungian *conjunctio*?
- the garden: perhaps start with Lorna Crozier's *The Garden Going on Without Us*, balanced between domestic and wild nature, but tilted toward wilderness. Her famous "Sex Lives of the Vegetables" performing a kind of homage as it translates natural energy in terms of human eros. The old gardening gloves (in "Gloves"), the symbol that divides hand from world, becoming—paradoxically—the agent of connection. From there, move back to Marjorie Pickthall, Ethelwyn Wetherald, and Susanna

Moodie, and sideways to Robert Kroetsch's "Seed Catalogue." After genetic engineering, the seed is a political site as well as a natural one.

- Peter Sanger's terse, gnomic craft tuned to the spare subalpine landscapes of Atlantic Canada and to the iron relics of old smithies. Think about the importance of his collaboration in these projects (*Arborealis* and *Ironworks*) with photographer Thaddeus Holownia. Does poetry tend to turn from painting to photography when it leans away from impressionism and toward phenomenology?

- the practice of natural history and the practice of poetry. There is more to be learned from a study of the pressure that intimate and accurate observation places on language and form. Go back to early naturalists such as Ethelwyn Wetherald, Archibald Lampman, Seranus, and Charles G. D. Roberts, and bring these into resonance with current poets writing fine-grained perceptual work such as Brian Bartlett, Elizabeth Philips, Maureen Scott Harris, Jane Munro, Sue Sinclair, Jan Conn, and Tim Bowling.

- the shift from an ethos of mastery embedded in the colonial mindset to one of loss. George Grant, and the *via negativa* as discerned by Dennis Lee and Tim Lilburn are central here. The interior of that elegiac position is elaborated in the poetry and philosophy of Jan Zwicky. These call for a radical rethinking of the situation and allow for a redemptive mode of knowing called "lyric." Does her category of the "domestic" offer the possibility of occupying history differently? Zwicky's work seems like an essential metaphilosophy setting out ways in which key concepts can be reconstrued (music, history, wisdom, metaphor, poetry, and thinking itself) in the light of poetic modes of knowing. A figure as important as Grant in terms of conceptual shift, and an acute, heart-stopping poet.

- the aviary and the bestiary: it would be fascinating to follow the appearance of different species as seen through the lens of different poets. Follow especially white-throated sparrow, whippoorwill, sturgeon, moose, buffalo, and salmon through shifting ideas of wilderness.

- the poetry of the industrialized bush: poetry such as Peter Trower's brings into eloquent juxtaposition the romance of the logger (hearkening back to bunkhouse ballads such as those of Robert Swanson and Robert W. Service) with the devastation of the forest. His stance of complicit witness includes an informed account of the progress of technology: oxen to donkey engine to logging railway to chainsaw to logging road and truck. Interesting to place Trower's work alongside the celebration of conquering technology in E. J. Pratt's "The Last Spike."

- the regions: Is "Canadian" even a useful term? Place the pan-Canadian idea against the eloquent evocations of region in such poets as Charles Lillard and Tim Bowling (West Coast), Andrew Suknaski (Prairies), Phil Hall (rural Ontario), and Tom Dawe (Newfoundland). Ask the pointed question, and open the Pandora's box, of what is happening in French Canada.

- eco-feminism: investigate the theoretical and political poetics set forth by such thinkers as Daphne Marlatt, Di Brandt, and Pamela Banting. Is there, within the feminist perspective, an especially effective corrective to the colonial mindset?

- the seasons: start with Patrick Lane's deep symbolism in *Winter*. In our poetry, as in our conversation, the passage of the seasons is ever in the wings when it's not onstage. It comes from living in a country where, as Alden Nowlan remarked, the climate can kill you.

A last word. The environmental crisis has, until this point, been the unnamed elephant (or, perhaps more appropriately, great auk) in the room. All of us, as citizens of the planet, are called to amend our lives, to live less exploitatively and consumptively. And some, as artists of language—that is, poets— are also called to develop the sense organ that language listens with, to ensure that, as the effects of environmental degradation become more evident in decades to come, it is attending at a deep level. Even if, when it moves from listening to speaking, all it can utter is elegy. Even if it is all lament.

Don McKay

NOTES

1 Stan Dragland, *Floating Voice: Duncan Campbell Scott and the Literature of Treaty 9* (Toronto: Anansi, 1994), 5.
2 Dragland, 252.
3 Susan Glickman, *The Picturesque and the Sublime: A Poetics of the Canadian Landscape* (Montreal: McGill-Queen's University Press, 1998), vii.
4 David Hinton, trans., "Introduction," *The Selected Poems of Wang Wei* (New York: New Directions, 2006), xv.
5 William Wordsworth, *The Prelude* I: 374–400.
6 Dennis Lee, "Cadence, Country, Silence," *Body Music* (Toronto: Anansi, 1998), 14.
7 Lee, "Cadence, Country, Silence," 18.
8 Christopher Dewdney, "Author's Preface," *Predators of the Adoration* (Toronto: McClelland and Stewart, 1983), 7.
9 Lee, "Cadence, Country, Silence," 21.

 *The Poems*

THOMAS CARY (1751–1823)
from *Abram's Plains*

What tho' no mines their gold pour through thy stream,
Nor shining silver from thy waters gleam;
Equal to these, the forests yield their spoils,
And richly pay the skilful hunter's toils.
The beaver's silken fur to grace the head,
And, on the soldier's front assurance spread;
The martin's sables to adorn the fair,
And aid the silk-worm to set off her air.
Gems of *Golconda* or *Potosi's* mines,
Than these not more assist her eyes' designs.
The jetty fox to majesty adds grace,
And of grave justice dignifies the place;
The bulky buffalo, tall elk, the shaggy bear,
Huge carriboo, fleet moose, the swift-foot deer,
Gaunt wolf, amphibious otter, have their use,
And to thy worth, O first of floods! conduce.
For thee the sylvans of the forest bleed,
And, to the ax, their long-worn honors cede.
The sturdy oak, the lofty mountain-pine,
Their branching limbs and trunks mature resign;
Whilst Ceres, bounteous, from her gran'ries pours,
On craving realms, her grain in golden showers.
Nor is it want of climate or of soil
Thy shores not more the Muscovite's yet foil:
Our infant world asks but time's fost'ring hand,
Its faculties must by degrees expand.
Nor must thy own resources be past by,
Resources that within thy bosom lie;
The heavy porpus and the silly seal,
Their forfeit lives yield to the club or steel;
Soon of their skins and fat, reduc'd to oil,
The skilful fishers the dead victims spoil.
Here too the whale rolls his unwieldy form,
Laughs at the blust'ring winds and mocks the storm;

Gamesome, the billows far behind him throws,
And from his nostrils, a salt tempest blows:
Till, close beset, swift flies the barbed dart,
Down prone the monster dives to shun the smart;
The fishers, active, yield the smoking line,
The boats, like light'ning, cut the liquid brine;
Oft-times borne down beneath the briny wave,
Both boats and men share one wide watry grave:
His onward way, his doubles they pursue,
'Till, spent his strength, he panting floats in view;
Midst seas of blood wrathful his nostrils smoke,
An isle, his bare broad back lies to the stroke.
Now strong harpooners dart the iron death,
The monster force to yield his forfeit breath:
E'en while the waves he lashes into storm,
A monstrous mass floats motionless his form.
The grampus, of less bulk, stays his swift course,
Arrested on his way by iron force.
The fierce sea-cow, tho' cloth'd in stoutest mail,
Finds, 'gainst man's arts, his strength of small avail.
The salmon, cod, thy wave in myriads pours,
And, on far worlds, plenty redundant show'rs.
Next these the Naiades yield, for home supply,
Numbers, of various name and various dye.
The bass, rich flavor'd, high to pamper lust,
The pout or cat of no less luscious gust;
The speckled trout choice native of the lake,
'Tis thine the skilful angler's art to wake.
Thee silver white,* and thou bedropt with gold,*
The dusky eel, in circling volumes roll'd;
The bony shad, the poor man's bounteous friend,
E'er summer-suns dry roads and plenty send.
The weighty sturgeon, rank with native oil,
High fed from the fat river's slimy soil;
The autumn smelt, whose constant bite, tho' small,
E'er fix'd the ice, relief affords to all;
The winter tomi-cod when with feeble blaze,

From the bleak archer, Sol shoots oblique rays;
Then, from the ice-cot, on the frozen stream,
Through murky night, like meteors, fires gleam;
There, gather'd crouds, from the pierc'd solid flood,
With fleshy baits, attract the finny brood.

*The White-fish, and what the Canadians call the Poisson-doré or
Gold-fish.*
(1789)

ADAM ALLAN (1757–1823)

A Description of the Great Falls, of the River Saint John, in the Province of New Brunswick

Yes, "the commanding muse my chariot guides,
Which o'er the dubious cliff securely rides:
And pleas'd I am no beaten road to take,
But first the way to new discov'ries make."
                                        —Dryden.

A placid river, gliding easy on
To its dire Fall, o'er a huge bed of stone;
Into an abyss,—dreadful! even to thought,
Where caves immense by whirlpools are wrought;
And where huge trees, by annual freshes brought,
Are by incessant motion ground to nought.
See, where obstruction checks the torrent's way,
The part's announc'd by a vast mount of spray;
Where, as the sun its daily course pursues,
Reflects an arch of the most beauteous hues;
Combining elegance with scenes of horror,
Delight, and wonder, with most awful terror.
From this dread gulf of never-ending noise,
Resembling that where devils but rejoice,
The waters rush, like lava from the pits
Of fam'd Vesuvius, and Mount Etna's lips;
Foaming with rage, it forward presses on
From fall to fall, o'er variegated stone;
'Tween banks stupendous! seeming to the eye
An eagle's flight, when tow'ring to the sky.
This wond'rous chasm takes the crescent form,
The better its rude majesty to 'dorn;
So that, where'er you ramble for a view,
Each change of station shows you something new;
Verse colours faintly when strain'd from fiction,
Truth, here alone, has govern'd this description.

Now on the wings of fancy let me rove,
To paint the Fall, and margin of the grove,

In depth of winter,—when the river's bound,
And op'nings rarely but at falls are found.
How chang'd the scene!—each horror now is fled,
And frost's chill hand enchanting prospects made;
Now ev'ry tree is crystall'd on the shore:
The Fall, too, now most gorgeously appears,
Since purer waters aid its bold career;
Strong banks of ice contract its former bounds,
And under ice it echoes hollow sounds:
Around the verge what curious objects rise
To feed the fancy, and to feast the eyes!
Pilasters, arches, pyramids, and cones,
Turrets enrich'd with porticos and domes;
In artless order,—form'd by surge and spray,
And crystalline-garnet hues their rich array;
A dazzling cascade ground throughout the whole
Strikes deep with pleasure the enraptur'd soul.

(1798)

Ann Cuthbert Knight (1788–1860)
from *A Year in Canada*

PART SECOND

2.

Now while the frost still hangs on evening's train,
And mild at morn the melting south-wind blows,
'Tis time the maple's luscious juice to drain;
Sweet through the new-made wound the liquid flows.
The trees are pierced,—the vessels placed below,
Slow o'er th' inserted wedge the sap distils,
Beneath the cauldron crackling faggots glow,
And thick'ning o'er the fire the sugar boils,
Guiltless its sweets, for here no wretched Lybian toils.

(1816)

Adam Hood Burwell (1790–1849)
from *Talbot Road*

Now, first of all, on Talbot Road, began
The settlement, one solitary man;
An arduous task – unaided and alone,
The place a wilderness, and scarcely known;
But he, unmindful of surrounding toils,
Mock'd fortune's every frown – but caught her smiles—
He pierc'd the woods, his devious way he found,
And on the banks of Kettle Creek sat down.
Then bow'd the forest to his frequent stroke;—
There from his hearth ascended hallowed smoke;
Angels look'd down, propitious from above,
And o'er his labors breath'd celestial love:—
"Go on and prosper, for thine eyes shall see
The steps of thousands, soon to follow thee;
Go on and prosper, for the fostering hand
Of heaven, shall plant this highly favor'd land."
Now fame's loud, brazen trump began to sound,
The tidings flew thro' all the countries round...
From far and near, all flock'd the truth to know,
But found their expectations quite below
What now their eyes beheld. "O blissful land,"
They cried, "sure nature has with lavish hand
Scatter'd her sweets—how rich these vallies lie,
How soft the purling streams meander by!
How lofty, towering, these deep forests rise,
These pines, majestic, intercept the skies!
What stately columns, that, aspiring run
To heaven's blue arch, and hide the noon-day sun!
Sure, Liberty must call this favorite soil
Her own, and o'er the whole benignly smile;
How fitted to fair freedom's chosen race!
How might the goddess here her sons embrace!
Then why should it neglected, waste remain?
No—here's an offer—we'll return again;—
We will return again, and fetch our sons,

Our goods, our cattle, wives, and little ones.
Here long and happy days are kept in store,
And plenty teems—What can we look for more?"...

Now, ceaseless, crowd the emigrants along,
And moving families the country throng;
The fertile banks of Otter Creek, some take;
Some Talbot Road, and some prefer the lake;
While others claim'd a midway space between,
And all produced an animating scene.
Meantime the woodman's axe, with ardor plied,
Tumbles the tow'ring pines from side to side;
Fells the huge elms, and, with tremendous crash,
Brings down the steadfast oak, and lofty ash;
Which, pil'd , and interpil'd, present around,
A heap of chaos on th' encumber'd ground.
Not more, should Boreas from his windy hall,
Arm'd with fell ire, his blust'ring forces call,
And send them, howling, o'er the sylvan plain,
While headlong fly the rifted trees amain.
In heaps on heaps the shivered timbers lie,
A scene of terror to the astonish'd eye.
So crackling, crashing, thund'ring, plunging down,
The stateliest forest trees o'erspread the ground;
So roar'd, from day to day, their constant stroke,
So evening clos'd and so the morning broke.
Then rose the cabin rude, of humblest form,
To shield from rain, and guard against the storm;
Logs pil'd on logs, 'till closing overhead—
With ample sheets of bark of elms o'erspread,
And rough-hewn planks, to make a homely floor,
A paper window, and a blanket door....

Now Autumn's glowing suns with scorching ray,
Dried the fall'n timber, as exposed it lay,
Fit for the office of consuming fire,
Which soon shall execute the sentence dire.
The Woodman issues with a flaming brand,
Pluck'd from the hearth, brisk blazing in his hand;

Amongst the leafy brushwood fast he plies,
When lo! A hundred brilliant spires arise,
Columns of flame, and denser smoke that shrouds
The mid-day sun, and mingles with the clouds.
Wide wasting conflagration spreads around,
And quickly bares the bosom of the ground.
Herculean labors next demand the arm
Well nerv'd (such labors must begin the farm)
To pile the pond'rous logs, and clean the soil,
Which is perform'd not but with hardest toil...

Now, through the shades of the autumnal night,
The flaming log-heaps cast a glaring light
In contrast deep—the clouds, of sable hue,
Spread their dense mantle o'er the ethereal blue;
Above is pitchy blackness—all below
Wide flashing fires—Around, far other show—
Majestic trees, whose yet unfaded bloom,
In pale reflection, gives a sylvan gloom—
A dubious maze, which leads th' uncertain sight
To the drear confines of eternal night,
As it might seem:—While midst the raging fires,
That upward shoot a thousand forky spires,
Th' assiduous laborer plies his ready hands
To trim the heaps, and fire th' extinguish'd brands.

(1828)

Standish O'Grady (1793–1846)
from *The Emigrant*

Thou barren waste; unprofitable strand,
Where hemlocks brood on unproductive land,
Whose frozen air on one bleak winter's night
Can metamorphose *dark brown hares to white!*
Whose *roads* are *rivers*, o'er your fountains
See icebergs form your shining mountains,
And drifted snow, from arctic regions,
Gives sure employment to Canadians;
Here roads n'er known for many a summer,
Are now passt o'er by each new-comer,
All wrought one night, nor made of stone or gravel,
Complete withal and next day fit to travel,
Here forests crowd, unprofitable lumber,
O'er fruitless lands indefinite as number;
Where birds scarce light, and with the north winds veer
On wings of wind, and quickly disappear,
Here the rough Bear subsists his winter year,
And licks his paw and finds *no better fare*;
Here fishes swarm, now by reaction,
Congealed as ice seem petrifaction:
Till hottest ray with multiplying power
Dissolves and grants one genial shower.
In winter here, where all alike contrive,
And still withal few animals survive,
Till summer's heat, so potent and so quick,
Enough to make the *Crocodile grow sick*;
With vile mosquitoes, lord deliver us,
Whose stings could *blister a Rhinoceros.*
If on the living insects are thus fed,
How ill must fare the worms when we are dead!
Each pest conspires,—how idle is precaution,
We're eat by these or perish by exhaustion!
One month we hear birds, shrill and loud and harsh,

The plaintive bittern sounding from the marsh;
The next we see the fleet-winged swallow,
The duck, the woodcock, and the ice-birds follow;
Then comes, drear clime, the lakes all stagnant grow,
And the wild wilderness is rapt in snow.

(1842)

ADAM KIDD (1802–1831)
from *The Huron Chief*

The scene—the place—the happy hour—
Reminded much of MILTON'S bower:
Where first the parent of mankind
    Conducted Eve—with beauty blushing,
And feelings pure, and unconfined,
    As yon pellucid stream, now gushing
From the lovely arbour's side,
Clear as was then Euphrate's tide.

And here is seen the caraboo,
The elk, and wild deer, roving through
The silent forest's deep'ning shade—
    Nor distant is the swan—renewing
Pride, which for herself was made—
    Now, in the liquid mirror viewing
A graceful form—much whiter still
Than snow flakes on the Alpine hill.

While others feel the magic hand
Of love, their every thought command—
My 'raptured soul delights to trace,
    The charms which beauty round discloses,
Throughout this sweet, romantic place,
    To where the lily calm reposes,
Now on its half reclining stem,
Supporting Nature's purest gem.

And how the eye delights to see,
The humming-bird,[1] from tree to tree
So nimbly flit, till it can find
    Some blushing rose, with nectar in it,
Where, on a wing more fleet than wind,
    It banquets for a little minute,
Then quickly off it darting goes,
To seek elsewhere another rose.

And oh! how charming is the bliss—
So seldom felt—so pure as this,
Where in the forest's bosom far,
   From Europe's crimes, and Europe's errors,
Beneath the glowing western star,
   The Indian dwells secure from terrors[2]—
And by his streams, or by his lakes,
His path of independence takes.

NOTES

1 This is one of the prettiest little creatures among the feathered tribe. There are many species of them; but the smallest seems no larger than the wild black bee, which it imitates in feeding on the purest flowers. The richest fancy of the most luxuriant painter could never invent any thing to be compared to the beautiful tints with which this little miniature insect bird is arrayed. The wings are a deep green, and throw a variety of shades. The fine downy feathers on its head are embellished with the purest yellow, the most perfect azure, and dazzling red. When feeding, it appears immoveable, though continually on the wing, having its long fine bill dipped into the heart of the most delicate rose without the slightest injury, while its eyes appear like little diamonds sparkling in the morning sunbeam. It is very restless, and seldom perches for more than a few seconds at a time.

2 We and our kindred tribes—observe the Indians—lived in peace and harmony with each other before the white people came into this country—our Council-house extended far to the north and far to the south. In the middle of it we would meet from all parts to smoke the pipe of peace together.

WILLIAM KIRBY (1817–1906)
from *The U.E.*, *"Niagara"*

Now sailed the cloudless moon through seas of light
And dimmed the sleepless stars that watch the night,
As swiftly turning from the sandy lane
The riders crossed a spacious rolling plain,
Hedged by the lofty screen of dusky woods
That hide Niagara's deep-embedded floods.
White clouds of mist rolled upward on the breeze,
Swept o'er the brink, and dripped among the trees;
While earth and air, in tremor all around,
Shook in dread cadence to the rumbling sound
That rises up from Nature's troubled womb,
With war unbroken till the day of doom.
They hurried on; the woody veil withdrew,
The wondrous vision swept full into view;
Niagara's twin-born cataracts descend,
And eye and ear with their contention rend.
A spot of chaos, from Creation's day
Left unsubdued, to show the world alway
What was the earth ere God's commandment ran
That light should be, and order first began.

The riders halt, and for a moment stay,
While Ranger John half chid the brief delay.
Though often seen before, with fresh desire
The glorious vision still they each admire.
Spread o'er the south, a furious tumbling sea
Rolls down the steep incline, as wild and free
As when with tossing heads and flowing manes
The desert steeds in herds sweep o'er the plains,?
As in th'Olympic Stadium's final round
The chariot wheels revolve with thundering sound,
While veiled in clouds of dust the champions fly,
And shouts and turmoil shake the earth and sky!

Thus down the rocky rapids, side by side,
A thousand foaming currents madly ride;
Now mingling, now dividing, each and all

Still swifter hurry to the final goal.
There, waves that washed Superior's rocky strand,
And rolled transparent o'er her silver sand,
So pure and limpid, that they seem to bear
The bark canoe afloat in very air,
Now, lashed to madness, o'er the rapids ran,
Yoked to the darker waves of Michigan;
St Clair's shoal streams, and Huron's haunted floods
That trembled round the Manitoulin woods,
And fretful Erie's waters, in dismay
Sweep white with terror down the shelvy way.

In vain, Goat Island, dank, and grim with scars
Of an eternity of watery wars,
With stony shoulder stems the rushing tides
That right and left his dripping shore divides.
They 'scape his grasp, and o'er the jutting brink
Sheer down on either hand impetuous sink;
The vail of waters rending, as they go
'Mid storms of mist into the gulf below,
Where, face to face, the sundered torrents pour
In rival cataracts, with deafening roar,
Mingle their sprays, and with their mighty war
Shake earth's deep centre with eternal jar.

That dread abyss! What mortal tongue may tell
The seething horrors of its watery hell!
Where, pent in craggy walls that gird the deep,
Imprisoned tempests howl, and madly sweep
The tortured floods, drifting from side to side
In furious vortices, that circling ride
Around the deep arena; or, set free
From depths unfathomed, bursts a boiling sea
In showers of mist and spray, that leap and bound
Against the dripping rocks; while loud resound
Ten thousand thunders, that as one conspire
To strike the deepest note of Nature's lyre.

(1859)

ALEXANDER MCLACHLAN (1818–1896)
The Hall of Shadows

The sun is up, and through the woods
    His golden rays are streaming;
The dismal swamp and swale so damp
    With faces bright are beaming.
Down in the windfall by the creek
    We hear the partridge drumming,
And strange bright things on airy wings
    Are all around us humming.

The merry school boys in the woods
    The chipmunk are pursuing,
And, as he starts, with happy hearts
    They're after him hallooing.
The squirrel hears the urchins' cheers—
    They never catch him lagging—
And on the beech, beyond their reach,
    Hear how the fellow's bragging!

The red-bird pauses in his song,
    The face of man aye fearing,
And flashes like a flame along
    The border of the clearing.
The humming-bird above the flow'r
    Is like a halo bending,
Or like the gleams we catch in dreams,
    Of heav'nly things descending.

List to the humming of the bee
    Among the tufted clover!
This day, like thee, I'll wander free,
    My little wildwood rover!
Through the groves of beech and maple green,
    And pines of lofty stature,
By this lone creek once more we'll seek
    The savage haunts of nature.

See! there a noble troop of pines
    Has made a sudden sally,

And all, in straight unbroken lines,
    Are rushing up the valley;
Now round about that lonely spring
    They gather in a cluster,
Then off again, till on the plain
    The great battalions muster.

And there the little evergreens
    Are clust'ring in the hollows,
And hazels green with sumachs lean
    Among the weeping willows;
Or sit in pride the creek beside,
    Or through the valley ramble,
Or up the height in wild delight
    Among the rocks they scramble.

And here a gorge all reft and rent,
    With rocks in wild confusion,
As they were by the wood-gods sent
    To guard them from intrusion;
And gulfs all yawning wild and wide,
    As if by earthquakes shatter'd;
And rocks that stand, a grizzly band,
    By time and tempest batter'd.

Some great pines, blasted in their pride,
    Above the gorge are bending,
With rock elms from the other side
    Their mighty arms extending;
And midway down the dark descent
    One fearful hemlock's clinging—
His headlong fall he would prevent,
    And grapnels out is flinging.

One ash has ventured to the brink,
    And tremblingly looks over
That awful steep, where shadows sleep,
    And mists at noonday hover.
But farther in the woods we go,
    Through beech and maple alleys,

'Mid elms that stand like patriarchs grand
   In long dark leafy valleys.

Away! away from blue-eyed day,
   The sunshine and the meadows,
We find our way at noon of day
   Within the Hall of Shadows.
How like a great cathedral vast,
   With creeping vines roof'd over,
While shadows dim, with faces grim,
   Far in the distance hover

Among the old cathedral aisles
   And gothic arches bending,
And ever, in the sacred piles,
   The twilight gloom's descending.
Yet, let me turn where'er I will,
   A step is aye pursuing;
And there's an eye upon me still
   That's watching all I'm doing.

And in the center there's a pool,
   And by that pool is sitting
A shape of Fear, with shadows drear,
   Forever round her flitting.
Why is her face so full of woe,
   So hopeless and dejected?
Sees she but there, in her despair,
   Naught but herself reflected?

Is it the gloom within my heart,
   Or ling'ring superstition,
Which draws me here three times a year
   To this weird apparition?
I cannot tell what it may be:
   I only know that seeing
That shape of Fear draws me more near
   The secret Soul of Being.
(1874)

CHARLES SANGSTER (1822–1893)
from *The St. Lawrence and the Saguenay*

LXXIX.

In golden volumes rolls the blessed light
Along the sterile mountains. Pile on Pile
The granite masses rise to left and right:
Bald, stately bluffs that never wear a smile;
Where vegetation fails to reconcile
The parchèd shrubbery and stunted trees
To the stern mercies of the flinty soil.
And we must pass a thousand bluffs like these,
Within whose breasts are locked a myriad mysteries.

LXXX.

Here is a barren crag, at whose brown feet
Patiently sits the church and gleams the spire.
Commerce has found this a deserved retreat;
Here groan the mills, and there, the household fire
Sends up its smoke above the struggling briar
And dwarfish evergreens that grow between
The stubborn rocks—that grow but to expire.
Not here the thrifty farmer's face serene—
The lumberer alone lends life to the grim scene.

LXXXI.

No further evidence of life, save where
The young whales bask their broad backs in the sun,
Or the gay grampus, sportive as a hare,
Leaps and rejoices, playfully as one
In youth who sees some holiday begun.
Perhaps a crowded steamer, passing by,
Lights up the scene a moment. Trebly dun
The shades of sullen loneliness that lie
On rugged L'Ance l'eau when no living thing is nigh.

LXXXII.

Over the darkening waters! on through scenes
Whose unimaginable wildness fills
The mind with joy insatiate, and weans

The soul from earth, to Him whose Presence thrills
All Beauty as all Truth. These iron Hills!
In what profusion did He pile them here,
Thick as the flowers that blossom where the rills
Chant to the primal woods. Year after year
In solitude eternal, rapt in contemplation drear.

LXXXIII.

Dreaming of the old years before they rose
Triumphant from the deep, whose waters roll'd
Above their solemn and unknown repose;
Dreaming of that bright morning, when of old,
Beyond the Red Man's memory, they told
The Secrets of the Ages to the sun,
That smiled upon them from his throne of gold;
Dreaming of the bright stars and loving moon,
That first shone on them from the Night's impressive noon:

LXXXIV.

Dreaming of the long ages that have passed
Since then, and with them that diminished race
Whose birchen fleets these inky waters glassed,
As they swept o'er them with the wind's swift pace.
Of their wild legends scarce remains a trace;
Thou hold'st the myriad secrets in thy brain,
Oh! stately bluffs! As well seek to efface
The light of the bless'd stars, as to obtain
From thy sealed, granite lips, tradition or refrain!

LXXXV.

But they are there, though man may never know
Their number or their beauty. Pass the eye
Along the ever-looming scene, where'er we go,
Through these long corridors of rock and sky—
What startling barriers, rising sullenly
From the dark deeps, like giants, seem to place
An adamantine gateway, close and high,
To bar our progress; meet them face to face,
The magic doors fly open, and the rocks recede apace.

(1856)

GEORGE MARTIN (1822–1900)
The Jewelled Trees

I.

On the verge of the month of the white new year,
When friend to friend gives heartiest cheer,
The rain and the frost for a night and a day
Have cunningly worked alternately.
They have thickened the crust of the dazzling snow
Over whose surface the cold winds blow;
They have fringed the eaves with their old device,
Enormous daggers of glittering ice;
And the nails in the walls, where in summer time
The scarlet-runners were wont to climb,
They have crowned with gems more bright, more fair,
Than eastern queens on their bosoms wear.
But scarcely a glance do we waste on these,
For our wonder is fixed on the jewelled trees;
Never before, in all their days,
Have they borne such beauty for mortal gaze;
On them the frost and the rain have wrought
A splendour that could not be sold or bought,
Heavily laden from foot to crown,
Like fairest of brides with heads bowed down,
In park and square, demurely they stand,—
Stand by the wayside all over the land.
Thick-crusted with pearls of marvellous size,
Whose lustre rebukes our aching eyes.

II.

Thus for a night and a day have they stood,
Modest and chaste in their virginhood;
But are they as happy, as joyful at heart,
As when, in green vesture, they gladly took part
In all the fresh bliss that to spring-time they owed,—
In all the hot pleasure that summer bestowed?
"Nay, verily, nay!" I hear them repeat;
The blood in our veins, even down to our feet,

Is gelid and still,—we are sick unto death;
Oh send us, ye heavens! Oh send us a breath
Of warmth that will bear all these jewels away!
These fetters that we for a night and day
Have borne in silence with infinite pain!
Oh give us our freedom! our bare arms again!"

III.

A wind that had slept all this time in the south,
In an orange grove that was faint from drouth,
Heard the soft plaint of the jewelled trees,
And came in the guise of a gentle breeze,—
Came, and with kisses tenderly
Unbound the captives, and set them free.
Their crystalline chains were broken asunder,
Filling all earth with a blinding wonder;—
With a crash and a flash and a musical sound,
Like a shower of stars they fell to the ground;
And, freed from their bondage, the grateful trees
In their bare brown arms caressed the breeze,
Caressed the wind that came from the south,
From the orange grove that was faint from drouth;
And they wept for joy, their thanks they wept,
While the wind lay still in their arms and slept.

(1889)

CHARLES MAIR (1838–1927)
The Last Bison

Eight years have fled since, in the wilderness,
I drew the rein to rest my comrade there—
My supple, clean-limbed pony of the plains.
He was a runner of pure Indian blood,
Yet in his eye still gleamed the desert's fire,
And form and action both bespoke the Barb.
A wondrous creature is the Indian's horse;
Degenerate now, but from the "Centaurs" drawn—
The apparitions which dissolved with fear
Montezuma's plumed Children of the Sun,
And throned rough Cortez in his realm of gold!

A gentle vale, with rippling aspens clad,
Yet open to the breeze, invited rest.
So there I lay, and watched the sun's fierce beams
Reverberate in wreathed ethereal flame;
Or gazed upon the leaves which buzzed o'erhead,
Like tiny wings in simulated flight.
Within the vale a lakelet, lashed with flowers,
Lay like a liquid eye among the hills,
Revealing in its depths the fulgent light
Of snowy cloud-land and cerulean skies.
And rising, falling, fading far around,
The homeless and unfurrowed prairies spread
In solitude and idleness eterne.

And all was silence save the rustling leaf,
The gadding insect, or the grebe's lone cry,
Or where Saskatchewan, with turbid moan,
Deep-sunken in the plain, his torrent poured.
Here Loneliness possessed her realm supreme,
Her prairies all about her, undeflowered,
Pulsing beneath the summer sun, and sweet
With virgin air and waters undefiled.
Inviolate still! Bright solitudes, with power
To charm the spirit—bruised where ways are foul—

Into forgetfulness of chuckling wrong,
And all the weary clangour of the world.

Yet, Sorrow, too, had here its kindred place,
As o'er my spirit swept the sense of change.
Here sympathy could sigh o'er man's decay;
For here, but yesterday, the warrior dwelt
Whose faded nation had for ages held,
In fealty to Nature, these domains.
Around me were the relics of his race—
The grassy circlets where his village stood,
Well-ruled by custom's immemorial law.
Along these slopes his happy offspring roved
In days gone by, and dusky mothers plied
Their summer tasks, or loitered in the shade.
Here the magician howled his demons up,
And here the lodge of council had its seat,
Once resonant, with oratory wild.
All vanished! perished in the swelling sea
And stayless tide of an enroaching power
Whose civil fiat, man-devouring still,
Will leave, at last, no wilding on the earth
To wonder at or love!
                              With them had fled
The bison-breed which overflowed the plains,
And, undiminished, fed uncounted tribes.
Its vestiges were here—its wallows, paths,
And skulls and shining ribs and vertabræ;
Gray bones of monarchs from the herds, perchance,
Descended, by De Vaca first beheld,
Or Coronado, in mad quest of gold.
Here hosts had had their home; here had they roamed,
Endless and infinite—vast herds which seemed
Exhaustless as the sea. All vanished now!
Of that wild tumult not a hoof remained
To scour the countless paths where myriads trod.

Long had I lain 'twixt dreams and waking, thus,
Musing on change and mutability,

And endless evanescence, when a burst
Of sudden roaring filled the vale with sound.
Perplexed and startled, to my feet I sprang,
And in amazement from my covert gazed,
For, presently, into the valley came
A mighty bison, which, with stately tread
And gleaming eyes, descended to the shore!
Spell-bound I stood. Was this a living form,
Or but an image by the fancy drawn?
But no—he breathed! and from a wound blood flowed,
And trickled with the frothing from his lips.
Uneasily he gazed, yet saw me not,
Haply concealed; then, with a roar so loud
That all the echos rent their valley-horns,
He stood and listened; but no voice replied!
Deeply he drank, then lashed his quivering flanks,
And roared again, and hearkened, but no sound,
No tongue congenial answered to his call—
He was the last survivor of his clan!

Huge was his frame! the famed Burdash, so grown
To that enormous bulk whose presence filled
The very vale with awe. His shining horns
Gleamed black amidst his fell of floating hair—
His neck and shoulders, of the lion's build,
Were framed to toss the world! Now stood he there
And stared, with head uplifted, at the skies,
Slow-yielding to his deep and mortal wound.
He seemed to pour his mighty spirit out
As thus he gazed, till my own spirit burned,
And teeming fancy, charmed and overwrought
By all the wildering glamour of the scene,
Gave to that glorious attitude a voice,
And, rapt, endowed the noble beast with song.

THE SONG

Hear me, ye smokeless skies and grass-green earth,
Since by your sufferance still I breathe and live!
Through you fond Nature gave me birth,

And food and freedom—all she had to give.
Enough! I grew, and with my kindred ranged
Their realm stupendous, changeless and unchanged,
        Save by the toll of nations primitive,
Who throve on us, and loved our life-stream's roar,
And lived beside its wave, and camped upon its shore.

They loved us, and they wasted not. They slew
        With pious hand, but for their daily need;
Not wantonly, but as the due
        Of stern necessity which Life doth breed.
Yea, even as earth gave us herbage meet,
So yielded we, in turn, our substance sweet
        To quit the claims of hunger, not of greed.
So stood it with us that what either did
Could not be on the earth foregone, nor Heaven forbid.

And, so, companioned in the blameless strife
        Enjoined upon all creatures, small and great,
Our ways were venial, and our life
        Ended in fair fulfilment of our fate.
No gold to them by sordid hands was passed;
No greedy herdsman housed us from the blast;
        Ours was the liberty of regions rife.
In winter's snow, in summer's fruits and flowers—
Ours were the virgin prairies, and their rapture ours!

So fared it with us both; yea, thus it stood
        In all our wanderings from place to place,
Until the red man mixed his blood
        With paler currents. Then arose a race—
The reckless hunters of the plains—who vied
In wanton slaughter for the tongue and hide,
        To satisfy vain ends and longings base.
This grew; and yet we flourished, and our name
Prospered until the pale destroyer's concourse came.

Then fell a double terror on the plains,
        The swift inspreading of destruction dire—
Strange men, who ravaged our domains

On every hand, and ringed us round with fire;
Pale enemies, who slew with equal mirth
The harmless or the hurtful things of earth,
        In dead fruition of their mad desire:
The ministers of mischief and of might,
Who yearn for havoc as the world's supreme delight.

So waned the myriads which had waxed before
    When subject to the simple needs of men.
As yields to eating seas the shore,
    So yielded our vast multitude, and then—
It scattered! Meagre bands, in wild dismay,
Were parted and, for shelter, fled away
        To barren wastes, to mountain gorge and glen.
A respite brief from stern pursuit and care,
For still the spoiler sought, and still he slew us there.

Hear me, thou grass-green earth, ye smokeless skies,
    Since by your sufferance still I breathe and live!
The charity which man denies
    Ye still would tender to the fugitive!
I feel your mercy in my veins—at length
My heart revives, and strengthens with your strength—
        Too late, too late, the courage ye would give!
Naught can avail these wounds, this failing breath,
This frame which feels, at last, the wily touch of death.

Here must the last of all his kindred fall;
    Yet, midst these gathering shadows, ere I die—
Responsive to an inward call,
    My spirit fain would rise and prophesy.
I see our spoilers build their cities great
Upon our plains—I see their rich estate:
        The centuries in dim procession fly!
Long ages roll, and then at length is bared
The time when they who spared not are no longer spared.

Once more my vision sweeps the prairies wide,
    But now no peopled cities greet the sight;
All perished, now, their pomp and pride:

In solitude the wild wind takes delight.
Naught but the vacant wilderness is seen,
And grassy mounds, where cities once had been.
    The earth smiles as of yore, the skies are bright,
Wild cattle graze and bellow on the plain,
And savage nations roam o'er native wilds again!

The burden ceased, and now, with head bowed down,
The bison smelt, then grinned into the air.
An awful anguish seized his giant frame,
Cold shudderings and indrawn gaspings deep—
The spasms of illimitable pain.
One stride he took, and sank upon his knees,
Glared stern defiance where I stood revealed,
Then swayed to earth, and, with convulsive groan,
Turned heavily upon his side and died.

(1890)

ISABELLA VALANCY CRAWFORD (1850–1887)
The Lily Bed

His cedar paddle, scented, red,·
He thrust down through the lily bed;

Cloaked in a golden pause he lay,
Locked in the arms of the placid bay.

Trembled alone in his bark canoe
As shocks of bursting lilies flew

Thro' the still crystal of the tide,
And smote the frail boat's birchen side;

Or, when beside the sedges thin
Rose the sharp silver of a fin;

Or, when a wizard swift and cold,
A dragon-fly beat out in gold

And jewels all the widening rings
Of waters singing to his wings;

Or, like a winged and burning soul,
Dropped from the gloom of an oriole

On the cool wave, as to the balm
Of the Great Spirit's open palm

The freed soul flies. And silence clung
To the still hours, as tendrils hung,

In darkness carven, from the trees,
Sedge-buried to their burly knees.

Stillness sat in his lodge of leaves;
Clung golden shadows to its eaves,

And on its cone-spiced floor, like maize,
Red-ripe, fell sheaves of knotted rays.

The wood, a proud and crested brave;
Bead-bright, a maiden, stood the wave.

And he had spoke his soul of love
With voice of eagle and of dove.

Of loud, strong pines his tongue was made;
His lips, soft blossoms in the shade,

That kissed her silver lips—hers cool
As lilies on his inmost pool—

Till now he stood, in triumph's rest,
His image painted in her breast.

One isle 'tween blue and blue did melt,—
A bead of wampum from belt

Of Manitou—a purple rise
On the far shore heaved to the skies.

His cedar paddle, scented, red,
He drew up from the lily bed,

All lily-locked, all lily-locked,
His light bark in the blossoms rocked.

Their cools lips round the sharp prow sang,
Their soft clasp to the frail sides sprang,

With breast and lip they wove a bar.
Stole from her lodge the Evening Star;

With golden hand she grasped the mane
Of a red cloud on her azure plain.

It by the peaked, red sunset flew;
Cool winds from its bright nostrils blew.

They swayed the high, dark trees, and low
Swept the locked lilies to and fro.

With cedar paddle, scented, red,
He pushed out from the lily bed.

(1905) [1884]

from *Malcolm's Katie*

from PART II

The South Wind laid his moccasins aside,
Broke his gay calumet of flow'rs, and cast
His useless wampum, beaded with cool dews,
Far from him northward; his long ruddy spear,
Flung sunward, whence it came, and his soft locks
Of warm, fine haze grew silver as the birch.
His wigwam of green leaves began to shake;
The crackling rice-beds scolded harsh like squaws;
The small ponds pouted up their silver lips;
The great lakes ey'd the mountains, whisper'd "Ugh!"
"Are ye so tall, O chiefs? Not taller than
Our plumes can reach," And rose a little way,
As panthers stretch to try their velvet limbs
And then retreat to purr and bide their time.
At morn the sharp breath of the night arose
From the wide prairies, in deep-struggling seas,
In rolling breakers, bursting to the sky;
In tumbling surfs, all yellow'd faintly thro'
With the low sun—in mad, conflicting crests,
Voic'd with low thunder from the hairy throats
Of the mist-buried herds; and for a man
To stand amid the cloudy roll and moil,
The phantom waters breaking overhead,
Shades of vex'd billows bursting on his breast,
Torn caves of mist wall'd with a sudden gold—
Resealed as swift as seen—broad, shaggy fronts,
Fire-ey'd, and tossing on impatient horns
The wave impalpable—was but to think
A dream of phantoms held him as he stood.
The late, last thunders of the summer crash'd
Where shrieked great eagles, lords of naked cliffs.
The pulseless forest, lock'd and interlock'd
So closely, bough with bough, and leaf with leaf,
So serf'd by its own wealth, that while from high
The moons of summer kiss'd its green-glossed locks;

And round its knees the merry West Wind danc'd;
And round its ring, compacted emerald;
The south wind crept on moccasins of flame;
And the red fingers of th' impatient sun
Pluck'd at its outmost fringes—its dim veins
Beat with no life—its deep and dusky heart,
In a deep trance of shadow, felt no throb
To such soft wooing answer: thro' its dream
Brown rivers of deep waters sunless stole;
Small creeks sprang from its mosses, and amaz'd,
Like children in a wigwam curtain'd close
Above the great, dead heart of some red chief,
Slipp'd on soft feet, swift stealing through the gloom,
Eager for light and for the frolic winds.
In this shrill moon the scouts of winter ran
From the ice-belted north, and whistling shafts
Struck maple and struck sumach—and a blaze
Ran swift from leaf to leaf, from bough to bough,
Till round the forest flashed a belt of flame
And inward lick'd its tongues of red and gold
To the deep, tranied, inmost heart of all.
Rous'd the still heart—but all too late, too late.
Too late, the branches welded fast with leaves,
Toss'd, loosen'd, to the winds—too late the sun
Poured his last vigour to the deep, dark cells
Of the dim wood. The keen, two-bladed Moon
Of Falling Leaves roll'd up on crested mists,
And where the lush, rank boughs had foil'd the sun
In his red prime, her pale, sharp fingers crept
After the wind and felt about the moss,
And seem'd to pluck from shrinking twig and stem
The burning leaves—while groaned the shudd'ring wood.

(1884)

ETHELWYN WETHERALD (1857–1940)
Unheard Niagaras

We live among unheard Niagaras.
The force that pushes up the meadow grass,
That swells to ampler roundness ripening fruit,
That lifts the brier rose, were it not mute,
Would thunder o'er the green earth's sunlit tracts
More loudly than a myriad cataracts.

(1902)

The Hornèd Larks in Winter

Where the tufted red-root
  Rises from the snow,
See the flock of hornèd larks
  Crouching low,
Beating, shaking all the seeds
From the dry pods of the weeds,
Calling from the knolls and furrows
  As they go.

Lovers of the plowed field
  And the open sun,
Pacing thoughtfully the ruts
  One by one.
On each delicate small head
Black and white are closely wed,
And the horn-like tufts are lowered
  When they run.

Serious little fellows!
  Who would e'er surmise
That such grave field labourers
  Could arise,
Shaking from their yellow throats
Ravishing cloud-surrounded notes,
Flinging up the joy of springtime
  To the skies.

(1931)

SUSAN FRANCES HARRISON [SERANUS] (1859–1935)
   Rhapsodie (II)

Ring'd round with the dark green St. Laurent our isle as a jewel is set,
Moss'd agate in emerald rimm'd with an amethyst rare,
One link in the leafy green chain, one star in the stone coronet,

That crowns and encircles the brow of the peerless and proud rivulet,
A diadem Deity-plac'd—and a mortal's despair!
Ring'd round with the dark green St. Laurent our isle as a jewel is set,

While glowing with feverish garnet, its sands sparkle bright in the wet,
And clear as Brazilian topaz its summit declare
One link in the leafy green chain, one star in the stone coronet.

The lichen upon it is writing in God's orange own alphabet,
And dimly we measure its message, while past all compare
Ring'd round with the dark green St. Laurent our isle as a jewel is set.

And here as we stand on its summit, glad warders on grey parapet,
A thousand such jewels are sparkling in midsummer air;
One link in the leafy green chain, one star in the stone coronet,

One gem, and but one—of a thousand—is this whereon rest has been
   met,
And dimly we worship its beauty, while shining and fair,
Ring'd round with the dark green St. Laurent our isle as a jewel is set,
One link in the leafy green chain, one star in the stone coronet.

(1891)

A Canadian Anthology
(Of Flowers)

As once the Greek Meleager wove in verse
A chaplet for the bards of his own land,
Theocritus, and Simmias, Plato too,
All, all of the flowers, with ivy, cypress, grape,
Roses of Sappho, crocus, cyclamen—
So, for the dear Unknown across the seas,
And under Afric stars, and where the smoke
Of pulsing geysers rises in Maori land,
And even where Ganges rolls its lamp-lit flood,
For all who make the Empire (and all are friends),
I make a song in Canada to-day,
The song of her own flowers, not England's, nor
Another's, but her own. See—I have plucked
In fancy, some of the ivory blood-root buds
And twined with them the yellow violet,
No shrinking blossom this, but strong and erect
From sturdy clumps, encompassed by its leaves
Of fearless mien, protectress too of one
Like to itself, but timid, scented, white—
Viola blanda is her gentle name;
And further in the forest paths I sought
And found (for you) the ruby-tinted bells
Of sweet Linnæa, with perchance a stalk
Grey-curved and curious, of Indian Pipe,
Pale Monotropa, loving not the sun
Yet nurtured near the Trillium, all in threes,
Bravest of blossoms born in moist mid-May,
The children's choice, the nation's favourite,
Giving its light to darkest interlace
Of fallen log and fern. Still other prize
I have for you—in windy open fields
Blow saffron lilies and Asclepias
The orange Butterfly-Weed, Lupinus blue;
Calypso, Arethusa, Orchids twain,
I'll find, be sure, with Kypris' Moccasin-Flower,

The Painted Cup, all redolent of Spain,
Gay Castilleia, Sarracenia
Or Pitcher-Plant in hooded vesture drest,
Weird marvel of the marsh and irised pools;
Rhodora's clusters purple-rose in hue,
Andromeda, and Kalmia, Wintergreen;
Mitchella's scarlet berries, and the odorous
Arbutus, I must have, and the wild Calla
Gleaming in streamlets like a patch of snow,
And where the clearing slides along the rail
Pink Epilobium spires I'll gather in
With blackberry and vivid Golden-Rod,
Still on the prairie waves the fair Wind-Flower,
Anemone, but so unlike the frail
Anemone nemorosa of the wood!
And these are not all. Our Northern Rivers yield
Tall spikes of Cardinal flower and sumach bright,
And on the mountain slopes, corollas rare
(Celestial azure, crystal-cinctured) grow,
With gentian and azaleas. Maiden-hair
From dripping cliffs, and birch bark satin-smooth,
I must not miss, nor Nuphar's lovely cup;
Waxen Nymphæa and the Dragon-Root,
Wild rice, and Indian hemp, and plumed beach-grass,
Polygala's fringes and the fairy star
Of Trientalis whorled in emerald—
Must I not wait for these, Dicentra too,
And pearly "everlastings" and the spoils
Of fruited moss and cinnamon fungi, mats
Of hemlock twigs and tassels of the larch?
Yet are there more. What of the radiant lanes
Where warm peach-petals colour the fragrant air
For miles and miles of old Niagara's strand—
Not only for the rich, not glassed or walled
But full in sight for all. What of the bloom
Where eastern orchards burst their bonds in spring,
(And apples grow more rosy toward the sea);
And then—the misty berries of the North,

Blue as an infant's eye and kindly spread
O'er leagues Laurentian, plateau, stone, and dyke!
These will I add, and many a marvel more,
And I will dream that he, Meleager, came
And saw these wonders, and, working in his mind
Came Envy, Malice, and all Uncharitableness,
Fears, lest his own Anthology be found
Wanting, till later, better feelings filled
His heart; at last he spake—I hear the names
Of Græcia's Nymphs and Goddesses given to flowers
Growing in this far land, new land of snows
And boundless waters—I marvel much at this.
—And I, divining, answered—It is true,
And true of other things, for, like the Greek,
We love all waters. Mariners all are we,
Each one a proud Odysseus sailing thro'
The island channels or on craggy shores
Building the beacons that shall lead us home
Across the many-rivered, rocky plain,
Spangled with lakes and foaming waterfalls.
Mirth-merry at the thought I gave him roots
Of Aquilegia, gallant, spurred and gay—
Of Erythronium, saying—"Go and plant
These (if you have them not) in Ithaca
And watch if they flourish." But for all the rest
They are for all the friends in distant climes,
For all who make the Empire (plucked by one,
A lover of her country, coast to coast)
For whom this floral wreath I weave to-day
Bound with a branch of crimson Maple Leaf,
And may my loving Coronal of Song
"Be for all such as love these holy things."

(2000) [1928]

WILFRED CAMPBELL (1860–1918)
Indian Summer

Along the line of smoky hills
    The crimson forest stands,
And all the day the blue-jay calls
    Throughout the autumn lands.

Now by the brook the maple leans
    With all his glory spread,
And all the sumachs on the hills
    Have turned their green to red.

Now by great marshes wrapt in mist,
    Or past some river's mouth,
Throughout the long, still autumn day
    Wild birds are flying south.

(1889)

How One Winter Came in the Lake Region

For weeks and weeks the autumn world stood still,
    Clothed in the shadow of a smoky haze;
The fields were dead, the wind had lost its will,
And all the lands were hushed by wood and hill,
    In those grey, withered days.

Behind a mist the blear sun rose and set,
    At night the moon would nestle in a cloud;
The fisherman, a ghost, did cast his net;
The lake its shores forgot to chafe and fret,
    And hushed its caverns loud.

Far in the smoky woods the birds were mute,
    Save that from blackened tree a jay would scream,
Or far in swamps the lizard's lonesome lute
Would pipe in thirst, or by some gnarlèd root
    The tree-toad trilled his dream.

From day to day still hushed the season's mood,
    The streams stayed in their runnels shrunk and dry;
Suns rose aghast by wave and shore and wood,
And all in the world, with ominous silence, stood
    In weird expectancy:

When one strange night the sun like blood went down,
    Flooding the heavens in a ruddy hue;
Red grew the lake, the sere fields parched and brown,
Red grew the marshes where the creeks stole down,
    But never a wind-breath blew.

That night I felt the winter in my veins,
    A joyous tremor of the icy glow;
And woke to hear the north's wild vibrant strains,
While far and wide, by withered woods and plains,
    Fast fell the driving snow.

(1890)

CHARLES G. D. ROBERTS (1860–1943)
The Clearing

Stumps, and harsh rocks, and prostrate trunks all charred,
    And gnarled roots naked to the sun and rain,—
    They seem in their grim stillness to complain,
And by their plaint the evening peace is jarred.
These ragged acres fire and the axe have scarred,
    And many summers not assuaged their pain.
    In vain the pink and saffron light, in vain
The pale dew on the hillocks stripped and marred!

But here and there the waste is touched with cheer
    Where spreads the fire-weed like a crimson flood
And venturous plumes of goldenrod appear;
    And round the blackened fence the great boughs lean
With comfort; and across the solitude
    The hermit's holy transport peals serene.

(1891)

from "Ave!"
(An Ode for Shelley Centenary, 1892)

I

O tranquil meadows, grassy Tantramar,
    Wide marshes ever washed in clearest air,
Whether beneath the sole and spectral star
    The dear severity of dawn you wear,
Or whether in the joy of ample day
    And speechless ecstasy of growing June
You lie and dream the long blue hours away
        Till nightfall comes too soon,
Or whether, naked to the unstarred night,
You strike with wondering awe my inward sight,—

II

You know how I have loved you, how my dreams
    Go forth to you with longing, through the years
That turn not back like your returning streams
    And fain would mist the memory with tears,
Though the inexorable years deny
    My feet the fellowship of your deep grass,
O'er which, as o'er another, tenderer sky,
        Cloud phantoms drift and pass,—
You know my confident love, since first, a child,
Amid your wastes of green I wandered wild.

III

Inconstant, eager, curious, I roamed;
    And ever your long reaches lured me on;
And ever o'er my feet your grasses foamed,
    And in my eyes your far horizons shone.
But sometimes would you (as a stillness fell
    And on my pulse you laid a soothing palm)
Instruct my ears in your most secret spell;
        And sometimes in the calm
Initiate my young and wondering eyes
Until my spirit grew more still and wise.

IV

Purged with high thoughts and infinite desire
   I entered fearless the most holy place,
Received between my lips the secret fire,
   The breath of inspiration on my face.
But not for long these rare illumined hours,
   The deep surprise and rapture not for long.
Again I saw the common, kindly flowers,
     Again I heard the song
Of the glad bobolink, whose lyric throat
Pealed like a tangle of small bells afloat.

V

The pounce of mottled marsh-hawk on his prey;
   The flicker of sand-pipers in from sea
In gusty flocks that puffed and fled; the play
   Of field-mice in the vetches,—these to me
Were memorable events. But most availed
   Your strange unquiet waters to engage
My kindred heart's companionship; nor failed
     To grant this heritage,—
That in my veins forever must abide
The urge and fluctuation of the tide.

VI

The mystic river whence you take your name,
   River of hubbub, raucous Tantramar,
Untamable and changeable as flame,
   It called me and compelled me from afar,
Shaping my soul with its impetuous stress.
   When in its gaping channel deep withdrawn
Its waves ran crying of the wilderness
     And winds and stars and dawn,
How I companioned them in speed sublime,
Led out a vagrant on the hills of Time!

VII

And when the orange flood came roaring in
   From Fundy's tumbling troughs and tide-worn caves,

While red Minudie's flats were drowned with din
    And rough Chignecto's front oppugned the waves,
How blithely with the refluent foam I raced
    Inland along the radiant chasm, exploring
The green solemnity with boisterous haste;
      My pulse of joy outpouring
To visit all the creeks that twist and shine
From Beauséjour to utmost Tormentine.

VIII

And after, when the tide was full, and stilled
    A little while the seething and the hiss,
And every tributary channel filled
    To the brim with rosy streams that swelled to kiss
The grass-roots all awash and goose-tongue wild
    And salt-sap rosemary,—then how well content
I was to rest me like a breathless child
      With play-time rapture spent,—
To lapse and loiter till the change should come
And the great floods turn seaward, roaring home.

IX

And now, O tranquil marshes, in your vast
    Serenity of vision and of dream,
Wherethrough by every intricate vein have passed
    With joy impetuous and pain supreme
The sharp, fierce tides that chafe the shores of earth
    In endless and controlless ebb and flow,
Strangely akin you seem to him whose birth
      One hundred years ago
With fiery succour to the ranks of song
Defied the ancient gates of wrath and wrong.

X

Like yours, O marshes, his compassionate breast,
    Wherein abode all dreams of love and peace,
Was tortured with perpetual unrest.
    Now loud with flood, now languid with release,
Now poignant with the lonely ebb, the strife

Of tides from the salt sea of human pain
That hiss along the perilous coasts of life
     Beat in his eager brain;
But all about the tumult of his heart
Stretched the great calm of his celestial art.

XI

Therefore with no far flight, from Tantramar
     And my still world of ecstasy, to thee,
Shelley, to thee I turn, the avatar
     Of Song, Love, Dream, Desire, and Liberty;
To thee I turn with reverent hands of prayer
     And lips that fain would ease my heart of praise,
Whom chief of all whose brows prophetic wear
     The pure and sacred bays
I worship, and have worshipped since the hour
When first I felt thy bright and chainless power.

(1892)

The Skater

My glad feet shod with the glittering steel
I was the god of the wingéd heel.

The hills in the far white sky were lost;
The world lay still in the wide white frost;

And the woods hung hushed in their long white dream
By the ghostly, glimmering, ice-blue stream.

Here was a pathway, smooth like glass,
Where I and the wandering wind might pass

To the far off palaces, drifted deep.
Where Winter's retinue rests in sleep.

I followed the lure, I fled like a bird,
Till the startled hollows awoke and heard

A spinning whisper, a sibilant twang,
As the stroke of the steel on the tense ice rang;

And the wandering wind was left behind
As faster, faster I followed my mind;

Till the blood sang high in my eager brain,
And the joy of my flight was almost pain.

Then I stayed the rush of my eager speed
And silently went as a drifting seed,—

Slowly, furtively, till my eyes
Grew big with the awe of a dim surmise,

And the hair of my neck began to creep
At hearing the wilderness talk in sleep.

Shapes in the fir-gloom drifted near.
In the deep of my heart I heard my fear.

And I turned and fled, like a soul pursued,
From the white, inviolate solitude.

(1901)

BLISS CARMAN (1861–1929)
A Vagabond Song

There is something in the autumn that is native to my blood!
Touch of manner, hint of mood;
And my heart is like a rhyme,
With the yellow and the purple and the crimson keeping time.

The scarlet of the maples can shake me like a cry
Of bugles going by.
And my lonely spirit thrills
To see the frosty asters like a smoke upon the hills.

There is something in October sets the gypsy blood astir;
We must rise and follow her,
When from every hill of flame
She calls and calls each vagabond by name.

(1896)

Vestigia

I took a day to search for God,
And found Him not. But as I trod
By rocky ledge, through woods untamed,
Just where one scarlet lily flamed,
I saw His footprint in the sod.

Then suddenly, all unaware,
Far off in the deep shadows, where
A solitary hermit thrush
Sang through the holy twilight hush—
I heard His voice upon the air.

And even as I marvelled how
God gives us Heaven here and now,
In a stir of wind that hardly shook
The poplar leaves beside the brook—
His hand was light upon my brow.

At last with evening as I turned
Homeward, and thought what I had learned
And all that there was still to probe—
I caught the glory of His robe
Where the last fires of sunset burned.

Back to the world with quickening start
I looked and longed for any part
In making saving Beauty be...
And from that kindling ecstasy
I knew God dwelt within my heart.

(1921)

Pauline Johnson (Tekahionwake) (1861–1913)
The Flight of the Crows

The autumn afternoon is dying o'er
  The quiet western valley where I lie
Beneath the maples on the river shore,
  Where tinted leaves, blue waters and fair sky
  Environ all; and far above some birds are flying by

To seek their evening haven in the breast
  And calm embrace of silence, while they sing
Te Deums to the night, invoking rest
  For busy chirping voice and tired wing—
And in the hush of sleeping trees their sleeping cradles swing.

In forest arms the night will soonest creep,
  Where sombre pines a lullaby intone,
Where Nature's children curl themselves to sleep,
  And all is still at last, save where alone
  A band of black, belated crows arrive from lands unknown.

Strange sojourn has been theirs since waking day,
  Strange sights and cities in their wanderings blend
With fields of yellow maize, and leagues away
  With rivers where their sweeping waters wend
  Past velvet banks to rocky shores, in cañons bold to end.

O'er what vast lakes that stretch superbly dead,
  Till lashed to life by storm-clouds, have they flown?
In what wild lands, in laggard flight have led
  Their aerial career unseen, unknown,
  Till now with twilight come their cries in lonely monotone?

The flapping of their pinions in the air
  Dies in the hush of distance, while they light
Within the fir tops, weirdly black and bare,
  That stand with giant strength and peerless height,
To shelter fairy, bird and beast throughout the closing night.

Strange black and princely pirates of the skies,
   Would that your wind-tossed travels I could know!
Would that my soul could see, and seeing, rise
   To unrestricted life where ebb and flow
   Of Nature's pulse would constitute a wider life below!

Could I but live just here in Freedom's arms,
   A kingly life without a sovereign's care!
Vain dreams! Day hides with closing wings her charms,
   And all is cradled in repose, save where
   Yon band of black, belated crows still frets the evening air.

(1913) [1888]

The Camper

Night 'neath the northern skies, lone, black, and grim:
Naught but the starlight lies 'twixt heaven, and him.

Of man no need has he, of God, no prayer;
He and his Deity are brothers there.

Above his bivouac the firs fling down
Through branches gaunt and black, their needles brown.

Afar some mountain streams, rockbound and fleet,
Sing themselves through his dreams in cadence sweet,

The pine trees whispering, the heron's cry,
The plover's passing wing, his lullaby.

And blinking overhead the white stars keep
Watch o'er his hemlock bed—his sinless sleep.

(1913) [1891]

ARCHIBALD LAMPMAN (1861–1899)
Freedom

Out of the heart of the city begotten
    Of the labour of men and their manifold hands,
Whose souls, that were sprung from the earth in her morning,
No longer regard or remember her warning,
    Whose hearts in the furnace of care have forgotten
        Forever the scent and the hue of her lands;

Out of the heat of the usurer's hold,
    From the horrible crash of the strong man's feet;
Out of the shadow where pity is dying;
Out of the clamour where beauty is lying,
    Dead in the depth of the struggle for gold;
        Out of the din and the glare of the street;

Into the arms of our mother we come,
    Our broad strong mother, the innocent earth,
Mother of all things beautiful, blameless,
Mother of hopes that her strength makes tameless,
    Where the voices of grief and of battle are dumb,
        And the whole world laughs with the light of her mirth.

Over the fields, where the cool winds sweep,
    Black with the mould and brown with the loam,
Where the thin green spears of the wheat are appearing,
And the high-ho shouts from the smoky clearing;
    Over the widths where the cloud shadows creep;
        Over the fields and the fallows we come;

Over the swamps with their pensive noises,
    Where the burnished cup of the marigold gleams;
Skirting the reeds, where the quick winds shiver
On the swelling breast of the dimpled river,
    And the blue of the king-fisher hangs and poises,
        Watching a spot by the edge of the streams;

By the miles of the fences warped and dyed
    With the white-hot noons and their withering fires,
Where the rough bees trample the creamy bosoms

Of the hanging tufts of the elder blossoms,
   And the spiders weave, and the grey snakes hide,
      In the crannied gloom of the stones and the briers;

   Over the meadow lands sprouting with thistle,
      Where the humming wings of the blackbirds pass,
Where the hollows are banked with the violets flowering,
And the long-limbed pendulous elms are towering,
   Where the robins are loud with their voluble whistle,
      And the ground sparrow scurries away through the grass,

   Where the restless bobolink loiters and woos
      Down in the hollows and over the swells,
Dropping in and out of the shadows,
Sprinkling his music about the meadows,
   Whistles and little checks and coos,
      And the tinkle of glassy bells;

   Into the dim woods full of the tombs
      Of the dead trees soft in their sepulchres,
Where the pensive throats of the shy birds hidden,
Pipe to us strangely entering unbidden,
   And tenderly still in the tremulous glooms
      The trilliums scatter their white-winged stars;

   Up to the hills where our tired hearts rest,
      Loosen, and halt, and regather their dreams,
Up to the hills, where the winds restore us,
Clearing our eyes to the beauty before us,
   Earth with the glory of life on her breast,
      Earth with the gleam of her cities and streams.

   Here we shall commune with her and no other;
      Care and the battle of life shall cease;
Men her degenerate children behind us,
Only the might of her beauty shall bind us,
   Full of rest, as we gaze on the face of our mother,
      Earth in the health and the strength of her peace.

(1888)

In November

With loitering step and quiet eye,
Beneath the low November sky,
I wandered in the woods, and found
A clearing, where the broken ground
Was scattered with black stumps and briers,
And the old wreck of forest fires.
It was a bleak and sandy spot,
And, all about, the vacant plot
Was peopled and inhabited
By scores of mulleins long since dead.
A silent and foresaken brood
In that mute opening of the wood,
So shrivelled and so thin they were,
So grey, so haggard, and austere,
Not plants at all they seemed to me,
But rather some spare company
Of hermit folk, who long ago,
Wandering in bodies to and fro,
Had chanced upon this lonely way,
And rested thus, till death one day
Surprised them at their compline prayer,
And left them standing lifeless there.

There was no sound about the wood
Save the wind's secret stir. I stood
Among the mullein-stalks as still
As if myself had grown to be
One of their sombre company,
A body without wish or will.
And as I stood, quite suddenly,
Down from a furrow in the sky
The sun shone out a little space
Across that silent sober place,
Over the sand heaps and brown sod,
The mulleins and dead goldenrod,

And passed beyond the thickets grey,
And lit the fallen leaves that lay,
Level and deep within the wood,
A rustling yellow multitude.

And all around me the thin light,
So sere, so melancholy bright,
Fell like the half-reflected gleam
Or shadow of some former dream;
A moment's golden reverie
Poured out from every plant and tree
A semblance of weird joy, or less,
A sort of spectral happiness;
And I, too, standing idly there,
With muffled hands in the chill air,
Felt the warm glow about my feet,
And shuddering betwixt cold and heat,
Drew my thoughts closer, like a cloak,
While something in my blood awoke,
A nameless and unnatural cheer,
A pleasure secret and austere.

(1895)

To the Ottawa River

O slave, whom many a cunning master drills
   To lift, or carry, bind, or crush, or churn,
   Whose dammed and parcelled waters drive or turn
The saws and hammers of a hundred mills,
Yet hath thy strength for our rebellious ills
   A counsel brave, a message sweet and stern,
   Uttered for them that have the heart to learn:
Yea to the dwellers in the rocky hills,
The folk of cities, and the farthest tracts,
   There comes above the human cry for gold
The thunder of thy chutes and cataracts:
   And lo! contemptuous of the driver's hold,
Thou movest under all thy servile pacts
   Full-flowing, fair, and stately as of old.

(1900)

On the Companionship with Nature

Let us be much with Nature; not as they
That labour without seeing, that employ
Her unloved forces, blindly without joy:
Nor those whose hands and crude delights obey
The old brute passion to hunt down and slay;
But rather as children of one common birth,
Discerning in each natural fruit of earth
Kinship and bond with this diviner clay.
Let us be with her wholly at all hours,
With the fond lover's zest, who is content
If his ear hears, and if his eye but sees;
So shall we grow like her in mould and bent,
Our bodies stately as her blessèd trees,
Our thoughts as sweet and sumptuous as her flowers.

(1900)

FREDERICK G. SCOTT (1861–1944)
The Unnamed Lake

It sleeps among the thousand hills
  Where no man ever trod,
And only nature's music fills
  The silences of God.

Great mountains tower above its shore,
  Green rushes fringe its brim,
And o'er its breast for evermore
  The wanton breezes skim.

Dark clouds that intercept the sun
  Go there in Spring to weep.
And there, when Autumn days are done,
  White mists lie down to sleep.

Sunrise and sunset crown with gold
  The peaks of ageless stone,
Where winds have thundered from of old
  And storms have set their throne.

No echoes of the world afar
  Disturb it night or day,
But sun and shadow, moon and star,
  Pass and repass for ay.

'Twas in the grey of early dawn
  When first the lake we spied,
And fragments of a cloud were drawn
  Half down the mountain side.

Along the shore a heron flew,
  And from a speck on high,
That hovered in the deepening blue,
  We heard the fish-hawk's cry.

Among the cloud-capt solitudes
  No sound the silence broke,

Save when, in whispers down the woods,
    The guardian mountains spoke.

Through tangled brush and dewy brake,
    Returning whence we came,
We passed in silence, and the lake
    We left without a name.

(1897)

DUNCAN CAMPBELL SCOTT (1862–1947)
The Height of Land

Here is the height of land:
The watershed on either hand
Goes down to Hudson Bay
Or Lake Superior;
The stars are up, and far away
The wind sounds in the wood, wearier
Than the long Ojibwa cadence
In which Potàn the Wise
Declares the ills of life
And Chees-que-ne-ne makes a mournful sound
Of acquiescence. The fires burn low
With just sufficient glow
To light the flakes of ash that play
At being moths, and flutter away
To fall in the dark and die as ashes:
Here there is peace in the lofty air,
And Something comes by flashes
Deeper than peace;—
The spruces have retired a little space
And left a field of sky in violet shadow
With stars like marigolds in a water-meadow.

Now the Indian guides are dead asleep;
There is no sound unless the soul can hear
The gathering of the waters in their sources.
We have come up through the spreading lakes
From level to level,—
Pitching our tents sometimes over a revel
Of roses that nodded all night,
Dreaming within our dreams,
To wake at dawn and find that they were captured
With no dew on their leaves;
Sometimes mid sheaves
Of bracken and dwarf-cornel, and again
On a wide blueberry plain
Brushed with the shimmer of a bluebird's wing;

A rocky islet followed
With one lone poplar and a single nest
Of white-throat-sparrows that took no rest
But sang in dreams or woke to sing,—
To the last portage and the height of land—:
Upon one hand
The lonely north enlaced with lakes and streams,
And the enormous targe of Hudson Bay,
Glimmering all night
In the cold arctic light;
On the other hand
The crowded southern land
With all the welter of the lives of men.
But here is peace, and again
That Something comes by flashes
Deeper than peace,—a spell
Golden and inappellable
That gives the inarticulate part
Of our strange being one moment of release
That seems more native than the touch of time,
And we must answer in chime;
Though yet no man may tell
The secret of that spell
Golden and inappellable.

Now are there sounds walking in the wood,
And all the spruces shiver and tremble,
And the stars move a little in their courses.
The ancient disturber of solitude
Breathes a pervasive sigh,
And the soul seems to hear
The gathering of the waters at their sources;
Then quiet ensues and pure starlight and dark;
The region-spirit murmurs in meditation,
The heart replies in exaltation
And echoes faintly like an inland shell
Ghost tremors of the spell;
Thought reawakens and is linked again
With all the welter of the lives of men.

Here on the uplands where the air is clear
We think of life as of a stormy scene,—
Of tempest, of revolt and desperate shock;
And here, where we can think, on the bright uplands
Where the air is clear, we deeply brood on life
Until the tempest parts, and it appears
As simple as to the shepherd seems his flock:
A Something to be guided by ideals—
That in themselves are simple and serene—
Of noble deed to foster noble thought,
And noble thought to image noble deed,
Till deed and thought shall interpenetrate,
Making life lovelier, till we come to doubt
Whether the perfect beauty that escapes
Is beauty of deed or thought or some high thing
Mingled of both, a greater boon than either:
Thus we have seen in the retreating tempest
The victor-sunlight merge with the ruined rain,
And from the rain and sunlight spring the rainbow.

The ancient disturber of solitude
Stirs his ancestral potion in the gloom,
And the dark wood
Is stifled with the pungent fume
Of charred earth burnt to the bone
That takes the place of air.
Then sudden I remember when and where,—
The last weird lakelet foul with weedy growths
And slimy viscid things the spirit loathes,
Skin of vile water over viler mud
Where the paddle stirred unutterable stenches,
And the canoes seemed heavy with fear,
Not to be urged toward the fatal shore
Where a bush fire, smouldering, with sudden roar
Leaped on a cedar and smothered it with light
And terror. It had left the portage-height
A tangle of slanted spruces burned to the roots,
Covered still with patches of bright fire
Smoking with incense of the fragment resin

That even then began to thin and lessen
Into the gloom and glimmer of ruin.
'Tis overpast. How strange the stars have grown;
The presage of extinction glows on their crests
And they are beautied with impermanence;
They shall be after the race of men
And mourn for them who snared their fiery pinions,
Entangled in the meshes of bright words.

A lemming stirs the fern and in the mosses
Eft-minded things feel the air change, and dawn
Tolls out from the dark belfries of the spruces.
.How often in the autumn of the world
Shall the crystal shrine of dawning be rebuilt
With deeper meaning! Shall the poet then,
Wrapped in his mantle on the height of land,
Brood on the welter of the lives of men
And dream of his ideal hope and promise
In the blush sunrise? Shall he base his flight
Upon a more compelling law than Love
As Life's atonement; shall the vision
Of noble deed and noble thought immingled
Seem as uncouth to him as the pictograph
Scratched on the cave side by the cave-dweller
To us of the Christ-time? Shall he stand
With deeper joy, with more complex emotion,
In closer commune with divinity,
With the deep fathomed, with the firmament charted,
With life as simple as a sheep-boy's song,
What lies beyond a romaunt that was read
Once on a morn of storm and laid aside
Memorious with strange immortal memories?
Or shall he see the sunrise as I see it
In shoals of misty fire the deluge-light
Dashes upon and whelms with purer radiance,
And feel the lulled earth, older in pulse and motion,
Turn the rich lands and inundant oceans
To the flushed color, and hear as now I hear
The thrill of life beat up the planet's margin

And break in the clear susurrus of deep joy
That echoes and reëchoes in my being?
O Life is intuition the measure of knowledge
And do I stand with heart entranced and burning
At the zenith of our wisdom when I feel
The long light flow, the long wind pause, the deep
Influx of spirit, of which no man may tell
The Secret, golden and inappellable?

(1916)

The Wood by the Sea

I dwell in the wood that is dark and kind
    But afar off tolls the main,
Afar, far off I hear the wind,
    And the roving of the rain.

The shade is dark as a palmer's hood,
    The air with balm is bland:
But I wish the trees that breathe in the wood
    Were ashes in God's hand.

The pines are weary of holding nests,
    Are aweary of casting shade;
Wearily smoulder the resin crests
    In the pungent gloom of the glade.

Weary are all the birds of sleep,
    The nests are weary of wings,
The whole wood yearns to the swaying deep,
    The mother of restful things.

The wood is very old and still,
    So still when the dead cones fall,
Near in the vale or away on the hill,
    You can hear them one and all,

And their falling wearies me:
    If mine were the will of God,—O, then
The wood should tramp to the sounding sea,
    Like a marching army of men!

But I dwell in the wood that is dark and kind,
    Afar off tolls the main;
Afar, far off I hear the wind
    And the roving of the rain.

(1916)

D. E. HATT (1869–1942)
Sitka Spruce

Sitka Spruce is fine of grain,
      And Sitka Spruce is tough,
To carry weight and stand the strain
      There grows no better stuff:
It thrives upon Queen Charlotte Isles
      And lifts its head on high,
When summer's sun upon it smiles
      Or winter rages by.

Sitka Spruce is straight and clear,
      And Sitka Spruce is light,
That aviator knows no fear
      It girds into the fight;
For borne on wings that tire not,
      He hurtles on the foe
Until he finds a vital spot
      And sends him down below.

Sitka Spruce the Allies need,
      And Sitka Spruce must get;
The loggers answer: "With all speed
      This need shall now be met."
And when the logger speaks his mind
      It is not empty boast—
The Allied nations soon shall find
      The thing they need the most.

(1919)

Mosquitoes

There's a breed of big mosquitoes
      Living in Queen Charlotte Isles
That can buzz a fancy chorus
      You could hear for many miles,
They pack a red-hot needle
      Like the kind the doctors use
And play the mischief with you
      When you want to take a snooze.

They buzz outside your window
      And they buzz as well inside,
They bore right through your blankets
      And perforate your hide,
They are champion blood-suckers
      And they always seem to choose
That time to take their supper
      When you want to take a snooze.

They have a great capacity
      For drinking human gore
The more they get the more they want
      To drink a little more,
It takes a real professional
      To speak a layman's views
Of these blood-thirsty pirates
      When they will not let him snooze.

The more you try to get to sleep
      The wider you're awake
And more mosquitoes tackle you
      For every slap you make;
It certainly is bad enough
      To drive a man to booze
The way the villains bite him
      When he tries to take a snooze.

You may rise and light your candle
      And go at them with a swat,

But as soon as you are back in bed
    They start again red-hot;
To conquer these infernal pests
    Just try this little ruse,
According to directions,
    When you want to take a snooze.

Four ply of wire netting
    Should be put around your bed,
A canvas bag tied tightly
    Around your neck and head,
Put on two suits of oilskins
    A pair of thick gum shoes,
Roll up in four thick blankets,
    Shut your eyes and take your snooze.

(1919)

Robert W. Service (1874–1958)
The Pines

We sleep in the sleep of the ages, the bleak, barbarian pines;
The gray moss drapes us like sages, and closer we lock our lines,
And deeper we clutch through the gelid gloom where never a sunbeam
    shines.

On the flanks of the storm-gored ridges are our black battalions
    massed;
We surge in a host to the sullen coast, and we sing in the ocean blast;
From empire of sea to empire of snow we grip our empire fast.

To the niggard lands were we driven, 'twixt desert and floes are we
    penned;
To us was the Northland given, ours to stronghold and defend;
Ours till the world be riven in the crash of the utter end;

Ours from the bleak beginning, through the æons of death-like sleep;
Ours from the shock when the naked rock was hurled from the hissing
    deep;
Ours through the twilight ages of weary glacier creep.

Wind of the East, Wind of the West, wandering to and fro,
Chant your songs in our topmost boughs, that the sons of men may
    know
The peerless pine was the first to come, and the pine will be last to go!

We pillar the halls of the perfumed gloom; we plume where the eagles
    soar;
The North-wind swoops from the brooding Pole, and our ancients
    crash and roar;
But where one falls from the crumbling walls shoots up a hardy score.

We spring from the gloom of the canyon's womb; in the valley's lap we
    lie;
From the white foam-fringe, where the breakers cringe, to the peaks
    that tusk the sky,
We climb, and we peer in the crag-locked mere that gleams like a
    golden eye.

Gain to the verge of the hog-back ridge where the vision ranges free:
Pines and pines and the shadow of pines as far as the eye can see;
A steadfast legion of stalwart knights in dominant empery.

Sun, moon and stars give answer; shall we not staunchly stand
Even as now, forever, wards of the wilder strand,
Sentinels of the stillness, lords of the last, lone land?

(1907)

The Spell of the Yukon

I wanted the gold, and I sought it;
  I scrabbled and mucked like a slave.
Was it famine or scurvy—I fought it;
  I hurled my youth into a grave.
I wanted the gold, and I got it—
  Came out with a fortune last fall,—
Yet somehow life's not what I thought it,
  And somehow the gold isn't all.

No! There's the land. (Have you seen it?)
  It's the cussedest land that I know,
From the big, dizzy mountains that screen it
  To the deep, deathlike valleys below.
Some say God was tired when He made it;
  Some say it's a fine land to shun;
Maybe; but there's some as would trade it
  For no land on earth—and I'm one.

You come to get rich (damned good reason);
  You feel like an exile at first;
You hate it like hell for a season,
  And then you are worse than the worst.
It grips you like some kinds of sinning;
  It twists you from foe to friend;
It seems it's been since the beginning;
  It seems it will be to the end.

I've stood in some mighty-mouthed hollow
  That's plumb-full of hush to the brim;
I've watched the big, husky sun wallow
  In crimson and gold, and grow dim,
Till the moon set the pearly peaks gleaming,
  And the stars tumbled out, neck and crop;
And I've thought that I surely was dreaming,
  With the peace o' the world piled on top.

The summer—no sweeter was ever;
  The sunshiny woods all athrill;
The grayling aleap in the river,
  The bighorn asleep on the hill.

The strong life that never knows harness;
  The wilds where the caribou call;
The freshness, the freedom, the farness—
  O God! how I'm stuck on it all.

The winter! The brightness that blinds you,
  The white land locked tight as a drum,
The cold fear that follows and finds you,
  The silence that bludgeons you dumb.
The snows that are older than history,
  The woods where the weird shadows slant;
The stillness, the moonlight, the mystery,
  I've bade 'em good-by—but I can't.

There's a land where the mountains are nameless,
  And the rivers all run God knows where;
There are lives that are erring and aimless,
  And deaths that just hang by a hair;
There are hardships that nobody reckons;
  There are valleys unpeopled and still;
There's a land—oh, it beckons and beckons,
  And I want to go back—and I will.

They're making my money diminish;
  I'm sick of the taste of champagne.
Thank God! when I'm skinned to a finish
  I'll pike to the Yukon again.
I'll fight—and you bet it's no sham fight;
  It's hell!—but I've been there before;
And it's better than this by a damsite—
  So me for the Yukon once more.

There's gold, and it's haunting and haunting;
  It's luring me on as of old;
Yet it isn't the gold that I'm wanting
  So much as just finding the gold.
It's the great, big, broad land 'way up yonder,
  It's the forests where silence has lease;
It's the beauty that fills me with wonder,
  It's the stillness that fills me with peace.

(1907)

E. J. PRATT (1882–1964)
The Ice-Floes

Dawn from the Foretop! Dawn from the Barrel!
A scurry of feet with a roar overhead;
The master-watch wildly pointing to Northward,
Where the herd in front of *The Eagle* was spread!
Steel-planked and sheathed like a battleship's nose,
She battered her path through the drifting floes;
Past slob and growler we drove, and rammed her
Into the heart of the patch and jammed her.
There were hundreds of thousands of seals, I'd swear,
In the stretch of that field—'white harps' to spare
For a dozen such fleets as had left that spring
To share in the general harvesting.
The first of the line, we had struck the main herd;
The day was ours, and our pulses stirred
In that brisk, live hour before the sun,
At the thought of the load and the sweepstake won.

We stood on the deck as the morning outrolled
On the fields its tissue of orange and gold,
And lit up the ice to the north in the sharp,
Clear air; each mother-seal and its 'harp'
Lay side by side; and as far as the range
Of the patch ran out we saw that strange,
And unimaginable thing
That sealers talk of every spring—
    The 'bobbing-holes' within the floes
That neither wind nor frost could close;
Through every hole a seal could dive,
And search, to keep her brood alive,
A hundred miles it might well be,
For food beneath that frozen sea.
Round sunken reef and cape she would rove,
And though the wind and current drove
The ice-fields many leagues that day,
We knew she would turn and find her way
Back to the hole, without the help

Of compass or log, to suckle her whelp—
Back to that hole in the distant floes,
And smash her way up with her teeth and nose.
But we flung those thoughts aside when the shout
Of command from the master-watch rang out.
Assigned to our places in watches of four—
    Over the rails in a wild carouse,
    Two from the port and starboard bows,
Two from the broadsides—off we tore,
In the breathless rush for the day's attack,
With the speed of hounds on a caribou's track.
With the rise of the sun we started to kill,
A seal for each blow from the iron bill
Of our gaffs. From the nose to the tail we ripped them,
    And laid their quivering carcasses flat
On the ice; then with our knives we stripped them
    For the sake of the pelt and its lining of fat.
With three fathoms of rope we laced them fast,
    With their skins to the ice to be easy to drag,
With our shoulders galled we drew them, and cast
    Them in thousands around the watch's flag.
Then, with our bodies begrimed with the reek
    Of grease and sweat from the toil of the day,
    We made for The Eagle, two miles away,
At the signal that flew from her mizzen peak.
And through the night, as inch by inch
    She reached the pans with the 'harps' piled high,
    We hoisted them up as the hours filed by
To the sleepy growl of the donkey winch.

Over the bulwarks again we were gone,
With the first faint streaks of a misty dawn;
Fast as our arms could swing we slew them,
Ripped them, 'sculped' them, roped and drew them
To the pans where the seals in pyramids rose
Around the flags on the central floes,
Till we reckoned we had nine thousand dead
By the time the afternoon had fled;
And that an added thousand or more

Would beat the count of the day before.
So back again to the patch we went
To haul, before the day was spent,
Another load of four 'harps' a man,
To make the last the record pan.
And not one of us saw, as we gaffed, and skinned,
And took them in tow, that the north-east wind
Had veered off-shore; that the air was colder;
    That the signs of recall were there to the south,
The flag of *The Eagle,* and the long, thin smoulder
    That drifted away from her funnel's mouth.
Not one of us thought of the speed of the storm
    That hounded our tracks in the day's last chase
(For the slaughter was swift, and the blood was warm),
    Till we felt the first sting of the snow in our face.

We looked south-east, where, an hour ago,
    Like a smudge on the sky-line, someone had seen
The Eagle, and thought he had heard her blow
    A note like a warning from her sirene.
We gathered in knots, each man within call
    Of his mate, and slipping our ropes, we sped,
Plunging our way through a thickening wall
    Of snow that the gale was driving ahead.
We ran with the wind on our shoulder; we knew
That the night had left us this only clue
Of the track before us, though with each wail
That grew to the pang of a shriek from the gale,
Some of us swore that *The Eagle* screamed
Right off to the east; to others it seemed
On the southern quarter and near, while the rest
    Cried out with every report that rose
    From the strain and the rend of the wind on the floes
That *The Eagle* was firing her guns to the west.
And some of them turned to the west, though to go
    Was madness—we knew it and roared, but the notes
Of our warning were lost as a fierce gust of snow
    Eddied, and strangled the words in our throats.
Then we felt in our hearts that the night had swallowed

All signals, the whistle, the flare, and the smoke
To the south; and like sheep in a storm we followed
    Each other; like sheep we huddled and broke.
Here one would fall as hunger took hold
Of his step; here one would sleep as the cold
Crept into his blood, and another would kneel
Athwart the body of some dead seal,
And with knife and nails would tear it apart,
To flesh his teeth in its frozen heart.
And another dreamed that the storm was past,
    And raved of his bunk and brandy and food,
And *The Eagle* near, though in that blast
    The mother was fully as blind as her brood.
Then we saw, what we feared from the first—dark places
Here and there to the left of us, wide-yawning spaces
Of water; the fissures and cracks had increased
    Till the outer pans were afloat, and we knew,
As they drifted along in the night to the east,
    By the cries we heard, that some of our crew
Were borne to the sea on those pans and were lost.
    And we turned with the wind in our faces again,
    And took the snow with its lancing pain,
Till our eye-balls cracked with the salt and the frost;
Till only iron and fire that night
    Survived on the ice as we stumbled on;
As we fell and rose and plunged—till the light
    In the south and east disclosed the dawn,
And the sea heaving with floes—and then,
The Eagle in wild pursuit of her men.

And the rest is as a story told,
    Or a dream that belonged to a dim, mad past,
Of a March night and a north wind's cold,
    Of a voyage home with a flag half-mast;
Of twenty thousand seals that were killed
    To help to lower the price of bread;
Of a muffled beat…of a drum…that filled
    A nave…at our count of sixty dead.

(1923)

Sea-Gulls

For one carved instant they flew
The language had no simile—
Silver, crystal, ivory
Were tarnished. Etched upon the horizon blue,
The frieze must go unchallenged, for the lift
And carriage of the wings would stain the drift
Of stars against a tropic indigo
Or dull the parable of snow.

Now settling one by one
Within green hollows or where curled
Crests caught the spectrum from the sun,
A thousand wings are furled.
No clay-born lilies of the world
Could blow as free
As those wild orchids of the sea.

(1932)

from *Towards the Last Spike*

On the North Shore a reptile fell asleep—
A hybrid that the myths might have conceived,
But not delivered, as progenitor
Of crawling, gliding things upon the earth.
She lay snug in the folds of a huge boa
Whose tail had covered Labrador and swished
Atlantic tides, whose body coiled itself
Around the Hudson Bay, then curled up north
Through Manitoba and Saskatchewan
To Great Slave Lake. In continental reach
The neck went past the Great Bear Lake until
Its head was hidden in the Arctic Seas.
This folded reptile was asleep or dead:
So motionless, she seemed stone dead—just seemed:
She was too old for death, too old for life,
For as if jealous of all living forms
She had lain there before bivalves began
To catacomb their shells on western mountains.
Somewhere within this life-death zone she sprawled,
Torpid upon a rock-and-mineral mattress.
Ice-ages had passed by and over her,
But these, for all their motion, had but sheared
Her spotty carboniferous hair or made
Her ridges stand out like the spikes of molochs.
Her back grown stronger every million years,
She had shed water by the longer rivers
To Hudson Bay and by the shorter streams
To the great basins to the south, had filled
Them up, would keep them filled until the end
Of Time.

       Was this the thing Van Horne set out
To conquer? When Superior lay there
With its inviting levels? Blake, Mackenzie,
Offered this water like a postulate.
'Why those twelve thousand men sent to the North?

Nonsense and waste with utter bankruptcy.'
And the Laurentian monster at the first
Was undisturbed, presenting but her bulk
To the invasion. All she had to do
Was lie there neither yielding nor resisting.
Top-heavy with accumulated power
And overgrown survival without function,
She changed her spots as though brute rudiments
Of feeling foreign to her native hour
Surprised her with a sense of violation
From an existence other than her own—
Or why take notice of this unknown breed,
This horde of bipeds that could toil like ants,
Could wake her up and keep her irritated?
They tickled her with shovels, dug pickaxes
Into her scales and got under her skin,
And potted holes in her with drills and filled
Them up with what looked like fine grains of sand,
Black sand. It wasn't noise that bothered her,
For thunder she was used to from her cradle—
The head-push and nose-blowing of the ice,
The height and pressure of its body: these
Like winds native to clime and habitat
Had served only to lull her drowsing coils.
It was not size or numbers that concerned her.
It was their foreign build, their gait of movement.
They did not crawl—nor were they born with wings.
They stood upright and walked, shouted and sang;
They needed air—that much was true—their mouths
Were open but the tongue was alien.
The sounds were not the voice of winds and waters,
Nor that of any beasts upon the earth.
She took them first with lethargy, suffered
The rubbing of her back—those little jabs
Of steel were like the burrowing of ticks
In an elk's hide needing an antler point,
Or else left in a numb monotony.
These she could stand but when the breed

Advanced west on her higher vertebrae,
Kicking most insolently at her ribs,
Pouring black powder in her cavities,
And making not the clouds but her insides
The home of fire and thunder, then she gave
Them trial of her strength: the trestles tottered;
Abutments, bridges broke; her rivers flooded:
She summoned snow and ice, and then fell back
On the last weapon in her armoury—
The first and last—her passive corporal bulk,
To stay or wreck the schedule of Van Horne.

(1952)

The Good Earth

Let the mind rest awhile, lower the eyes,
Relieve the spirit of its Faustian clamour:
An atom holds more secrets than the skies;
Be patient with the earth and do not cram her

With seed beyond the wisdom of her soil.
She knows the foot and hoof of man and ox,
She learned the variations of their toil—
The ploughshare's sensitivity to rocks.

Gather the stones for field and garden walls,
Build cellars for your vegetable stores,
Forgo the architecture of your halls,
Until your hands have fashioned stable doors.

She likes the smell of nitrates in her stalls,
She hates a disciplined tread, the scorching roar
At the grain's roots: she is nervous at the calls
Of men in panic at a strike of ore.

Patient she is in her flesh servitude,
Tolerant to curry ticklings of the harrow,
But do not scratch past her agrarian mood
To cut the calcium in her bone and marrow.

Hold that synthetic seed, for underneath
Deep down she'll answer to your horticulture:
She has a way of germinating teeth
And yielding crops of carrion for the vulture.

(1958)

MARJORIE PICKTHALL (1883–1922)
When Winter Comes

Rain at Muchalat, rain at Sooke,
And rain, they say, from Yale to Skeena,
And the skid-roads blind, and never a look
Of the Coast Range blue over Malaspina,
And west winds keener
Than jack-knife blades,
And rocks grown greener
With the long drip-drip from the cedar shades
On the drenched deep soil where the footsteps suck,
And the camp half-closed and the pay-roll leaner,—
Say, little horse, shall we hunt our luck?

Yet…I don't know…there's an hour at night
When the clouds break and the stars are turning
A thousand points of diamond light
Through the old snags of the cedar-burning,
And the west wind's spurning
A hundred highlands,
And the frost-moon's learning
The white fog-ways of the outer islands,
And the shallows are dark with the sleeping duck,
And life's a wonder for our discerning,—
Say, little horse, shall we wait our luck?

(1922)

Inheritance

Desolate strange sleep and wild
Came on me while yet a child;
I, before I tasted tears,
Knew the grief of all the years.

I, before I fronted pain,
Felt creation writhe and strain,
Sending ancient terrors through,
My small pulses, sweet and new.

I, before I learned how time
Robs all summers at their prime,
I, few seasons gone from birth,
Felt my body change to earth.

(1922)

Kenneth Leslie (1892–1974)
Tasseled Thought

I've walked about since birth;
Yet, when I stoop to eat
The tasseled wheat
I put roots in the earth,
And, finding there my home,
Coolly I burn
And greenly like a fern,
My feet in the soft loam.
It is then disesteem
To make pretence I am not
A tasseled thought,
A smouldering leafy dream.

But, though my soil is deeper
Than a tree's
And even the walled seas
Are not my keeper
And my keen mind must feed
On hurrying stars
(Distance and days no bars
To my mad need)
Vainly from earth I turn
Out where the ether stirs;
Deeper than hers
For me no secrets burn.

(1934)

from *By Stubborn Stars*

Day slipped out of the web of her fogwet gown
and buried her bright face in the pale sheen
of the maple leaves and pushed her fingers down
in the damp moss under the deeper green
of the darkling spruce and found a cool mind
and turned and looked back through the lucent panes
of maple leaves at the sky she had left behind
and traced each pointed leaf and its intricate veins.
Lying there she shook with a sudden mirth
and waited awhile without breathing a breath
and nestled closer into the hollow earth
and knew a bliss that would have welcomed death,
knowing she could not deeper drink delight,
and she dreamed there of shadow and of night.

(1938)

W. W. E. Ross (1894–1966)
Fish

A fish dripping
sparkling drops
of crystal water,
pulled from the lake;
long has it dwelt
in the cool water,
in the cold water
of the lake.

Long has it wandered
to and fro
over the bottom
of the lake
among mysterious
recesses
there in the semi-
light of the water;

now to appear
surprised, aghast,
out of its element
into the day—
out of the cold
and shining lake
the fish dripping
sparkling water.

(1930)

The Snake Trying

The snake trying
to escape the pursuing stick,
with sudden curvings of thin
long body. How beautiful

and graceful are his shapes!
He glides through the water away
from the stroke. O let him go
over the water

into the reeds to hide
without hurt. Small and green
he is harmless even to children.
Along the sand

he lay until observed
and chased away, and now
he vanishes in the ripples
among the green slim reeds.

(1968) [1930–1939]

F. R. Scott (1899–1985)
Laurentian Shield

Hidden in wonder and snow, or sudden with summer,
This land stares at the sun in a huge silence
Endlessly repeating something we cannot hear.
Inarticulate, arctic,
Not written on by history, empty as paper,
It leans away from the world with songs in its lakes
Older than love, and lost in the miles.

This waiting is wanting.
It will choose its language
When it has chosen its technic,
A tongue to shape the vowels of its productivity.

A language of flesh and of roses.

Now there are pre-words,
Cabin syllables,
Nouns of settlement
Slowly forming, with steel syntax,
The long sentence of exploitation.

The first cry was the hunter, hungry for fur,
And the digger for gold, nomad, no-man, a particle;
Then the bold commands of monopoly, big with machines,
Carving its kingdoms out of the public wealth;
And now the drone of the plane, scouting the ice,
Fills all the emptiness with neighbourhood
And links our future over the vanished pole.

But a deeper note is sounding, heard in the mines,
The scattered camps and the mills, a language of life,
And what will be written in the full culture of occupation
Will come, presently, tomorrow,
From millions whose hands can turn this rock into children.

(1954)

Flying to Fort Smith

The spread of silver wing
    Gathers us into long lanes of space.
We peer through panes of glass.

The plain of lakes below
    Is bound with bands of green
Fringed by darker green
    Pocked with drops of ponds.

Everywhere
    A huge nowhere,
Underlined by a shy railway.

Snaking brown streams
    At every islanded corner
Widen their reaches
    Leaving blue pools behind.

An arena
    Large as Europe
Silent
    Waiting for contest

Underground
    In the coins of rock
Cities sleep like seeds.

(1964)

RAYMOND KNISTER (1899–1932)
Boy Remembers in the Field

What if the sun comes out
And the new furrows do not look smeared?

This is April, and the sumach candles
Have guttered long ago.
The crows in the twisted apple limbs
Are moveless and dark.

Drops on the wires, cold cheeks,
The mist, the long snorts, silence...
The horses will steam when the sun comes;
Crows, go, shrieking.

Another bird now; sweet...
Pitiful life, useless,
Innocently creeping
On a useless planet
Again.

If any voice called, I would hear?
It has been the same before.
Soil glistens, the furrow rolls, sleet shifts, brightens.

(1949) [1923]

The Hawk

Across the bristled and sallow fields,
The speckled stubble of cut clover,
Wades your shadow.

Or against a grimy and tattered
Sky
You plunge.

Or you shear a swath
From trembling tiny forests
With the steel of your wings—

Or make a row of waves
By the heat of your flight
Along the soundless horizon.

(1949) [1924]

CHIEF DAN GEORGE (1899–1981)
from *My Heart Soars*

No longer
    can I give you a handful of berries as a gift,
no longer
    are the roots I dig used as a medicine,
no longer
    can I sing a song to please the salmon,
no longer
    does the pipe I smoke make others sit with me in friendship
no longer
    does anyone want to walk with me to the blue mountain to pray,
no longer
    does the deer trust my footsteps
   •

If you talk to animals they will talk with you
and you will know each other.

If you do not talk to them you will not know them,
and what you do not know you will fear.

What one fears one destroys.
   •

O earth
for the strength
in my heart
I thank Thee.

O cloud
for the blood
in my body
I thank Thee.

O fire
for the shine
in my eyes
I thank Thee.

O sun
for the life
you gave to me
I thank Thee.

(1974)

Robert Finch (1900–1995)
Silverthorn Bush

I am a dispossessed Ontario wood
That took the circling weather as my crown,
Now noise makes havoc of my whispered mood
And enterprise has laughed my towers down.

Is there a poem where I blossom still?
Do paintings keep my solitude secure?
Somewhere remote adventure must distil
Part of its fragrance from an air so pure.

I am the springing memory of my past
In vagabond and child who held me dear,
Theirs is the surest witness that I last
In buds of mine that I no longer bear.

If you can overtake their truant youth
Ask them to flash my secret on your sight,
They heard my pensive river spill its truth
And felt my hidden fibres tug the light.

The riddle is how disappearance puts
A dusty end to a green revery
Yet leaves me nourished by so many roots
That I shall never cease ceasing to be.

(1966)

MARTHA OSTENSO (1900–1963)
Lexicon

There are dark, human things
You know not, simple grasses,
Colder than the cold wings
Of the lone wild duck that passes·
Hereover in the late Fall;
Warmer than the warm stain
On the thorn where the tall
Stag winced in swift pain;
Harder than the strange stone
That grows not e'en a brier,
Softer than the mist blown
Athwart marsh-fire.
I have learned dark things
You know not, simple grasses,—
Teach me what your cricket sings
Until my learning passes.

(1924)

The Return

Oh, strong and faithful and enduring
As my mother's face,
The sowing of the years has wrought
No change in you, no ill,
Wild field that I loved! The generous grace
Of ragweed and of nettle caught
In the ruddy fall of sun
And in the silvering of rain enveils you still,
And here and there a warm rut of the dun
And patient earth with small, slow life is stirring.

Your stiff, pale grass and weedy flowers
Still proudly grow
Innocent of being beautiless—
(Even a little vain,
Trusting no leafed thing could be low
That the sky-born rain would bless)
And Oh! the sunny smell of you—
Of brittling stems, sweet spears long-matted lain
In spider weft and gold-pricked dust and dew
Through the dream and languidness of humming
    hours.

Under the blackbird swartly flying
From west to east,
Under the reach of the lark from north to south
You are my field—the same
Brown curve along the sky—even the least
Brown blade the same. To lay my mouth
On the quiet of your dew sweet face
And hear the deep earth of you call my name—
This is to know that I have found my place—
And the empty years have ended all their crying.

(1924)

L. A. Mackay (1901–1982)
Snow Story

Suddenly light shone out from the dark window
and he moved more cautiously over the creaking snow.
Low boughs laid on his lips a cold finger
and sprang back, as the silence dropped, with a soft whir.
The shadow mink, by his moving step startled
skimmed like a thrown stone over the glitter. Cold
sucked at his muscles; powdery breath bit in his nostrils.
He listened at the clearing's edge. The house was still.
Deep in the cold dunes he swung north, in a cautious
drifting down, stealthily, on the blind side of the house.
Unheard he hid by the chimney, crept past the corner,
and laid stiff fingers on the capped latch of the door.
Suddenly thrust. The door swung; the snow tumbled
in from the banked drift, and the swift light spread
over the level swells, blank. The new-comer
stepped stiffly into the house; and the soft air
lapped at his eyelids. The last ember shivered,
flared in the cold gust, fell. Not a spark stirred.
He closed the door, stood for a heavy instant
listening in the soft dark, then with a grunt
squirmed out of his coat, and turned towards the dead embers.
There was a gliding rustle in the frosty firs
or so he thought. But already the sharp bramble
slipped snake-toothed from the earthy edge of the hearth-sill
had trapped his ankles; the hard searching root-tip
plunged in his heart, as the fresh leaves brushed his lip.

(1938)

A. J. M. Smith (1902–1980)
The Lonely Land

Cedar and jagged fir
uplift sharp barbs
against the gray
and cloud-piled sky;
and in the bay
blown spume and windrift
and then, bitter spray
snap
at the whirling sky;
and the pine trees
lean one way.

A wild duck calls
to her mate,
and the ragged
and passionate tones
stagger and fall,
and recover,
and stagger and fall,
on these stones—
are lost
in the lapping of water
on smooth, flat stones.

(1943)

R. G. EVERSON (1903–1992)
L'Orignal

The bull moose, only a startling rod or so away from me,
looked to be about nine feet long,
maybe six feet above the trampled-down snow
and he would be about a thousand pounds
even though starved gaunt. He was murder-angry, had eaten
all the undergrowth and above him all twigs and branches
within reach, so that the little forest on his island was trimmed
evenly along the lower parts of the trees
according to the undulations of the land.

This ballet-skirts appearance of the island had drawn my curiosity
as I crossed the lake on the way home with my new axe—
to encounter the terrifying sight at close range of l'orignal
as the French long ago named the bull moose, having never
seen so strange an animal in Europe. (The Indians called him
        mongswa,
from which the English took the name, twig-eater).

The moose had probably been chased to this island
in the deep of winter. Nearby me on the lake lay a dead wolf
frozen at full length and partly drifted over.
I figured that the moose had used the island as a fort.
Even after the wolves gave up and went away,
he may have stayed browsing—but the island had trapped him.

The late-winter sun, heating shore rocks,
had circled the island with a thin-crusted moat,
too weak for a getaway. Dimly seeing me out there
among pressure ridges and sugar snow,
the moose presumably took me for one of those wolves,
so he charged.

Immediately he splintered through the ice and disappeared.
When he came up on a tide of icicles and water,
he kept trying to get at me, slamming with sharp hooves.
Then he swam feebly back through the floes.

I walked half way around his little island
and bellied ashore over the thin ice, pushing
my axe ahead of me. I cut down a poplar,
pushing it inland as the moose staggered toward me.
The falling treetop confronted his weak charge.
The monster began to nibble on the delicate twigs.

I hacked down enough weed trees to nourish him
until breakup, when he could swim to mainland.
Then I crawled over the weak shore ice again
and walked along the lake in the last of the day.

(1983)

EARLE BIRNEY (1904–1995)
David

I

David and I that summer cut trails on the Survey,
All week in the valley for wages, in air that was steeped
In the wail of mosquitoes, but over the sunalive week-ends
We climbed, to get from the ruck of the camp, the surly

Poker, the wrangling, the snoring under the fetid
Tents, and because we had joy in our lengthening coltish
Muscles, and mountains for David were made to see over,
Stairs from the valleys and steps to the sun's retreats.

II

Our first was Mount Gleam. We hiked in the long afternoon
To a curling lake and lost the lure of the faceted
Cone in the swell of its sprawling shoulders. Past
The inlet we grilled our bacon, the strips festooned

On a poplar prong, in the hurrying slant of the sunset.
Then the two of us rolled in the blanket while round us the cold
Pines thrust at the stars. The dawn was a floating
Of mists till we reached to the slopes above timber, and won

To snow like fire in the sunlight. The peak was upthrust
Like a fist in a frozen ocean of rock that swirled
Into valleys the moon could be rolled in. Remotely unfurling
Eastward the alien prairie glittered. Down through the dusty

Skree on the west we descended, and David showed me
How to use the give of shale for giant incredible
Strides. I remember, before the larches' edge,
That I jumped on a long green surf of juniper flowing

Away from the wind, and landed in gentian and saxifrage
Spilled on the moss. Then the darkening firs
And the sudden whirring of water that knifed down a fern-hidden
Cliff and splashed unseen into mist in the shadows.

III

One Sunday on Rampart's arête a rainsquall caught us,
And passed, and we clung by our blueing fingers and bootnails
An endless hour in the sun, not daring to move
Till the ice had steamed from the slate. And David taught me

How time on a knife-edge can pass with the guessing of fragments
Remembered from poets, the naming of strata beside one,
And matching of stories from schooldays...We crawled astride
The peak to feast on the marching ranges flagged

By the fading shreds of the shattered stormcloud. Lingering
There it was David who spied to the south, remote
And unmapped, a sunlit spire on Sawback, an overhang
Crooked like a talon. David named it the Finger.

That day we chanced on the skull and the splayed white ribs
Of a mountain goat underneath a cliff, caught
On a rock. Around were the silken feathers of hawks.
And that was the first I knew that a goat could slip.

IV

And then Inglismaldie. Now I remember only
The long ascent of the lonely valley, the live
Pine spirally scarred by lightning, the slicing pipe
Of invisible pika, and great prints, by the lowest

Snow, of a grizzly. There it was too that David
Taught me to read the scroll of coral in limestone
And the beetle-seal in the shale of ghostly trilobites,
Letters delivered to man from the Cambrian waves.

V

On Sundance we tried from the col and the going was hard.
The air howled from our feet to the smudged rocks
And the papery lake below. At an outthrust we baulked
Till David clung with his left to a dint in the scarp,

Lobbed the iceaxe over the rocky lip,
Slipped from his holds and hung by the quivering pick,
Twisted his long legs up into space and kicked
To the crest. Then, grinning, he reached with his freckled wrist

And drew me up after. We set a new time for that climb.
That day returning we found a robin gyrating
In grass, wing-broken. I caught it to tame but David
Took and killed it, and said, "Could you teach it to fly?"

VI

In August, the second attempt, we ascended The Fortress.
By the forks of the Spray we caught five trout and fried them
Over a balsam fire. The woods were alive
With the vaulting of mule-deer and drenched with clouds all the
        morning,

Till we burst at noon to the flashing and floating round
Of the peaks. Coming down we picked in our hats the bright
And sunhot raspberries, eating them under a mighty
Spruce, while marten moving like quicksilver scouted us.

VII

But always we talked of the Finger on Sawback, unknown
And hooked, till the first afternoon in September we slogged
Through the musky woods, past a swamp that quivered with frog-song,
And camped by a bottle-green lake. But under the cold

Breath of the glacier sleep would not come, the moon-light
Etching the Finger. We rose and trod past the feathery
Larch, while the stars went out, and the quiet heather
Flushed, and the skyline pulsed with the surging bloom

Of incredible dawn in the Rockies. David spotted
Bighorns across the moraine and sent them leaping
With yodels the ramparts redoubled and rolled to the peaks,
And the peaks to the sun. The ice in the morning thaw

Was a gurgling world of crystal and cold blue chasms,
And seracs that shone like frozen saltgreen waves.

At the base of the Finger we tried once and failed. Then David
Edged to the west and discovered the chimney; the last

Hundred feet we fought the rock and shouldered and kneed
Our way for an hour and made it. Unroping we formed
A cairn on the rotting tip. Then I turned to look north
At the glistening wedge of giant Assiniboine, heedless

Of handhold. And one foot gave. I swayed and shouted.
David turned sharp and reached out his arm and steadied me
Turning again with a grin and his lips ready
To jest. But the strain crumbled his foothold. Without

A gasp he was gone. I froze to the sound of grating
Edge-nails and fingers, the slither of stones, the lone
Second of silence, the nightmare thud. Then only
The wind and the muted beat of unknowing cascades.

VIII

Somehow I worked down the fifty impossible feet
To the ledge, calling and getting no answer but echoes
Released in the cirque, and trying not to reflect
What an answer would mean. He lay still, with his lean

Young face upturned and strangely unmarred, but his legs
Splayed beneath him, beside the final drop,
Six hundred feet sheer to the ice. My throat stopped
When I reached him, for he was alive. He opened his gray

Straight eyes and brokenly murmured, "over…over."
And I, feeling beneath him a cruel fang
Of the ledge thrust in his back, but not understanding,
Mumbled stupidly, "Best not to move," and spoke

Of his pain. But he said "I can't move…If only I felt
Some pain." Then my shame stung the tears to my eyes
As I crouched, and I cursed myself, but he cried
Louder, "No, Bobbie! Don't ever blame yourself.

I didn't test my foothold." He shut the lids
Of his eyes to the stare of the sky, while I moistened his lips

From our water flask and tearing my shirt into strips
I swabbed the shredded hands. But the blood slid

From his side and stained the stone and the thirsting lichens,
And yet I dared not lift him up from the gore
Of the rock. Then he whispered, "Bob, I want to go over!"
This time I knew what he meant and I grasped for a lie

And said, "I'll be back here by midnight with ropes
And men from the camp and we'll cradle you out." But I knew
That the day and the night must pass and the cold dews
Of another morning before such men unknowing

The ways of mountains could win to the chimney's top.
And then, how long? And he knew…and the hell of hours
After that, if he lived till we came, roping him out.
But I curled beside him and whispered, "The bleeding will stop.

You can last." He said only, "Perhaps…For what? A wheelchair,
Bob?" His eyes brightening with fever upbraided me.
I could not look at him more and said, "Then I'll stay
With you." But he did not speak, for the clouding fever.

I lay dazed and stared at the long valley,
The glistening hair of a creek on the rug stretched
By the firs, while the sun leaned round and flooded the ledge,
The moss, and David still as a broken doll.

I hunched to my knees to leave, but he called and his voice
Now was sharpened with fear. "For Christ's sake push me over!
If I could move…or die…." The sweat ran from his forehead
But only his head moved. A hawk was buoying

Blackly its wings over the wrinkled ice.
The purr of a waterfall rose and sank with the wind.
Above us climbed the last joint of the Finger
Beckoning bleakly the wide indifferent sky.

Even then in the sun it grew cold lying there….And I knew
He had tested his holds. It was I who had not….I looked
At the blood on the ledge, and the far valley. I looked
At last in his eyes. He breathed, "I'd do it for you, Bob."

IX

I will not remember how or why I could twist
Up the wind-devilled peak, and down through the chimney's empty
Horror, and over the traverse alone. I remember
Only the pounding fear I would stumble on It

When I came to the grave-cold maw of the bergschrund…reeling
Over the sun-cankered snowbridge, shying the caves
In the névé…the fear, and the need to make sure It was there
On the ice, the running and falling and running, leaping

Of gaping greenthroated crevasses, alone and pursued
By the Finger's lengthening shadow. At last through the fanged
And blinding seracs I slid to the milky wrangling
Falls at the glacier's snout, through the rocks piled huge

On the humped moraine, and into the spectral larches,
Alone. By the glooming lake I sank and chilled
My mouth but I could not rest and stumbled still
To the valley, losing my way in the ragged marsh.

I was glad of the mire that covered the stains, on my ripped
Boots, of his blood, but panic was on me, the reek
Of the bog, the purple glimmer of toadstools obscene
In the twilight. I staggered clear to a firewaste, tripped

And fell with a shriek on my shoulder. It somehow eased
My heart to know I was hurt, but I did not faint
And I could not stop while over me hung the range
Of the Sawback. In blackness I searched for the trail by the creek

And found it…My feet squelched a slug and horror
Rose again in my nostrils. I hurled myself
Down the path. In the woods behind some animal yelped.
Then I saw the glimmer of tents and babbled my story.

I said that he fell straight to the ice where they found him,
And none but the sun and incurious clouds have lingered
Around the marks of that day on the ledge of the Finger,
That day, the last of my youth, on the last of our mountains.

(1942)

Bushed

He invented a rainbow but lightning struck it
shattered it into the lake-lap of a mountain
so big his mind slowed when he looked at it

Yet he built a shack on the shore
learned to roast porcupine belly and
wore the quills on his hatband

At first he was out with the dawn
whether it yellowed bright as wood-columbine
or was only a fuzzed moth in a flannel of storm
But he found the mountain was clearly alive
sent messages whizzing down every hot morning
boomed proclamations at noon and spread out
a white guard of goat
before falling asleep on its feet at sundown

When he tried his eyes on the lake   ospreys
would fall like valkyries
choosing the cut-throat
He took then to waiting
till the night smoke rose from the boil of the sunset

But the moon carved unknown totems
out of the lakeshore
owls in the beardusky woods derided him
moosehorned cedars circled his swamps and tossed
their antlers up to the stars
then he knew   though the mountain slept   the winds
were shaping its peak to an arrowhead
poised

And now he could only
bar himself in and wait
for the great flint to come singing into his heart
(1952)

DOROTHY ROBERTS (1906–1993)
Private

On our Sunday afternoon walk in the green woods
In the underbough damp and brown we found the fungi
Overboiling from a log of sooty rot

Into this orange, yellow, coral even—
But not made out of earth or out of heaven,
Not like the airy leaves or the earthy root.

Who will praise fungi on Sunday?—lobed like a brain,
Brilliant, of no airiness or rooted reaching,
But deeply composed with decay for a private sun.

(1959)

CHARLES BRUCE (1906–1971)
Fall Grass

This is the season when the darkest grass
Flows in its deepest waves, on fading stubble;
The time of cloud; and cattle brought to stable
At dusk; and moonlit water still as glass...

Smoke in the mornings, and always a crow caws
On wagging wings. Across the first strewn litter
Of leaves a squirrel scurries, and children loiter
In roadside pastures after ripening haws.

Time to be thoughtful: time to be getting on
With threshing, and fall plowing; time to gather
Eelgrass, for banking house...A frail white feather
Of frost shines in the grass blades and is gone.

Slowly the days grow colder, the long nights fall;
Plows turn the stubble, fires are tended, and apples
Mellow in cellars; and under the roots of maples
Mice are burrowing. And the high geese call.

(1951)

Orchard in the Woods

Red spruce and fir have crossed the broken lines
Where ragged fences ran; ground-juniper
Covers the sunny slope where currant bushes
Blackened their hanging clusters in green leaves.
Where oats and timothy moved like leaning water
Under the cloud sweep of August wind,
The crop is stunted alders and tall ferns.

Above the cellar's crust of falling stone
Where timbered walls endured the treacherous
Traffic of frost and sunlight, nothing stands...
Under the wreckage of the vanished barn
A woodchuck burrows. Where the dooryard was,
The matted grass of years encloses now
Two horseshoes and a rusted wagon-tire.

Only the apple trees recall the dream
That flowered here—in love and sweat and growth,
Anger and longing. Tough and dark and wild,
Grown big of stump, rough in the bark and old,
They still put forth a light ironic bloom
Against the green utility of spruce.

Clearing and field and buildings gone to waste—
But in the fall, a gunner going home
Will halt a moment, lift a hand to reach
One dusky branch above the crooked track,
And, thinking idly of his kitchen fire,
Bite to the small black shining seeds and learn
The taste of ninety seasons, hard and sweet.

(1951)

John Glassco (1909–1981)
Catbird
for Marian Scott

'Airoee…
eh 'rhehu 'vrehu
eh villia villia 'vrehu, eh villa 'vrehu
        eh velù villiu villiu villiu!
'tse dàigh   dàigh dàigh
'tse-de-jay 'tse-de-jay 'tsee-'tsee 'tsirritse 'tsirritse
        'tsirao 'twitsee
'wìtitsee 'wètitsee 'wètitsee wit 'yu woity woity woity
téeah wéeah, te-wéeah-weeàh
k' tuf à tuf à tuf à tuf à tuf à te kerry
k'rry k'rry k'rry, tū!
ka 'kea kowa, keka keka!
'tw'ait, 'tw'it. Tw'at.

Cràow! 'Tsh'àow!

Quèah? Pueàh!
soit soit soit, twee twee 'twittitsee
kooka prea prea prea, preoi, preait, preoit,
        preeai preoo, pirriweet, peto peto peto

Pràigh! Pràigh!
pip te waigh à tshewa
pip te woi wee, 'tshippewatt 'wurr-wurr.

Sooteet sooteet sooteet

'airoee? airoee…

Cr'àow! 'Tsh'àow!

'tship.
(1971) [1963]

A. M. KLEIN (1909–1972)
Beaver

He lifts his middle-aged cabby face from roots,
hears the far ferment of the fall. *The time!*
Soon drunk with juice of timber, he smiles logs:
the joy of habitat.

Twigs, branches, bitten bole–they teeth him and tusk him;
mud webs his feet, he shines as if with sweat;
now in deep water builds his forest, fruited
with fish, by currents breezed, by quivering quiet.

Come frost, and ice his mud!
                    Come flakeful fall
his herbage hibernate!
                    Come flurrying months
and whitely roof him over his crystal plinths:
he waits the spring—a merman animal.

(1952)

Malcolm Lowry (1909–1957)
The Glaucous Winged Gull

The hook nosed angel with spring plumage
Hunter of edible stars, and sage
Catsbane and defiler of the porch,
Dead sailor, finial, and image
Of freedom in morning blue, and strange torch
At twilight, stranger world of love,
Old haunter of the Mauretania,
Snowblinded once, I saved. And hove
Out of the rainbarrel, back at heaven
A memory stronger than childhood even
Or freighters rolling to Roumania.

(1962) [1947]

Dorothy Livesay (1909–1996)
Pioneer

He laboured, starved, and ploughed:
In these last days
Cities roar where his voice
In lonely wilderness first sang out praise.

He sits with folded hands
And burns to see
How he has ravaged earth
Of her last stone, her last, most stubborn tree.

(1932)

"Haunted House"

If people cannot stay in this sun field
Of wayward grass,
If people cannot live
Where ghost winds pass,
Wild raspberries know how.

Deep in July
The thick down-hanging canes
Bring mockery to the house half fallen down
With roof awry:
Wild raspberries are sweet with wind
And the bees' hum
Around this green sun field
Where footsteps never come.

If people go away
Or even fear to pass,
Wild raspberries and grass
Are here to stay.

(1932)

GREGORY J. POWER (1909–1997)
Bogwood

The year we plowed the river field, we found
Deep in the silt, the warped and blackened bones
Of ancient trees; and most of them were sound,
Though every bit as heavy as the stones.
Among them there were ribs, backbones, and knees,
Thin fingers that had held green leaves, or fed
White blossoms to the wind, lost springs, when these
Made magic here. For days we harvested
These bones of trees from soft, black furrows where
The land was wet; and when the field was done
We left them in loose tangles, here and there,
To season in the summer wind and sun.

Around the coast, old custom sets a time
For certain work, and in our neighbourhood,
When April comes we tidy up and lime;
December is the month for getting wood.
So, while the meadows slept, benumbed and white,
And skies were little more than half-awake,
We cut them into junks and they were light
As feathers now, but hard enough to break
An axeman's heart. One bitter night we burned
This wood that time had tempered in the mire.
It charmed those hours of rest, when we concerned
Ourselves with dreams, and made a ghostly fire,
Beyond its blue, transparent flame, we saw
The heat waves dancing in a parched July;
Its light transformed by some enchanted law,
Was hoarded sunlight from an age gone by.

(1989) [1930s–1940s]

ANNE WILKINSON (1910–1961)
A Poet's-Eye View

You are earth, loam, actual fields
And we the green reed growing from your body;
You are solid, we are porous, ringed with chatter,
Stalks that echo water
Running in your under-wordly springs;
Your ribs crack in the sun, ridge with rain,
We lie boneless when our tissues fade;
You are stiff against the wind, we
Bend, arc'd with ague, by the storm
Are properly bowed down a day
Then up a daisy, green stalk straight, unbroken;
You, the earth, are bound to earth's own axis,
We, who grow our down roots deep in you
Are multi-headed, spray out seed like dandipuff
To tickle the fabulous thin highborn skin of air
Before we fall, point every potent feather
Back into its spawning bed, your tethered body;
You are warped with rock, the woof of you
Is ore; in soul's rough weather
Rock splits open at the giant tremor of the soil;
We, the green ones, laugh and add an inch
For each storm's death, our knowing nonsense blowing
On and off the lode of your mortality.

(1951)

Nature Be Damned

I

Pray where would lamb and lion be
If they lay down in amity?
Could lamb then nibble living grass?
Lamb and lion both must starve;
For none may live if all do love.

II

I go a new dry way, permit no weather
Here, on undertaker's false green sod
Where I sit down beneath my false tin tree.
There's too much danger in a cloud,
In wood or field, or close to moving water.
With my black blood—who can tell?
The dart of one mosquito might be fatal;

Or in the flitting dusk a bat
Might carry away my destiny,
Hang it upside down from a rafter
In a barn unknown to me.

I hide my skin within the barren city
Where artificial moons pull no man's tide,
And so escape my green love till the day
Vine breaks through brick and strangles me.

III

I was witch and I could be
Bird or leaf
Or branch and bark of tree.

In rain and two by two my powers left me;
Instead of curling down as root and worm
My feet walked on the surface of the earth,
And I remember a day of evil sun
When forty green leaves withered on my arm.

And so I damn the font where I was blessed,
Am unbeliever; was deluded lover; never
Bird or leaf or branch and bark of tree.
Each, separate as curds from whey,
Has signature to prove identity.

And yet we're kin in appetite;
Tree, bird in the tree and I.
We feed on dung, a fly, a lamb
And burst with seed
Of tree, of bird, of man,
Till tree is bare
And bird and I are bone
And feaster is reborn
The feast, and feasted on.

IV

I took my watch beside the rose;
I saw the worm move in;
And by the tail I yanked him out
And stamped him dead, for who would choose
To leave alive a sin?

The pale rose died of grief. My heel
Had killed its darling foe,
Worm that cuddles in the heart
To ravish it. If worm not tell
How should rose its fairness know?

V

Once a year in the smoking bush
A little west of where I sit
I burn my winter caul to a green ash.
This is an annual festival,
Nothing to stun or startle;
A coming together—water and sun
In summer's first communion.

Today again I burned my winter caul
Though senses nodded, dulled by ritual.

One hundred singing orioles
And five old angels wakened me;
Morning sky rained butterflies
And simple fish, bass and perch,
Leapt from the lake in salutation.
St. Francis, drunk among the daisies,
Opened his ecstatic eye.

Then roused from this reality I saw
Nothing, anywhere, but snow.

(1968) [c. 1957]

WILFRED WATSON (1911–1998)
Sermon on Bears

1.

I would have you think on the mystery of bears,
and how they feed in the wild mountains, poets of our wilderness.
You will see the bushes with the hearts scooped out of them—
salmon-berry, wild raspberry, kinnikinic
miserably violated. I had not expected to find
that when an infinitesimal stalk of moss is broken,
the mountain suffered

2.

We set aside sanctuaries for these animals,
for every nation has its own sense of the sacred.
We cherish these brutes, not from impure appetite,
as English lords kept poets instead of whores,
but from our tameness, because, being utterly unwild,
we honour the strangeness of this brutal fur,
the beast we never are

3.

It is a truth that with stupidity—only the young
in it are lovable; and this truth repeats with bears.
The adult is mother-irritable, jealous-irascible.
I have seen a bear with a cloud of mosquitoes
covering its head—but the pathos of bears
is comfortless. You cannot wipe away the look
of treason from their eyes, but must leave them
to their blindness, and to their flies
and to the kindness of winter

4.

I fear our parks of mercy compromise this fur—
the pity of pity is its conscienceless cruelty—
there is a tendency in all natural creatures
to become monstrous, as if monstrosity
were the ultimate goal of unchecked nature;
and here among the bears this tendency is left free

to burst their forms in a grief for which there
is no natural relief. Would it not be better
to let our hunters decorate this fur with the death
which never brought any creature real loss,
             despite the will which deals it?

5.

These animals become our paupers—and of all creatures
only man can support indigence with nobleness,
recognizing, as Yeats said, that shabbiness is the patina of the poor.
We have ecumenically decided that their poetry
is not ours, who cannot support the stiff elbow
of our civilization, as rats can, crows and other vermin.
Let us therefore abandon to this decision
those whom we cannot save—without a revision
of heart we obviously have no mind for;
knowing at the bottom of our hearts, that with progress
             all poetry ends

6.

Then, Mary, mother of Jesus, pray to your son
to intercede with the father of all life
to accept back again into his incomprehensible bosom
the majesty, the mystery of his creature the bear;
who cannot support upon so simple a bone
the turning of the machine we mismultiply on earth,
             its ultimate monster

(1986) [1961]

Irving Layton (1912–2006)
The Predator

The little fox
was lying in a pool of blood,
having gnawed his way out to freedom.

Or the farmhand,
seeing his puny, unprofitable size
had slugged him after with a rifle butt

And he had crawled
to the country roadside
where I came upon him, his fur dust-covered.

Hard to believe
a fox is ever dead, that he isn't
just lying there pretending with eyes shut.

His fame's against
him; one suspects him of anything,
even when there's blood oozing from the shut eyes.

His evident
self-enjoyment is against him also:
no creature so wild and gleeful can ever be done for.

But this fox was;
there's no place in the world any more
for free and gallant predators like him.

Eagle, lion,
fox and falcon; their freedom is their death.
Man, animal tamed and tainted, wishes to forget.

He prefers bears
in cages: delights to see them pace
back and forth, swatting their bars despondently.

Yet hates himself,
knowing he's somehow contemptible;
with knives and libraries the dirtiest predator of all.

Ghost of small fox,
hear me, if you're hovering close
and watching this slow red trickle of your blood:

Man sets even
more terrible traps for his own kind.
Be at peace; your gnawed leg will be well-revenged.

(1963)

Lake Selby

Definitely it's not polluted
since no germ would wish
to be found dead in it,
and also it's absolutely
safe for you and the kids
for however far you walk
into its lukewarm wetness
wavelets sedulously suck-suck
at your hips and navel: believe me
it's hardly worth trying
to drown in it; you'd only
be found sitting on your bottom
and the lake's, rope around
your neck or ankle,
stone heavy on your lap.

My son who is six flatly
refuses to swim in it
though wind and water
drive him crazy with joy,
especially water;
he calls the stuff squishing
through his toes 'sea food'
and wants none of its sliminess;
as he describes it
it's so many vile fingers
clutching clammily at his heels
he has to kick furiously
before they will release him
sputtering with rage
and spitting out mouthfuls
of tepid lakewater and weeds.

Yet the townsmen summering it
in stolid painted cottages
that each year tighten

around the lake like a noose
plunge into the shallow water
with cries of delight and gusto
ha-ha-ing to one another
and trying a hundred-and-one tricks
to amuse the less venturesome on shore;
for hours and hours I watch them
pretend they're bouncing porpoises
leviathans and comical octopi
or cruel-mouthed sharks
to make their beached wives and progeny
wave admiringly and praise;
afterwards, scrubbed clean of grime
and slime, smoking their pipes
they will sit and stare at the lake
which moon and silence have changed
into a silvered apparition
of some lost and perfect island
rising slowly to enchant them
between the dark elms and pines.

(1971)

George Johnston (1913–2004)
from "Under the Tree"

7.
God's good kind Earth, God's manybosomed Earth,
God's suffering ugly cunning beautiful
   Wounded creature of Earth,
The pit whence we were dug,
The garden in which we grope
   For love;
Kind Earth, our gorgeousness of blood,
Our fleeting pain of birdsong,
Our poised in air, our footsore, delicate,
Our lifted up in grief, our loosed in death,
   Carrion;
Darktongued Earth, tell our deeds to the dark.

(1966)

The Creature's Claim

I stare back at a gibbous moon and brood,
Hardly knowing the words that name my mood
Or the moon's mood, that shares the Earth with me,
Her stony stuff and creaturely history.

I brood over the creatureliness of Earth
This gibbous night, fifty years from my birth,
And feel her claim, not on my yielded life
But on my heart, cut out with a stone knife.

(1966)

Anne Marriott (1913–1997)
Sandstone

In this buff-gray cliff
Ash-crumbling under rock-blow,
Gouged by the sea's claws,
See the prints of the old generations.
Slice the stone cleanly, see
Webbed beach-leaf signature,
Ribbed shell-mark where now no shell is,
Soft wood time-turned flinty,
Bone of the unknown, unvisioned creature
Once as your bone.

Wind sucks broken sand with a terrible breathing,
Stone that shattered bone by bone is shattered,
Sea snatches out taloned green fingers
To shatter all;
Outjut of sandstone falls and is crumb and is dust.

Take the path, upward in stone,
To where strong trees bind encouraged soil together.
On atrophied fallen, forgotten,
Stands steady the supple new growth
Beyond the strained stretch of the clutching tide.

(1945)

Self-Guided Nature Trail

We left the sand
took a thin trail.
It was all childhood images at first
the fungus face
grinned out of the root
or made an umbrella for the gnome
the talking mouse
or poisoned the wicked witch.
Higher, bush densened, knotted into walls
huckleberries hexed us with their bright red eyes
ferns sharpened into swords.
Over our heads the sea-mist lingered
shaping trees
into heraldic totems
(figures that had slipped and shifted
for years in and out of my half-sleep)
but though we waited all we learned
were mythologies changing ten times in an hour.
Desperate, we searched out notices:
Skunk cabbage, largest leaf
of any native plant;
elder, leaves toothed and opposite;
red cedar—but no information that we sought.
At length we found the exit: at
the exact place where the trail began.

(1981)

DOUGLAS LEPAN (1914–1998)
The Green Man

Leaves twist out of his mouth, of his eyes, of his ears,
twine down over his thighs, spring out of his heels,
as he runs through the woods as a deer or an outlaw, or curled
up in moss and bracken, light speckling him feckless,
he watches the other animals, himself hidden
like an animal, although so strangely human
that if you surprise him you might think yourself looking
into the eyes of the mad but all-wise Merlin.

Boreal forest his most natural habitat
from the edge of our cities up to the tree-line
where at a summer's end in the spongy Mackenzie Delta
he glides through pale yellowing poplars before the snow flies
or at a Northwest River slips out of the spruce to play
with the huskies, chained on the shingle. His territory
spreads far and wide beneath the Bear. Morose
and frolic and savage his sports where the forests are.

But I have glimpsed him almost everywhere.
In pool-rooms and bargain basements. In the glance of the dark
prisoner in the dock, not knowing how to plead,
passionate the criss-cross light that sifts through leaves.
In pale changing-rooms at the atomic energy plant
the young technician is changed into a sylvan man,
shadowed with mystery, and suffering from the sap
like a young green tree, quick thrall of earth and frenzy.

And quick he runs through my dreams, so quick and grieving,
to banish grey calculations of tomorrow,
to banish old gods with gay assurance,
impatient of bounds and all mere definition,
but sometimes himself a god, now minor, marginal,
now reigning sovereign over an empty tomb,
the incised leaves on his flesh now wounds, now blood,
now flame. The forest reeks now with vermillion.

There is a shade that glides beneath the skyscrapers
and makes those papery steeples soar and tremble
like poplars in a breeze, a green man's shade
who came before Champlain, green traveler, trader,
debauchee, wearing around his neck
gull's feathers and four new sweetwater seas,
interpreting the woods to Europe and Europe to
the woods—till finally he was cooked and eaten.

His taciturnities were our title deeds,
his heart divided food that our hearts have fed on,
so many morsels from that seething pot,
some for the merchant princes in their lofty
boardrooms (a long long way from poor Etienne Brulé!),
but more for more ravenous hunters through other wastes,
lost, lost, and wild in utter inner dark
where the hunters and the circling hunted are the same.

And so I circle on the green man's tracks,
allured, bewildered by the bright green shoots
and headman's axe he holds, those baffling icons
(for all the subtle theories that I half believe in)
that lead me on and down. But past all doubt
there thrives an underworld where life and death
are woven. And it is bright and dark and savage,
as speckled and as rippling as a snakeskin.

Outlaw or god this cunning harlequin?
I feel him darkening my glittering veins,
he kennels in my loins, knows every crevice
of my half-breed heart, and yet eludes me still,
though rumours reach me of him fugitive,
laughing and drinking behind an empty warehouse,
disguised in rags, and tossing empty bottles
to splash and sparkle on the cindery railway-siding.

Scion of the undergrowth and underworld
but a prince of darkness in all daylight polity.

I could lead you on a perfect summer afternoon
into a clearing where the trees are still and lucid
and have you stare and listen till a rustle comes
of a serpent moving underneath the columns.
Light slows. Leaves tremble—with Marsyas' blood as much
as Apollo's brightness. Now break a branch, it bleeds.

Some nights and seasons are his own, and sacred.
Then dreams flow into the woods, woods flow
into dreams, the whole pent city dreaming of a carnal
wood, confluence that empties into the streets
with a scurry of leaves and carnival drums and flutes,
and torches that set fire to the leaves and the city, a blaze
of harlequin crimson, skyward, as quick he still winds
among the masquers mocking, a green man with green wounds.

(1982)

Black Bear

Sweet-mouth, honey-paws, hairy one!
you don't prowl much in the history books
but you sure figure when choker-men, donkey-men, shanty-men
    gather,
or pulp-savages, or top-riggers.
"I've seen me go up a tree so fast with one of them after me
I only had time to loosen my belt and give him my pants
or I'd been done for."
"When I came into the cook-house I knew there was something there.
And was there ever! A great big black bear.
He chased me round and round the table till I hauled off and hit the
dinner gong.
That shook him! He was out the door like a bat out of hell."
If only you could hear us talk, you would know how we love you
sweet-mouth, honey-paws, hairy one!

Cousin, comrade, and jester,
so like us as you pad along jocularly
looking for garbage and honey, and not leaving much trace,
dozing off (for a whole season—as who wouldn't want to?)
then when you waken, perhaps a little too devil-may-care,
not knowing your own strength, ready to carry a joke a little too far,
creature of moods, old man, young man, child,
sitting in a meadow eating blueberries by the bushful.

Don't you know how much we love you?
Old man, curled up in your lair? So come out and be killed, old man!
Sweet-mouth, honey-paws, hairy one!

(1982)

Patrick Anderson (1915–1979)
Landscape

Whether in snow scene or a green season
whether through whipping grass or foundering amongst swans
the emptiness is always the arena
where you are the one.

When bird like a bright pilot steers in the trees
or the snow's blossoms bulge in the shut pines
whatever is haunting there on the horizon
is wanting your mind.

Whether your journey is paved with the petals of flowers
or with the chords of waves on the piano sea,
amongst vowels of water or in the grammar of stones
the lovely is empty

until you, the one, the walker who talks to himself
move through the fields the forests and freely declare:
I am the man, the owner, the one who cares,
I am the answer.

Whoever you are this will define your heart
and what you are more will be shown by your further words,
whether you bring a poet to play a part
or a gun for the birds.

O welcome the medicine man with the gay moral
whose lovely politics are entirely love,
who says that he is responsible to these hills—
in him they shall move.

(1946)

Song of Intense Cold

One night when the stars are exploding like nails
comes Zero himself with his needle,
an icicle full of the cold cocaine
but as tall as the glittering steeple
that pins us down in the town.
One night when the stars are heavy as hail
he pushes the silver handle
and plunges in through the freckled skin
where the pulse of firelight trembles
the drug running round like the moon.
One night when the stars are dials
I see him stride in the meadow
and in his hand a glittering wire
he plugs in a rag of shadow,
and throws the switch till the whistling ditch
and the plough and the hill all sparkle
with light's electric evil,
and a sleeper cries, and a chipmunk dies,
his little guts turned to jewels
in the purse of his fearing fur.
And I wake when the stars are buzzing like flies
round snow's dumb windowboxes
and in the heavy grasses
the flowers turn to glass,
and find alight in the middle of the night
like a cage of lover's whispers
the great stove of the house
        though Zero plunges winter
        down through the blue December
        through the pitted hills and the chipmunk dead in his purse.

(1953)

P. K. PAGE (1916–)
Personal Landscape

Where the bog ends, there, where the ground lips, lovely
is love, not lonely.
                 Land is
love, round with it, where the hand is;
wide with love, cleared scrubland, grain
on a coin.
Oh, the wheatfield, the rock-bound rubble;
the untouched hills
                  as a thigh smooth;
the meadow.
Not only the poor soil lovely, the outworn prairie,
but the green upspringing,
the lark-land,
the promontory.

A lung-born land,
a breath spilling,
scanned by the valvular heart's
field glasses.

(1946)

Summer

I grazed the green as I fell
and in my blood
the pigments flowed like sap.
All through my veins the green
made a lacy tree.
Green in my eye grew big as a bell
that gonged and struck
and in a whorl of green in my ear
it spun like a ball.

Orphaned at once that summer
having sprung
full grown and firm with green,
chorused with fern.
Oh, how the lazy moths were soft upon
my feminine fingers,
how flowers foamed at my knees
all those green months.

Near reeds and rushes where the water lay
fat and lustred by the sun
I sang the green that was in my groin
the green
of lily and maidenhair and fritillary
from the damp wood
of cedar and cypress from the slow hill,
and the song, stained with the stain of chlorophyll
was sharp as a whistle of grass
in my green blood.

(1954)

Planet Earth

It has to be spread out, the skin of this planet,
has to be ironed, the sea in its whiteness;
and the hands keep on moving,
smoothing the holy surfaces.
        —In Praise of Ironing, *Pablo Neruda*

It has to be loved the way a laundress loves her linens,
the way she moves her hands caressing the fine muslins
knowing their warp and woof,
like a lover coaxing, or a mother praising.
It has to be loved as if it were embroidered
with flowers and birds and two joined hearts upon it.
It has to be stretched and stroked.
It has to be celebrated.
O this great beloved world and all the creatures in it.
It has to be spread out, the skin of this planet.

The trees must be washed, and the grasses and mosses.
They have to be polished as if made of green brass.
The rivers and little streams with their hidden cresses
and pale-coloured pebbles
and their fool's gold
must be washed and starched or shined into brightness,
the sheets of lake water
smoothed with the hand
and the foam of the oceans pressed into neatness.
It has to be ironed, the sea in its whiteness

and pleated and goffered, the flower-blue sea
the protean, wine-dark, grey, green, sea
with its metres of satin and bolts of brocade.
And sky—such an O! overhead—night and day
must be burnished and rubbed
by hands that are loving
so the blue blazons forth

and the stars keep on shining
within and above
and the hands keep on moving.

It has to be made bright, the skin of this planet
till it shines in the sun like gold leaf.
Archangels then will attend to its metals
and polish the rods of its rain.
Seraphim will stop singing hosannas
to shower it with blessings and blisses and praises
and, newly in love,
we must draw it and paint it
our pencils and brushes and loving caresses
smoothing the holy surfaces.

(1994)

MIRIAM WADDINGTON (1917–2004)
Understanding Snow

how hard it is
to understand
snow   how it is
a burning pillow
and a white
sea   a halo of
greeting   hello
from a far star
and a sudden-
ness of seeing

miracles   bands
of light curving
around us moving
inside us   and
even in spring
when grass covers
the snow winter
is not asleep
but waiting
folded and dark

about to sprout
from the plump
lap of summer
about to fountain
from the green jet
of maytime or
throw down from
its white tent
handfuls of
angry flowers

whole mouthfuls
of frost   paralyzed

stars   icefeathers
burning pillows
and white seas:
and on my empty
bed   lost summers
armfuls of soft
ownerless love

(1969)

. Dead Lakes

The dead lakes
of Sudbury
those passive
unstirring waters
without splash
without fish
without waterbugs
without breath.

The slag fires
of Sudbury
spill molten metal
on summer midnights
and the low lakes
of Sudbury
press deep into earth
under the towers
of shivering
mines.

I look down
in the dead waters
of Sudbury and
I think of Flaubert
with his crystal
Frenchness with
his one sentence
a day with his
passion for clarity
like the passion
of fish for a
living element.

And I search
for the living water

in the dead lakes
of Sudbury
and I search
for a living element
in the dead places
of my country.

(1972)

FRED COGSWELL (1917–2004)
Paleontology Lecture: Birds (Circa 2500 A.D.)

These balls of frozen feathers shared
The food on which our fathers fared.
But eggs they laid were much too small
To make a human meal at all,
And flesh upon their bones, though sweet,
Was not enough for men to eat.
So since their lives could fit no plan
Envisaged by economic man,
We left them in the wasteland drear
Outside the plastic hemisphere
We raised to hoard the sun's thin gold.
And so these creatures, dead of cold,
Are still preserved. Traditions say
(How true I do not know) that they,
Before they froze on frozen hills,
Made pleasant noises with their bills.

(1970)

A Grey World Lightened by Snow

Outside the window on a leafless bough
A spent Pine Grosbeak sits, no doubt at rest
Before it joins again its fellows in
The flock's bold pilgrimage through Winter snow
And sleety winds which brought it to this tree
Where a few frozen berries are clinging.

It may be this is no time for singing
For that lone bird is still. It grips the bough
Unmoving in its perch upon the tree
As if the beating of its carmine breast
Were through the feathers frozen like the snow
That has not melted where sharp claws sink in.

But its eyes are quick. They dart and move in
Response to whatever force is bringing
Things to notice, whether wind-driven snow,
The slightest shift of any twig or bough,
Or a paper cup that from one drift-crest
To another flutters from tree to tree.

This is a one-way viewing. Bird and tree
Are mine to watch, but that bird can't look in
Where warm and safe and fed I take my rest
While with my mind I am with it clinging
In a half-numb stupor to the grey bough
Of a grey world lightened only by snow.

But such a thought as mine may be, I know,
An example of human sophistry
Which claims words are most real, but the word "bough"
Is not less bough but more to those that in
Exigency take refuge there, bringing
No concepts to the space on which they rest.

If *life* is less the head than it's the breast,
Far more than I that bird realizes *snow*,

The time for silence, the time for singing,
The various uses of each shrub and tree,
The tang of cones that it sinks its beak in,
The sway and shift of every limber bough.

Fellow travelers, though apart, we rest,
Surrounded by recurrent thaw and snow
Here in time's tree, clinging to space's bough.

(1988)

AL PURDY (1918–2000)
Trees at the Arctic Circle
(*Salix Cordifolia—Ground Willow*)

They are 18 inches long
or even less
crawling under rocks
grovelling among the lichens
bending and curling to escape
making themselves small
finding new ways to hide
Coward trees
I am angry to see them
like this
not proud of what they are
bowing to weather instead
careful of themselves
worried about the sky
afraid of exposing their limbs
like a Victorian married couple

I call to mind great Douglas firs
I see tall maples waving green
and oaks like gods in autumn gold
the whole horizon jungle dark
and I crouched under that continual night
But these
even the dwarf shrubs of Ontario
mock them
Coward trees

And yet—and yet—
their seed pods glow
like delicate grey earrings
their leaves are veined and intricate
like tiny parkas
They have about three months
to make sure the species does not die

and that's how they spend their time
unbothered by any human opinion
just digging in here and now
sending their roots down down down
And you know it occurs to me
                 about 2 feet under
those roots must touch permafrost
ice that remains ice forever
and they use it for their nourishment
they use death to remain alive

I see that I've been carried away
in my scorn of the dwarf trees
most foolish in my judgements
To take away the dignity
                of any living thing
even tho it cannot understand
                the scornful words
is to make life itself trivial
and yourself the Pontifex Maximus
            of nullity
I have been stupid in a poem
I will not alter the poem
but let the stupidity remain permanent
as the trees are
in a poem
the dwarf trees of Baffin Island

Pangnirtung

(1967)

The Winemaker's Beat-Étude

I am picking wild grapes last year
in a field
      dragging down great lianas of vine
tearing at 20 feet of heavy infinite purple
having a veritable tug-o-war with Bacchus
who grins at me delightedly in the high branches
of one of those stepchild appletrees
unloved by anything but tent caterpillars
and ghosts of old settlers
become such strangers here
I am thinking what the grapes are thinking
become part of their purple mentality
that is
      I am satisfied with the sun and
eventual fermenting bubble-talk together
then transformed and glinting with coloured lights in
      a GREAT JEROBOAM
that booms inside from the land beyond the world
In fact
I am satisfied with my own shortcomings letting
myself happen then
            I'm surrounded by Cows
black and white ones with tails
At first I'm uncertain how to advise them
in mild protest or frank manly invective
then realize that the cows are right
it's me that's the trespasser
         Of course they are curious
perhaps wish to see me perform
      I moo off key
      I bark like a man
      laugh like a dog
      and talk like God
      hoping
they'll go away so Bacchus and I can get on with it

Then I get logical thinking if there was ever a
feminine principle cows are it and why not but
what would so many females want?
I address them like Brigham Young hastily
"No, that's out! I won't do it!
                    Absolutely not!"
Contentment steals back among all this femininity
thinking cows are together so much they must be nearly
all lesbians fondling each other's dugs by moonlight why
Sappho's own star-reaching soul shines inward and outward
from the soft Aegean islands in these eyes and
I am dissolved like a salt lick instantly oh
                    Sodium chloride!
                    Prophylactic acid!
                    Gamma particles (in suspension)!
                    Aftershave lotion!
                    Rubbing alcohol!
                    suddenly
I become the whole damn feminine principle so
happily noticing little tendrils of affection steal
out from each to each unshy honest encompassing
golden calves in Israel and slum babies in Canada and
a millionaire's brat left squalling on the toilet seat in
Rockefeller Center
                    Oh my sisters
                    I give purple milk!

(1968)

Red Leaves

—all over the earth
little fires starting up
especially in Canada
some yellow leaves too
buttercup and dandelion yellow
dancing across the hillside
I say to my wife
"What's the yellowest thing there is?"
"School buses"
a thousand school buses are double-
parked on 401 all at once

I suppose this is the one thing
your average level-headed Martian
or Venusian could not imagine
about Earth:
                    red leaves
and the way humans attach emotion
to one little patch of ground
and continually go back there
in the autumn of our lives
to deal with some of the questions
that have troubled us
on our leapfrog trip thru the Universe
for which there are really no answers
except at this tranquil season
of falling leaves
watching them a kind of jubilation
sometimes mistaken for sadness

(1990)

Margaret Avison (1918–2007)
Snow

Nobody stuffs the world in at your eyes.
The optic heart must venture: a jail-break
And re-creation. Sedges and wild rice
Chase rivery pewter. The astonished cinders quake
With rhizomes. All ways through the electric air
Trundle candy-bright discs; they are desolate
Toys if the soul's gates seal, and cannot bear,
Must shudder under, creation's unseen freight.
But soft, there is snow's legend: colour of mourning
Along the yellow Yangtze where the wheel
Spins an indifferent stasis that's death's warning.
Asters of tumbled quietness reveal
Their petals. Suffering this starry blur
the rest may ring your change, sad listener.

(1960)

Sparrows

Do tiny ruins, glimpsed triangles of parquet,
tempt stopover, or the shepherd's purse a-wag
or skeletal milk-weed? The frail millions
flit hither
blown like the wrack of hurricanes
along the barrel-ribs of sky.
Some will be off again
to tundra summer and the chill
promise of it and of death.

No bird-memorial commemorates
the prince of sparrows, in this their park
although our king in bronze
is here. The sparrows
in suet season, and through
carbon monoxide summer till
autumn's enlarged outdoors,
quick in their public middle age
keep hidden delicate and final things.

Only whiskered cats and the
hidden lover see their stillness, and
the devotees of cats.

(1989)

RAYMOND SOUSTER (1921–)
Weeping Willow

Nowhere a more
unabashed surrender
to the sun and wind.

Response to air delicate
as the most tinkling
shivering Chinese glass.

The stretching out
of a thousand fingers
to clutch the sun's
elusive ball of gold.

Roots reaching down
into their own
seven cities of beginning.

(1967)

Queen Anne's Lace

It's a kind of flower
that if you didn't know it
you'd pass by the rest of your life.

But once it's been pointed out
you'll look for it always,
even in places
where you know it can't possibly be.

You'll never tire
of bending over to examine,
of marveling at this
shyest filigree of wonder
born among grasses.

You'll imagine poems
as brief, as spare,
so natural with themselves
as to take your breath away.

(1974)

ELI MANDEL (1922–1992)
From the North Saskatchewan

when on the high bluff discovering
the river cuts below
                    send messages
we have spoken to those on the boats

I am obsessed by the berries they eat
all night odour of Saskatoon
and an unidentifiable odour
something baking
                    the sun
never reaches the lower bank

I cannot read the tree markings

today the sky is torn by wind:
a field after a long battle
strewn with corpses of cloud

give blessings to my children
speak for us to those who sent us here
say we did all that could be done
we have not learned
what lies north of the river
or past those hills that look like beasts

(1967)

DOUGLAS LOCHHEAD (1922–)
Open wide a wilderness

I.
Open wide
a wilder-
ness

with hemlock
balsam
dense

worm bark
for nut-
hatches

black and
white
warblers

veerie thin
silver from
silence

the paths
shrink
inward

mushrooms
push
old leaves

overnight
they
erect

& there are
windless
nights

for sitting
taking
cider

taking close
ways of
woods

unto us,
wrap too
the night

the river
hill
touching

stars, a
meteor
once

told children
in one
hot fling

all there
is
to know

in black book
of
universe

black book
of all
things.

II.
The open
wilder-
ness

each visit
each
year

each
a beginning
and closing

new terms
new shapes
of selves

& deeper we
dance
into

the maze
the
creeping

path so
unlike
anything

into soft
centre
labyrinth

gold maze
silver
flutes

birds on
a simple
casket

my parts
are
one

we are
to blink
and die

some minute
some now
in

the labyrinth
the tick-tock
wood

& what do
you say
to all

this open
and close-
ness

our shadow
dance where
damp limbs

piled and
rotting
lie

so much
like
half-tones

close-ups
of the world's
dead.

III.
Then there is
the
book black

untouched
unopened
unread

so much
a cage
of gold

hiding a
devil bird
living

on pheasant
heads
but,

O, this wilder-
ness
opens

and closes
like pages
and covers

& strange
faces
portray

lurkings
& dark clouds
closed paths

the central
wilderness
labyrinthian

now grasps
for
death

it was all
too
easy

to find

to find
this dark centre
of labyrinth.

(1975)

Elizabeth Brewster (1922–)
Starlings

I remember one autumn
There was a surplus of starlings,
And they used to shoot them
In the early morning.
Later, walking through the campus,
We stumbled on dead starlings,
Heaped up feathered bodies.
Somebody told me it must have been a dream,
One of those nightmares one has
On hot dark nights:
They wouldn't let all those birds lie rotting.
But it wasn't a dream.
I was there.

(1969)

Blueflag

So that I would not pick the blueflag
in the midst of the pond
(and get my clothes wet)
my mother told me that it was poison.

I watched this beautiful, frightening flower
growing up from the water
from its green reeds,
washed blue, sunveined,
and wanted it more
than all the flowers I was allowed to pick,
wild roses, pink and smooth as soap,
or the milk-thin daisies
with butterblob centres.

I noticed that the midges
that covered the surface of the water
were not poisoned by the blueflag,
but I thought they must have
a different kind of life from mine.

Even now, if I pick one,
fear comes over me, a trembling.
I half expect to be struck dead
by the flower's magic

a potency seeping
from its dangerous blue skin
its veined centre.

(1972)

Alchemist

Man, the evil magician,
brews, in the perishable cauldron
of rock and sand,
a violent fiery potion,
melted lightning.

Foolish enchanter,
do not break
this great brown dish
with green edges
which has been in the family
all these years.
Where will you find another
to hold your children's supper?

(1972)

ANNE SZUMIGALSKI (1922–1999)
On Conquest

This day hunters to the cabin.
It's the season they explain.
Inviting themselves to supper.

Three of them—a father and two sons,
They bring flesh,

A cowmoose fallen in a cold swamp,
Her own place,

Where she rooted for wet tubers. Blood oozes
From the great Roman profile,
Cakes in the nostrils,

Is a thin brownish smear on the powder of autumn snow,
While the wind is a bluish smear in the air.

Frost enters the enormous head through the eyes.
Frost enters the huge foolish mouth.

The grinding-teeth become brittle with cold,
Fall away like the first defences of a stronghold.

They might be the yellow stones of a Roman wall.

Here in the breached town of the head
Whole streets of houses are razed.

Roads with their arches of insight
Obliterated by a fall of ashes.

And the lolling red tongue is a bridge
Let down for the conquest of that bony keep

The skull. From the hunter's nostrils
Clouds of white breath. Breath of the hunted

Has become steam lifting the lid of an iron pot
On an iron stove.

I serve bread. I serve tea, mushrooms and berries
Preserved in jars. After dinner we talk;

I tell them how you have tricked me with foreign
Photographs. They laugh at your work,

Explaining that the colours are not bright enough.
I complain that your black and white interiors,

Mostly young girls reading books
In the bay windows of brick houses,
Are mannered and precious.

They display their own loud prints
Of conquered game and drowned fishes
Hooked on stringers.

They fall asleep at last on the kitchen floor,
Hands and guns under their heads for pillows.

All at once it's a clear morning for this
End of the year, and they're gone,

Taking their bravado and their harsh laughter
With them. It has snowed again,

Just a sprinkle really, but enough to cover
Their footprints to and from the privy.

To cover the slide of the toboggan,
The scattered entrails.

Their forgotten breath
Has thickened the ice on our windows.

The remembrance of their eyes,
Dark and opaque as camera lenses,
Has reached into the corners of the room.

(1988)

MILTON ACORN (1923–1986)
The Goldenrods Are Coming Up

The goldenrods are coming up
Late in the year, in all neglected places;
Our neglect is care for them.

They are pushing through the wild grasses,
the wild grasses turning to grain.
Outside my doorstep there are three withered heads
Of wild alfalfa tangled with goldenrod—

Like three princes of an old family
Trying to hold their land
While their heads turn dull;
The goldenrod twists them with
Its every nod, working at
Their roots and stems
like a rising moneylender.

(1968) [c. 1963–1968]

Crabgrass

Beast with tentacular white worms
For fingers, pitting your life against mine—
Crabgrass! I've laboured belly-low with the hot hand of the sun
A branding iron on my back;
Crawling with a knife along resilient living wires
Like one lethal snake after another—
Though you're tough enough to turn the edge
On this mercantile tool I've got.

What do they know, up in their hobbyhouse
About you, crabgrass? I weep and want to plunge
Into earth and follow you, brother,
Who'd leave this ground no succulence.
It's not like them or you my brain grows,
For whom each curse fuels a new blessing.
These white and furious nerves refertilize
Where they've destroyed. I'll burn you,
Being sure to retain your ashes—
These thoughts coiling far as smoke;
Secreting mulch to restore this acre.

(1987) [c. 1970s]

RONA MURRAY (1924–2003)
The Death of the Bear

Moving through cool moonlight
in a quiet place
        he tested
his hairy weight
against rough bark and caught
at branch after branch until
    —surrounded by apples and drunk
    with night time apple fire—
        growing careless
        he pushed too far
    stuck his front paws in the trap

        and fell

When they came he stood
outlined against the sun
and   taller than any
        he cried a man's cry
        waved bloody stumps at them

The boys hugged themselves in their delight
but the men stared uneasily
        recalling tales
        of great bears dancing
        of surreptitious mating
        and birth of lordly cubs
        to far walking women

   They fetched a gun   and one
     whose fathers had been hunters
        shot
    into the open mouth

       Half his head blown off
       the bear dropped at their feet

He will not die   one said
and kicked the mangled head
until it looked into the sky
and they could see clouds
     reflected in a living eye

          Let's show him to the women

They drove back
to the village
in a pick-up truck

               Come and see
               the bear who cries
               with a man's voice
               and will not die

The women
          —huddled in sweaters
     against the autumn morning—
               looked and prodded
               peered into the wound
               the noise came from
     and said
               when the wind blew them back
               to breakfast and TV in their clutch of shacks

               Leave him to the children

(1981)

JOAN FINNIGAN (1925–2007)
November on the Orser Farm

Moonlight enlarges the folk-myths
of the split-rail fences,
early Canadian icons
falling into the jungle
of the farm gone to pasture,
going to ruin,
soon for the sub-dividers

in the orchard
the apple trees gather
in dark untutored congregations

black flames of firs
flash against the sky

the songs of the creek
and the birds
have dried in the throat
of the rattling wind

On the south side of the house
in a wild bee-fetching tangle
of Manitoba Maples,
black currant bushes, cherry trees,
raspberry canes,
the empty white bee-boxes
of the dead bee-keeper
drift like lost boats
down the moon-glade
the long empty lane to the road
is lengthened
by moonlight

in the dark fields above me
are sprung in scattered clusters
the first diaphanous daisies
of the sky.

(1976)

COLLEEN THIBAUDEAU (1925–)
Getting the High Bush Cranberries

I looked up suddenly and the sky
was full of them, sky
was on fire with them.

Following her directions I find
the purple maple
walk the mosslog
deeper into the bush
veer at the rushes
test for sinkholes
crawl the rabbitdropping undergrowth
straighten up
and the sky is full of them, sky
is on fire with them.

(got the fence up here
a long story
so it's beginning
to look like Story Book Farm
after all
after a lot of work
also we've been laying in
crab-apple jelly
wild-grape jam
wild-cranberry & the like
and Arthur was into the chokecherries
for the wine also
I brandied some wild-plums
which I will never do again
as you have to pierce each
dratted little plum
with a needle
it's so nice to be settled in
Do come & see us)

The Lake is directly in front of me but
High Bush Cranberries swaying muddle up
locations: dis
mayme   dis
turbme   dis
locate

years of the instinctive glance
for bears over the shoulder
I begin picking, shouting
out to Burning Lake:

This is only Watergate Year
It's not Year Whole World on Fire
Not that Year yet.

(1977)

ROBIN SKELTON (1925–1997)
Stone-Talk

Put your hand on
stone and listen, not

with your ear or your
mind but with your fingers,

to the changing
syllables that spell

out sentences you have not
met before

save in the scratch of
bark upon the hand,

the rasp of grass between
the naked toes,

and listen (through your
fingers, through the throb

of pulse, the hiss of
skin) to all the words

that are beyond the words
we think we know

and are the knowledge that
we think to words.

(1985)

JAMES REANEY (1926–2008)
The Crow

A fool once caught a crow
That flew too near even for his stone's throw.
Alone beneath a tree
He examined the black flier
And found upon its sides
Two little black doors.
He opened both of them.
He expected to see into
Perhaps a little kitchen
With a stove, a chair,
A table and a dish
Upon that table.
But he only learned that crows
Know a better use for doors than to close
And open, and close and open
Into dreary, dull rooms.

(1949)

The Morning Dew

Shake seed of light and thunder
From where you hang.
The Word without the Flesh.

The pastures, sloughs and trees all shine
Their leaves and grasses sown
With flashing tears.

Here is Absalom's hair in crystal terms
Feverish bonfire of the sensual body,
Bloodbob.

Sharp, sharp yellow teeth, sharp sharp
In the dark mouth blinking of the
Fox-haired queen.

Blue as the fields of flax in the summer
That dream of retting, spreading, drying,
White linen snow.

Green as the thoughtful ancient woods
Ash contemplation of linden tree thinking.
Paththrough.

The killdeer's nest is built of gold,
Cobwebs are blessed and Eden
Has caught these fields within her fold.

(1949)

PHYLLIS WEBB (1927–)
A Long Line of Baby Caterpillars

A long line of baby caterpillars
follow their leader from the house corner
heading dead on for the Japanese Plum Tree.

Take away my wisdom and my categories!

(1962)

from "A Question of Questions"

v.
for R.D.L.

The error lies in
the state of desire
in wanting the answers
wanting the red-crested
woodpecker to pose
among red berries
of the ash tree
wanting its names
its habitations
the instinct
of its ways for
my head-travelling
wanting its colours
its red, white, its black
pressed behind my eyes
a triptych
three-fold
and over
and wanting the bird
to be still and
wanting it moving
whiteflash of underwings
dazzling all questions
out of me, amazement
and outbreathing
become a form
of my knowing.

I move and it moves
into a cedar tree.
I walk and I walk.
My deceiving angel's
in-shadow joins me
paces my steps and threatens

to take my head
between its hands.
I keep walking.
Trying to think.
Here on the island
there is time
on the Isabella
Point Road.
We pass a dead
deer on the beach.
Bloated. It stinks.
The angel insists, 'Keep
walking. It has all the time
in the world. Is sufficient.
Is alone. Keep walking.'
it says and flies off
with my head.

What's left of me
remembers a funny song
also a headless
man on rockface
painted in red
by Indian finger spirits.

The red-crested woodpecker swoops down
and sits on my trunk. Posing.
Dryocopus pileatus. 'Spectacular, black,
Crow-sized woodpecker with a red *crest*,
great size, sweeping wingbeats, flashing
white underwing.' Pileated woodpecker.
Posing. Many questions.
'The diggings, large *oval* or *oblong* holes,
indicate its presence.'

Zen Master.

(1980)

John Smith (1927–)
The Birds Returned

The birds returned so often to the island, to one
particular tract of peat bog, that they lost the hang of
interbreeding with any other race than those
who felt at home with the savour of a special ground-spruce

so thick that a man—but there were no men—
could walk on top of it and not fall through.
Inevitably men arrived—the island was a way station
on the route to somewhere else. Then everything changed—

not by much, but enough to keep wariness
on wing, flying wider circles, landing rarely,
the savour of ground-spruce farther off

the more desired. These are depictions of perhaps the last
breeding pairs. The captions have faded. Stories
tell of a land of one prolific mountain, back

before difference, before things parted from their names.

(1993)

ROBERT KROETSCH (1927–)
from "Seed Catalogue"

2.

My father was mad at the badger: the badger was digging holes in the
potato patch, threatening man and beast with broken limbs (I quote).
My father took the double-barrelled shotgun out into the potato patch
and waited.

Every time the badger stood up, it looked like a little man, come out of
the ground. Why, my father asked himself—Why would so fine a fellow
live under the ground? Just for the cool of the roots? The solace of dark
tunnels? The blood of gophers?

My father couldn't shoot the badger. He uncocked the shotgun, came
back to the house in time for breakfast. The badger dug another hole.
My father got mad again. They carried on like that all summer.

> *Love is an amplification*
> *by doing/over and over.*
>
> *Love is a standing up*
> *to the loaded gun.*
>
> *Love is a burrowing.*

One morning my father actually shot at the badger. He killed a magpie
that was pecking away at a horse turd about fifty feet beyond and to the
right of the spot where the badger had been standing.

A week later my father told the story again. In that version he intended
to hit the magpie. Magpies, he explained, are a nuisance. They eat
robins' eggs. They're harder to kill than snakes, jumping around the
way they do, nothing but feathers.

Just call me sure-shot,
my father added.

(1977)

How I Joined the Seal Herd

I swear it was not   the hearing
itself   I first refused
it was   the sight of my ears

in the mirror: the sight
of my ears   was the first
clue: my head did not please me

the seals so loud   I could hardly
accept the message: she wanted
no other going/than to be gone   the

neat bed itself   strange in the
mirror, she   kneeling across the bed
to close the window: maybe

I have this wrong: but only then
I saw   my ears/the difference
she wanted to go   I heard

a loud snort   a throaty grunt:
it was the breeding season   the tide
low, the wind still: they'd be wary

I knew, the seals   lying together
in the hot sun   maybe 300 seals
I counted   slipping off my shoes

the effect was immediate   I learned
to let my body give   it was not I
who controlled the rocks   I learned

curling my stockinged toes   to the
granite cracks and edges: maybe
I have this wrong   but I knew

in the first instant   of my courage
I must undo my very standing/crawl
on the wet rocks, the sand   not

standing   ease down on my belly:
it was strange at first   looking up
at the world: but I arched my back

I turned my head and paused   what
was I doing there on the beach/   wait
the luminous eyes of a young   seal cow:

I, the long bull seal   bravely
guarding the rookery   alone
holding together a going world/   but

frankly, I wanted to get laid   she was
maybe five feet tall (long)   the cow:
I could see   she didn't like my clothes/

moving carefully   avoiding any fuss
I unbuttoned, I unzipped   squirmed
out of my shorts, my socks   it was, yes

quite frankly   love at first sight/
flicking, with my left hand   some sand
over my back   for an instant

I thought of my wallet   my driver's
license, my credit cards: she had dark
fur on her belly   a delicate nose:

she went towards the water   looking
back over her shoulder/   the water
looking iceberg cold   I wasn't quite ready

she was rushing me: men in their forties
I shouted after her   are awfully good
in bed (on a sandbank   I corrected myself)

alone   I lay in the sand, I lay
watching   the slow coming of each wave
to the merciful shore   I humped

down to the water's curl   I, yes
without thinking,   *without thinking*, I
dove   my ears shrank

back   to my badly designed skull: under
the water: opening my eyes   I saw
the school of herring   SNAP

I had one in my teeth   I surfaced
hungry   I let myself float head up
on the lifting waves   I hauled out

I lolled: the cow that nudged me
awake: she might have been just plain
curious   my ear flaps, my exterior testicles/

that crossed my mind   or slightly perverse
but the sun had warmed me again   we were both
well   I was still a man, I had to talk:

my nights are all bloody   I whispered
god, I am lonely   as a lover/my
naked body swims   in the leak of light

death has a breath too   it smells
of bedclothes   it smells of locked
windows   my nights are all drenched/

my body/I   saw she had no idea
well/that was nicer, even   than the
moist hunger   in her eyes

I brushed   at my grey beard/
my flipper   trying to make the hairs
look like   vibrissae (I believe is the word)

I wasn't quite ready when   the bull hit me
I whirled   caught his neck
in my teeth   roared at the sonofabitch

slammed my head   against his nose:
he was gone/   the cow had noticed
everything   I could tell/she would

dance now/first   dance, slapping
the rising tide   to a quick froth:
she/I   rolling the waves themselves

back to the sea   I dared beyond the
last limit   of whatever I thought
I was   where, exactly, I asked is—

my only question   and when she gave
herself/took   me out of the seen land
this, for the gone world   I sang:

America was a good lay   she nearly
fucked me to death, wow   but this
I'm a new man   (mammal, I corrected

myself) here   and yet I was going
too far   too far past everything
dispersed past   everything here/gone

dear, I whispered,   (words again,
words)   I wanted to say/I am
writing   this poem   with my life

I whispered,   I hope (the rising
tide had lifted my socks   had swum
them to where   I might reach)

dear, I whispered   I hope my children
(ours, I corrected myself)   their ears perfect
will look   exactly like both of us.

(1977)

D. G. JONES (1929–)
Snow Buntings

i)
I watched them from the road

At first
they didn't move
and when they didn't move
you couldn't see them

They were earth and snow

The birds were in a fallow field
and it was earth
and snow
and so you couldn't see them

They moved

And when they moved
they moved like snow
like earth and snow blown by the wind
above the furrows
and since they moved
and since you knew that they were birds
you saw them   '

Their advance was slow

They moved up, one by one
in bursts
and disappeared

The sun came flooding over field and road
and it was cold
the sun was like a sea
to flood a barren world

You must make them
out of earth and snow

ii)
In the spring
the birds nest on tundra

It is spring

and the flowers bloom
they are like pictures in the fairy books
thousands of little flowers

they make carpets
carpets of flowers and stone

They have tiny claws

and when they light upon the bushes
they are weightless stone
bursts of rough stone

iii)
They make love among the flowers

They are like nothing made of wood
or stone
they are like wood and stone
becoming something else
in mid-air sometimes

and the sun is warm

iv)
Time sings across the land

and they are born
like little skeletons with grotesque heads

tiny in the nest
they are a fragile
syntax, drying in the wind

and they are mouths, mouths
lost among the grasses and the arctic flowers

v)
It is summer in the land, the falcon
hangs in the sun

the falcon
drops like stone, like carved stone
explodes

without resentment on the timid bird

vi)
They drift across the barren days

like grain in birch
in bird's-eye-maple...seeds

like feathered seeds they drift along
blown by the wind

blown by the wind above the grass and stone

and the days are long

vii)
It is winter—you remember?

and the sun bursts
upon an ebb in splendour
over fields

and it's cold

The trees are black
like iron against the sunset
but the birds

move

the birds like earth and snow
come from the tundra
and they move

the birds come from the tundra
and like blizzards move

they circle in the sunlight
like a whirl of snow

The wind is very cold

viii)
The wind is cold. I must go home

Make them out of wood and stone
wood *in* stone, perhaps
or vice versa—can you do that?

You must think of the birds

In the beginning perhaps
there were birds

Let us say
ab initio
there were birds...

The fences trail across the hills

Where do they go
in the thin air, in the cold
among the barns and naked fields

where do they go
in the waste fields?

You must think of the birds

and make them as you will
wood or stone or broken clay
with a brown glaze

You must lie down in the dark
in the naked fields
You must think of the birds

and make them as you will

(1961)

STANLEY COOPERMAN (1929–1979)
The Rivals

Three otters
on a slant black stump,
the lake green
The mountains
green and white:
sunlight
struggles
over the east ridge,
water
holds its mist
and three otters
on a slant
    black
       stump
mock me
through a cold november morning.

I slap a paddle
    at the neutral trees
    that—upside down—
    agreeably shatter;
one otter
    ducks his head and stares:
before my outraged eyes
the beast
grows fatter
with trout I could have,
should have
taken.
and what I most resent
is that he gives me
joy.

Bloody animals!
I refuse
to grant the precedence
of fur,
continue
to deep water,
cast my lure,
but—after one strike—
the fish are gone.
Still…
Galila has her breakfast,
I my pride,
and I must be content.
Nothing else remains
but bright silence,
iridescent leaves,
the otter's swift and
comic dance,
the journey home.

(1976)

KENNETH McROBBIE (1929–)
Something Wild for Our Room

This wild thing in our room
        is a dark green fir-top
from a dying tree in a frozen swamp.
    Birds streamed out like smoke
as we cut, leaving behind presents
of upward pressure even as it fell
and wings within its darkness beating.

Something wild for our room, cut
        as the wild light went.
One side bushy, catching the firelight,
the other flattened through deep snow,
    where the two of us broke a path
dragging its black cloud behind.

The woods were being taken home
        upon the roofs of cars,
leaving lowered prairie's bare
silver of floor sliding backwards
beneath the ashes of descending sky.
    Our tree covered the side-windows, drummed
on the roof, rising in the highway wind.

Cornered in our room, shocking
        green, its concentration
of needles holds now our soft gifts.
    And we have made a star come out
among the still-living decorations:
boughs white-ringed by the sharp
claws of birds, the fibrous
shimmer of their memoryless eyes.

It was never wilder. Its dark cloud
        reformed behind us, shrinking

each time a door was slammed
as the floor grew green with sheddings.
    When we took hold to throw it out at last
        by its stripped bare branches,
angled, fierce wings whipped and scratched,
then sprang to embrace both of us.

(1979)

Richard Outram (1930–2005)
Turtle

Each desk had its own sink,
With a sharp formaldehyde stink;
They were handed round in a pail;
Under the leathern tail
We probed, thorough in this,
The cloacal orifice
For imminent parchment eggs;
We articulated the legs
And duly noted in each
Leg-pit at least one leech;
The feet like webbed mole's paws;
The surprisingly sharp claws;
The extended neck and beaked head
Like our little toe; dead, dead
On the bright tile where we watched
The dissected dark-blood-blotched,
Dangled heart muscle beat
Beat after spasmodic beat,
As if it was still alive.

Creature, we may survive
Our present human disgrace
Through truths that your carapace
Or plastron's mosaic conceal,
Here virtuous to reveal:
But scrabbling across a road,
Past the flat pattern of a toad,
It would seem only chance can
Save you from passing man
Who will, for something to do,
Drive expertly over you.

(1979)

Peter Trower (1930–)
Goliath Country

Birds circle bewildered
in a scathing grey rain
above this field of the fallen—
these huge slain.
Cawing puzzlement,
they sideslip and swoop.
The downed giants lie silent
in more than sleep.

There has been great havoc here—
an enormous slaughtering.
Some David has run amok
with a machinegun sling
leaving a broken green silence—
an apocalypse of wood
and a new void in the universe
where Goliaths once stood.

They will come to remove the bodies
where the echoes linger
in driven chariots, driven
by the hard ancient hunger.
Birds circle bewildered
like men long-travelled
who return to find their homes gone
and the town levelled.

(1974)

The Alders

They alders are the reoccupiers—
they come easily
and quick into skinned land
rising like an ambush
on raked ridges—
jabbing like whiskers up through the washedout
faces of neverused roads.

The alders are the forestfixers
bandaging brown wounds
with applegreen sashes—
filling in for the fallen
firs—
jostling up by the stumps
of grandfather cedars—
leaning slim to the wind
by logjammed
loggerleft streams.

The alders are the encroachers
seizing ground the greater trees owned
once
but no more.

It is the time of the alders
they come
like a bright upstart army
crowding the deadwood spaces
reaching
at last for the hand of the whole
unshadowed sun.

(1974)

RITA JOE (1932–2007)
The Art of Making Quillboxes

In July, August, September and October
When it is the warmest part of summer
Maskwi' is ripe for stripping
To make quillboxes.

We look for the tree
The trunk the size of the bucket
The bark is good, we carve and cut
It peels away, coming to me

Now we look for quills
We see a porcupine
And throw a cloth on his back
Jumping behind, he aims the arrow
As if to say, "Leave me alone"
He waddles away

Now we have maskwi and kowi
To make quillboxes
The art of my people standing the ages
The skill like no other.

maskwi—birchbark
kowi—quills

(1991)

ALDEN NOWLAN (1933–1983)
St. John River

The colour of a bayonet this river
that glitters blue and solid on the page
in tourist folders, yet some thirty towns
use it as a latrine, the sewerage
seeping back to their wells, and farmers maddened
by debt or queer religions winter down
under the ice, the river bottom strewn
with heaps of decomposing bark torn loose
from pulpwood driven south, its acid juice
killing the salmon. August, when the stink
of the corrupted water floats like gas
along these streets, what most astonishes
is that the pictures haven't lied, the real
river is beautiful, as blue as steel.

(1961)

The Bull Moose

Down from the purple mist of trees on the mountain,
lurching through forests of white spruce and cedar,
stumbling through tamarack swamps,
came the bull moose
to be stopped at last by a pole-fenced pasture.

Too tired to turn, or perhaps, aware
there was no place left to go, he stood with the cattle.
They, scenting the musk of death, seeing his great head
like the ritual mask of a blood god, moved to the other end
of the field, and waited.

The neighbours heard of it, and by afternoon
cars lined the road. The children teased him
with alder switches and he gazed at them
like an old, tolerant collie. The woman asked
if he could have escaped from a Fair.

The oldest man in the parish remembered seeing
a gelded moose yoked with an ox for plowing.
The young men snickered and tried to pour beer
down his throat, while their girl friends took their pictures.

And the bull moose let them stroke his tick-ravaged flanks,
let them pry open his jaws with bottles, let a giggling girl
plant a little purple cap
of thistles on his head.

When the wardens came, everyone agreed it was a shame
to shoot anything so shaggy and cuddlesome.
He looked like the kind of pet
women put to bed with their sons.

So they held their fire. But just as the sun dropped in the river
the bull moose gathered his strength
like a scaffolded king, straightened and lifted his horns
so that even the wardens backed away as they raised their rifles.
When he roared, people ran to their cars. All the young men
leaned on their automobile horns as he toppled.

(1962)

JOE ROSENBLATT (1933–)
Mansions

Aroused in deepest mansions of the night
trout change their skin inside a speckled chamber
before they levitate above the iridescent vapour;
and singing as though it were a lunar highball
my soul absorbs a little ether out in orbit.

A riffle bubbles, "Isn't every fish a visiting star?"
Afraid, I pour some wicked moonlight down the hatch:
a woman leers back at me from Heaven…
Entangled in my net, a daughter of the river shimmies
flouncing in a silver nightgown; she's finally my bride.

(1983)

Caterpillar Disarmed

they are fuzzy dreams in dream pajamas
they tease trout through radio signals
they suffer from a dual personality
they have buried angst   don't indulge them
they embrace the female principle
they are found delicious by blind flinches
they loom into your life
they are three-dimensional women
they want to be raised on a pedestal
they are jealous of tabbies
they are primitives among the power elite
gold is alien to them

they don't want to drown
they are born blind
they are not too easy to domesticate
they eat far too much mulch
they love the warm weather
they take shelter in the storm
they hate the rain on their fur
they are mortal
they have a short time on earth
they are a hedonist pod on a leaf
they resist the temptation to fly
they have met Uncle Nathan in a tabernacle
they serve as bread for his brides

(1983)

Peter Blue Cloud (Aroniawenrate)
For a Dog-Killed Doe

They say she cried her agony for a long time
as dog fangs tore her body apart,
> trapped
at the corner of a fence, too swollen with
an unborn fawn to leap and run any further.

The neighbour took her in a wheelbarrow,
ready to take her body outside the fence
and dump her in a gully. "She's no more
good," he said, not looking at me.

"She's still alright," I said, meaning
much more as I looked into her eyes,
still so alive-seeming.
> There were two
deaths standing close by.

> When I cut
her belly open, that which was dead
tumbled out as if to mimic birth.
Many nations passed through my mind
as I began skinning the body of her clan.

I sit eating the flesh of her young,
taking the strength of her never-to-be
motherhood. I feast solemnly,
> wishing
sadly that I could take her back
> to winter.

(1995)

M. Travis Lane (1934–)
  Field

Field:
is the detail of the field,
and the relations of the field
to fields—to fields
composing planes
                    that deliquensce
in decomposing, battered ferns
crisping like drying seaweeds, foam,
no—fluff. Like seedheads, or like feather puffs,
like dry mists hanging in the bush,
snagged wool.

That valley into that
long gulley where the stream comes out:
you have a map for what it was,
a farm—
where we found those rusted pails,
containers for the things contained,
their bottoms gone.

The road
is the colour of old brick, its ruts
popping with frogs.
They spatter into grass.
Bear tracks, dog, deer, moose, human—
nothing's here
but last week's newsprint,
invalid

and the chartreuse, purring, insect,
the machine
that so delicately picks,
as if with mandarin nails, its coarse
fistfuls of logs.

It changes everything, the field
made plain.
But raspberries creep into it,
small spruce.
They recompose.

(1989)

Trout Lily
Erythronium americanum, liliaceae

This is a small flower.
Its leaves are brown like bruises—no,
like remnants of a night
they rubbed off on the soil
when they speared through,
red needles, and grew fat.

Earth tongue: a leaf
so leopard-mottled that
it has no definition on the ground.
The flower:
six prongs
that make the shape of sound,
silent until the bee's knocks thud
and speak its essence to itself.

It is
no cure for our diseases, but its roots
bleed when you uproot it.
It speaks
for earth, itself, its private needs,
not us.

(2006)

HEATHER SPEARS (1934–)
How Animals See

This is terrible.
It says here
bees can't see yellow.
So the broom, the rape, even the dusty
stamen of the rose
are lurid puce, a shuddery ultra pink,
studied to perfection
over hot millennia how best
to please their lust
these bits
zooming in for the take
faceted fuzzy cells
the dancing optics of a vast
seduced intelligence.
And as for us
what the flower intends
is less than casual—
utter indifference.
Oh my notched, loved world, atlas of lies,
no longer fit to believe!
and not even mine, not private—
photographed, reassured—
Van Gough in Arles—
impassioned cadmiums!
Armfuls of buttercups
plundered in childhood
on the Musqueam flats!
And now this maple, frost of gold!
The bees are gone to hive,
in secret, they keep the real real,
their tiny manifold eye
closing in on
the actual valuable
planet, terrible in neon and violet.

(1991)

JOY KOGAWA (1935–)
Rain Day in Beacon Hill

From the woods weeping green
and the lone bird calling
to this new house in this new suburb
its walls dripping white paint from
a blue veined sky overcome with slush—

Two blocks away in the future shopping cemetery
under a soap and salt washed sun
brittle bulrushes stand sentinel
silent frogs dive in a drying slough
beaver frantically gnaws a tree
snapping turtle snaps in futility
mud puppy, microscopic water life
water spiders, skaters, snails
crawling twig things, tadpoles
disappear down the roadside drainage
as if they had never been.

(1985)

PAT LOWTHER (1935–1975)
Anemones

Under the wharf at Saturna
the sea anemones
open their velvet bodies

chalk black
        and apricot
                and lemon-white

they grow as huge
and glimmering
        as flesh chandeliers

under the warped
and salt-stained wharf
        letting down
                their translucent mouths
                                of arms

even the black ones
have an aura
like an afterimage of light

Under our feet
        the gorgeous animals
                are feeding
                        in the sky

(1977)

Elegy for the South Valley

1

South Valley Dam is silted up,
the slid scree of a whole mountain
is leaning there; some year
when the rains keep
on and on as they do
it will go, and the wind seethe
in the trees,
the cedars toss and toss
and the creek froth
over broken banks
and the work of men
will all be undone

2

We have no centuries
here a few generations
do for antiquity:
logging camps hidden
around the backs of mountains
shacks falling without sound
canyons with timber trestles
rotting to shreds
like broken spiderwebs
straight scars and planks
collapsed on the walls
of improbable mountains
mountains mountains
and the dam that served
a mine that serviced empire
crumbling slowly deep
deep in the bush
for its time
for this country
it's a pyramid

it's Tenochtitlan going back
to the bush and the rain

3
The gravel pit is eating
South Valley, the way you'd
eat a stalk of asparagus,
end to end, saving the tender
tip for last. It starts
at the highway end
gouging alder and huckleberry
off the creek banks;
dust loosed in the air
precipitates slowly on water
and smooth wet stones.
Each year the tooth marks
go deeper along the valley
higher into the green
overhanging falls and terraces
of water, shearing toward
the head of the south fork
where the dam leans
between time's jaws
waiting for either
the weight of its past
or the hard bite of the future
to bring it down unmade
and original gravel
bury its shards at last.

(1996) [1974]

E. D. Blodgett (1935–)
Doma

We gathered up the little lakes and took them home—the fish that
    sleep
beneath their surfaces, the trees along the shores that shelter them,
the birds that cast their sudden shadows on the water—lakes and their
environments were placed in our house, and we would sit within
their seasons, floors beneath us but of grass, and where the ceilings
    were
the skies of several lakes arose, the air more various: we lived
with them and they with us until it was that we became for them

their seasons in their passage, autumns radiant in their conclusions,
snow and rain we were, a moon that finds its light dispersed upon
the water through the longest nights, at one with stars that see
    themselves
afloat in us and on the lakes. And so we are a knowing that is
not seen with our eyes but visible within our bodies, nor
is it given other than as parable that writes itself
in that place where air in gusts moves past, the colour of the lakes

now this, now that, and you might say that all of it—the we as we
would think we were, the water, air and changes in the light—was on
the point of speaking, and if they did, to speak in tongues not their
    own,
and we would speak as water, lakes would murmur with the chant of
    rain
upon their faces, rain itself and sun in our mouths as our
words, all of us an analogue of all that is, and where
we thought the centre was is there, at home upon the shores of lakes.

(2003)

CHRISTOPHER WISEMAN (1936–)
Snaring Valley

Nobody comes here and leaves
unaltered. Such wildness
stops us dead except
for the pulse, except
for the heart's thick sliding.

Few know the real Snaring,
have followed the river
up to the far heights of it
where wolf-pack and grizzly
rule the tangle.

It is the place for the
lonely man to discover
his loneliness, to know
that he can never again
not be lonely.

The further you go up
Snaring Valley, the further
you move into the secret
corners of the mind,
the places you don't want

to admit to, where
you are open to shocks
beyond understanding,
to sharp inadequacies.
There is no defence.

The danger is great
when we are cut off
from time and recognize
nothing. The senses
struggle, lost and confused.

Yet we need this place
to keep us frightened,

to keep ourselves open.
Safely down, we thank
our stars, and by thanking

notice them and know
stars for the first time.
They are further away than
we could imagine, but also
closer, brighter. Closer.

See, they are inside us.

   Jasper National Park
(1982)

Lionel Kearns (1937–)
Trophy

There were no grouse that day
but because we were hunting
I had to shoot something
so I shot a jay
as blue as the autumn sky
as he sat on a branch above me
in the golden glow of those leaves
I was eight years old
and my father was teaching me
how to shoot grouse in the head
so as not to spoil the meat
But this killing was not for food
I wanted a trophy. One feather
I pulled from the bird's tail
as I held it warm and limp
in my hand. This feather
I put in my hunting hat
and I glanced at my father
and behind him I glimpsed
the jay's mate gliding, circling
through the tops of the trees
"Better shoot that one too"
said my father, "You shouldn't
leave her alone." But I couldn't
get a shot at her, and we left
with the knowledge that I was now
a small sure source of sorrow
in this world, and my father
who was teaching me said nothing

Where is that father? Under the old earth
Where is that place? Under the new lake
Where is that boy? Inside an old man
Where is that feather? Inside the boy's mind

(1978)

GLEN SORESTAD (1937–)
  Shitepoke

shikepoke/sloughpump
shike/poke slough/pump
shitepoke shitpoke
what does it matter now?

        shikepoke or sloughpump
        the memory fades   fades
        we name and then unname
        but it was our word   good enough
        for anyone but ornithologists
        who latinize the bird world

the plains Cree named it
moo-ku-hoo-sew
naming the evening sound
when an Indian says the name
you can smell summer slough

and the first French trader
named it *butor*   then plunged
his paddle deep to pass by

        does it really matter
        that this bird
        is really the yellow bittern
        (though no one I know
        ever heard or used this name)?

we didn't know that shitepoke
was some English settler's way
of naming the bird
that shits when it leaps
to flight from the slough

I can still hear
the pump-handle sound cut the evening
still mould in my throat
the shitepoke sound

shikepoke/sloughpump
you are my language my image
shike/poke slough/pump

(1979)

EDWARD A. LACEY (1937–1995)
Mossbacks

Once a year, in June, we'd meet them on the road
(old and abandoned, scarcely a road any more)
back of the cottage, winding up to the hill,
up from the swamp, bodies unused to land,
dragging wet reptile tails through the hot dust
—the snapping turtles, coming to lay their eggs.
Obviously ladies, then. How hard to think of them as females,
with those black oozing bodies, three feet long,
those horny shells, and claws so sharp they'd put a cat to shame,
clenched disapproving toothless mouths wearing the grim expression
of an Ontario Presbyterian, and able
to snap a stick in half if you held it in front of them.
And their gentlemen? Their males? Well of course we never met them;
down in the depths of the swamp they sulked and waited.
But I suppose, considering the female of the species,
They would be even uglier, if possible.
All sorts of myths grew on them, like moss:
that they lived 500 years and got ten feet long;
that they were capable of swallowing a duck,
killing a dog; and old women even spoke
of children swimming who had disappeared,
dragged under the murky water by those jaws.
They were our monsters, our dragons, and we loved
to tease them when we met them (prudently keeping our distances),
to jab sharp sticks behind their legs, or in their eyes,
blinding them, or to stand upon their backs,
or turn them over and watch the thick long neck
muscles bulge in desperation as the head
butted against the ground, hour after hour,
trying to right itself. Some people even trapped them
and made soup—tasty, they say—out of their innards,
keeping the shells at home as souvenirs.
And still they came, each year.

Clumping on through the dust,
all of one hundred yards an hour, at high speed.

Future mothers, going to do their duty,
and we were not going to stop them. Children attacked them,
dogs barked at them, cows trampled them, cars mashed them,
but on they carried, every June, carried on their mossy backs
the burden of the future of the snapper race.
All year in the cool swamp, winter and summer,
they lurked; you rarely saw them even sunning
—unlike their pleasant bourgeois painted-turtle cousins.
No, these were isolates, true anchorites,
penitents and contemplatives of nature.
Not being fish, they must have had to rise
to breathe occasionally, but their blackness in the black water
made them invisible; if the swamp had a soul,
they were the true expression of it. It was their element.

I suppose in winter they must have hibernated;
yet we knew so little of them, I can't affirm it
—the invisible neighbours, the snapping turtles.
In order to spawn, they must have had to mate,
but the idea is almost inconceivable
—like priests and nuns—these solitary hermits
making it? In that ooze? I could imagine
with my child's eye the dance in the deep, dark water,
the mating dance of the male snapping turtle.
But what did he do then? Did he mount upon her?
Surely that would crush her, even underwater.
Or did their shells meet, or their tails interlock?
Well, any kind of sex was always a mystery to me.

But mate they did, and out they came in June,
the mothers, dragging their tails behind them, onto the foreign land,
like the first land-fish in the Devonian Era
a half-billion years ago. Why? Were *they* there then too,
the snapping turtles? Armoured like old tanks
I see them, moving through strange soupy seas
of distant ages, crawling across the first dry land,
always in progress, always moving onward,
carrying the race, carrying the race.
What did earth look like to them, after a year or an eon

of water and blackness? Did the light dazzle their eyes?
Did the green upset them, and why did they always choose
to travel on the road, with all its hazards?
Why did they come at all? Ask the turtles.

And the egg-laying? No one ever saw it.
I suppose it happened at night. Once more, I could imagine
the heavy black mother, grimmer-mouthed than usual,
digging the hole (six inches deep) with her claws, then bracing herself
for the labour pains, the discharge of her burden, the assurance
of a future better world of turtledom.
The leathery eggs plop one by one into the hole.
She lies bleeding, empty, after her travail,
exhausted, rests a while. And then
the hole is filled and smoothed over by the heavy paws.
No one could ever tell afterwards where the eggs were laid.
You only knew, one day, where it has happened
if you were poking around with your dog on the hillside and came
    across
an open hole and a half-dozen curled up leathery
broken ping-pong balls; then you knew they'd hatched
and dug their way out—the baby turtles—but no use looking for them;
you'd never see them being born, and you'd never find them.
How did they get back to the water so unobtrusively?
Such a long distance? And, come to think of it,
you never saw the mothers crawling back, either.
—Only the upward progress of the race.
Snapping turtles. So many mysteries.

I caught a young one once, on a log, while boating,
kept it for a year in a refrigerator tray,
where it swam, or sat on a rock taking the sun,
and learned to eat raw hamburger from a matchstick
and bit my finger without drawing blood.
Was it a mother? I never knew its sex;
it used to crane its neck in obvious pleasure
when I stroked the bald black head. After a year
I let it go in the swamp. It swam away and dived
into its dark element. Back to the swamp.

The swamp is gone now, bulldozed away
for a marina and a cottage development,
and no doubt the snapping turtles are going too
into the past of the planet and the race.
The cruel, purposeless, meaningless life of the swamp.
Still these great alien things with shining eyes,
black dripping bodies cased in mossy horn,
slogging like wingless birds through the white dust,
clump through my mind. No facile sympathy
or easy fallacy of communication,
only this, that even then I understood
—inchoately perhaps, but understood—
as I must write this poem, they must spawn.

(1974)

John Thompson (1938–1976)
Poem of Absence

An odour of moon, or
mown hay, green
cord wood,

the moon a yellow coat
in the mist;

the green glass of the wine bottle
does not yield
the body of things, nor

cut maple, grass, weave
of moon;

the wind pulls down the apples,
a coon squats
and gorges in the corn:

the open, where are you in
the open?

(1995) [1966–68]

Ghazal V

Don't talk to me of trifles; I feel the dirt in these:
what brightens when the eye falls, goes cold.

I have so many empty beer bottles, I'll be rich:
I don't know what I'd rather be: the Great Bear, or stone.

I feel you rocking in the dark, dreaming also
of branches, birds, fire and green wood.

Sudden rain is sweet and cold. What darkens
those winds we don't understand?

Let's leave the earth to be; I'm asleep.
The slow sky shuts. Heaven goes on without us.

(1978)

John Newlove (1938–2003)
    The Well-Travelled Roadway

The dead beast, turned up
(brown fur on back and white
on the belly), lay on the roadway,
its paws extended in the air.

It was beautiful on the well-travelled roadway
with its dead black lips: God help me,
I did not even know what it was.
I had been walking into the city then,
early, with my own name in mind.

(1965)

In the Forest

In the forest
    down the cut roads
        the sides of them
gravel rolls
    thundering down,
        each small stone
a rock waterfall
    that frightens me
        sitting in my ditch.

I smoke my last
    cigarette rolled
        with bible paper,
listen to the stone,
    casting down,
        some of it bouncing
off my hunched shoulders.
    Above me the dark grass
        hangs over the edge
like a badly-fitted wig—
        10 feet above me.

I dream of the animals
    that may sulk there,
        deer snake and bear
dangerous and inviolable
    as I am not inviolable.
        Even the gentle deer
scare me at midnight,
    no one else for 100 miles,
        even the sucking snakes
small and lithe as syrup.
    The forest is not silent,
water smashes its way,
    rocks bounce, wind magnifies

its usual noise
    and my shivering fear
        makes something alive
move in the trees,
    shift in the grass
        10 feet above me.

I am too frightened
    to move or to stay,
        sweating in the wind.

An hour later
    I convulse unthinking,
and run, run, run down the cold road.

(1965)

J. Michael Yates (1938–)
from *The Great Bear Lake Meditations*

I return here. Like a man who has bombed a city and returns as a
tourist, I return here—a camera between me and the world. How to
wrest my wilderness from the teeth of all my cannibal cities. One man
of me goes ghostly through all the walls. He lives without substance
and has only nothing to say. The rest live as animals at a zoo. And over-
civilized men who gaze down the colours of an arctic lake. In the twilit
negative landscape, a self-conscious nothing moves away: a pike which
will die with a pike in its throat. Geographic and historic distances are
coevals. I can fall up the terrible blue canyons between the clouds.

•

I'm here to remember my animal, that ghost-beast of many shapes—
sometimes a solitary caribou, more often a bear. A man comes north
to become an animal, to turn the whole day toward food and a place to
sleep warm. Small cracks begin at the bases of marble angels that were
his ideas. His days come down like trees felled to feed an insatiable fire.
Like trees felled to raise a cabin whose windows and doors vanish a
little hour to hour.

•

The caribou are crossing. Someone has just come to town and said that
from the air you can't see the ground for the animals. Twenty or thirty
thousand of them. It's fifty below. Quickly the town begins to empty
as the long snake of smoking vehicles moves out the highway. When
they arrive at the appointed place, the animals are still behind a ridge.
Cars and trucks park in a long line at the shoulder of the road, engines
and heaters running; together they send a mile-long hackle of ice-fog
into the flawless winter sky. The waiting begins and could last for days
until something occurs to the milling animals. Always there are a few
men who won't wait. They leave their automobiles, sling their rifles
and make for the ridge-crest. After a while, there are shots. Then the
interval to clean the kill. Those still waiting grow excited, impatient,
expectant. The first to kill and clean his caribou drapes the carcass
around his shoulders and begins climbing the ridge toward the road,

the long antlers bouncing as he walks. The rack is higher than the hunter's head, and those waiting see this before they see the man beneath the animal against the horizon at the top of the ridge. Doors open and several race across the road. Shots. The man carrying the caribou drops the carcass, flattens himself behind it, and fires back at the line of cars. The sound of a bullet striking the metal or the glass of a vehicle is almost indistinguishable from the sound of a bullet entering the body of a caribou or a bear.

·

I'm coming soon to the end of me, to the edge, the drop-off, to the place where the tundra halts, even the mosses don't survive, and the ice presides for all seasons. The auditory landscape thins and my ears are going blind of silence. I'll strike through. Then drown in the clear cold water at the bottom of the fall. And try to know I'm drowning as I drown. I came up from the south, from the equator at the centre of all bone where the hot dark whispered into my animal listening. But there was something else, always something else, had to be, and I'm moving out from the hollows of the tree-root places into the gaining light, over the thunderous boulders of the river-bed which shatter one another in high water, I pierce the thickets of nerve at the bone and enter the hazy skies of flesh, the skies the colour of lichen on the deadfalls, pass the ligaments, wade the currents of muscle, then wait days, often, for the water to drop in the glacial braids, to prepare for a crossing. The mad arctic light of the outside finally finds me through the crusted snows of my skin. I'm coming soon to the end of me, to the membrane which contains all my mortal remains. The needle of my compass points always north like the finger of a prophet until I become north, and, like a shot swan, it bewilders in terrible circles. There is no object in the white landscape upon which to triangulate. Hunter and weapon merge, and the quarry whirls at the box-canyon wall to battle the nothing at all behind him.

(1970)

BILL BISSETT (1939–)

othr animals toys

i was givn a job kleening a cabin   up in northern
bc that had bin totalee livd in by a lot uv pack
rats   from th amount uv brokn dishes   rat shit n
blood   on th floor   i think ther had bin major
parteeing   rats i sd   whn i got th first whiff uv
th smell

n thees huge nests they built   coupul feet hi n
decoratid with sequins   n brite tiny stones they
had takn off toy animals that had bin in th cabin
bfor they got ther

i kleend an entire day   non stop   scrubbd carreed
hevee nests out 2 th garbage far away   hammerd thik
metal ovr all th holes that th pack rats had sawd
thru 2 get inside   they had gnawd a hole thru th
front door   evree time i wud slop anothr bucket uv
hot watr n solvent on th floors   i wud hope ths
wud dew it   kleen it   th blood n shit   th smell
scrub   scrub   slop   slop

in wun uv theyr nests   layerd so beautifulee   sequins
shining   brite green grass   i lookd in   THER WAS A
TOY MOUS that had nevr bin ther bfor   in th cabin
IT WAS THEYRS THE PACK RATS HAD BROUT THEYR OWN TOY
MOUS INTO TH CABIN   WITH THEM

i now knew that probablee most creatures on ths planet
love   n have toys   n xperiens speshul delite in
miniaturizing   portabul   magik essenses   remindrs

n i knew fr sure th pack rats had brout ths toy mous
with them   i had nevr seen it bfor   tiny n silvree
n hopeful looking

that nite   i was almost asleep   undr th blankit   i
herd a nois   sat up   n saw a huge pack rat staring at
me   i sd   get BACK   i closd all yr doors YU CUDINT
HAVE GOT IN HEER   i was veree loud

th pack rat noddid   n split back outside
(1992)

PATRICK LANE (1939–)
Buffalo Stones

This river was a wall to the wandering buffalo
who drifted here in the last of summers
before turning back to graze their way south
into the American guns and the hunters
who shipped their tongues to the east.
On the brooding hills above the blue
great stones remain. Around their base
wallows curve in deep depressions.
Above them marsh hawks wheel.

But forget the hunters and their steel,
the old ones who wish
the animals' return to these wide plains,
the farmers who turn the rare
skull to sky with their deep plows.
The bones are long since shipped to Minneapolis,
a dream of charcoal stolen from the sun.

Above this river a child slides a stone
and does not know his long smooth falling
is a history of death, his breath
a breaking that the wind will steal.
But I, who wish to speak with history,
will sing of this though kingbirds cry
and coyotes move like ghosts
across the rolling grasslands.
There is nothing to atone, there is
only a dreaming, a child climbing,
and a man above a river who still feels
the heart's revenge, the grieving and the earth
falling like a smooth stone into darkness.

(1983)

Winter 13

There is a brief thaw and now
everything is frozen. Outside
ptarmigan wander ceaselessly
trying to find a way back
to where they believe
there is release from cold.
Beneath them their white sisters
struggle under the clear crust.
In the rare moments
when they are still
they are mirrors of each other,
each of them dying, each of them
wanting the other's dilemma,
believing the cries of the others
are lies, something done
only to torment them.

(1990)

Cougar Men

They came out of the hills with their arms
hanging in fists. Across the fenders and the hood
the cougars rested their long yellow, the male
with his eyes closed, not staring at whatever was left,
and the female's open, her lips pulled back over
the teeth, the long ones broken off at the base
by what must have been a stone, flakes of quartz
glinting on her torn tongue. The hounds
tied to the door handles with short ropes
raged at the air, one thin bitch tearing at the end
of a tail, the hair stripping off into her mouth
and her spitting, leaping again at what was dead.
The people came to the station in two and threes
from the bars across the street, men mostly,
but women too, some with children. One was me,
a small boy with white hair as if I'd grown old
before my time. I reached for a head
and when no one stopped me, touched
my finger to the female's eye, the ball sinking
in. When I pulled away, the ball stayed as it was,
a cup now, holding the light of the autumn sun.
A bottle of whiskey was broken open
and the men took it in their fists and drank, wiping
their mouths with their wrists. *Don't get too close,
boy*, a man said, and kicked the bitch in the ribs—
her falling under the other dogs and rising again,
slavering, her high wail wet among the pack. The crowd
passed the long teeth among them and then, because
there was nothing else to do, returned to the bars
and streets, women pulling their children by the arms.
The cougar men tied the dogs into the truck box
and pulled away from the station,
the tails of the cougars dragging in the dust.
Then the street was empty, the sun
caught in the tired elms. It was Thursday, I think,

though I cannot be sure. It was a long time ago.
Those dogs and men are dead now, gone to bone,
but that eye I touched still holds the light
in what little is left of me in those far hills.

(1995)

DENNIS LEE (1939–)
from Civil Elegy

3

The light rides easy on people dozing at noon in Toronto, or
here it does, in the square, with the white spray hanging
upward in plumes on the face of the pool, and the kids and the thrum
    of the traffic,
and the people come and they feel no consternation, dozing at
lunchtime; even the towers comply.
And they prevail in their placid continuance, idly unwrapping their
    food
day after day on the slabs by the pool, warm in the summer sun.
Day after day the light rides easy.
Nothing is important.
But once at noon I felt my body's pulse contract and
balk in the space of the square, it puckered and jammed till nothing
worked—the whole brave willed design
an abstract pass at grandeur, and casting back and forth
the only resonance that held was in the Archer.
Great bronze simplicity! that muscled form still
moved in the aimless expanse, and tense and
waiting to the south I stood until the clangour in my forearms found
    its outlet.
And when it came I knew that stark heraldic form is not
great art. For it is real, great art is less than its necessity.
But it held; when the monumental space of the square
went slack, it moved in sterner space.
Was shaped by earlier space and it ripples with
wrenched stress, the bronze is flexed by
blind aeonic throes
that bred and met in a slow enormous impact,
and they are still at large for the force in the bronze churns
through it, and lunges beyond and also the Archer declares
that space is primal, raw, beyond control and drives toward a
living stillness, its own.

But if some man by the pool, doing his workaday
job in the city, hammering

type for credits or bread, or in for the day, wiped out in Long Branch
by the indelible sting of household acts of war,
or whatever; if a man strays into that
vast barbaric space it happens that he enters into
void and will go
under, or he must himself become void.

We live on occupied soil.
Across the barren Shield, immortal scrubland and our own,
where near the beginning the spasms of lava
settled to bedrock schist,
barbaric land, initial, our
own, scoured bare under
crush of the glacial recessions,
and later it broke the settlers, towing them
deeper and deeper each year beneath the
gritty sprinkle of soil, till men who had worked their farms for a
    lifetime
could snap in a month from simple cessation of will,
though the brute surroundings went on—the flagrant changes
of maple and sumach, the water in ripples of light,
the face of outcrop, the stillness, and up the slopes
a vast incessant green that drew the mind
beyond its tether, north, to muskeg and
stunted hackmatack, and then the whine of icy tundra north to the
    pole—
despotic land, inhuman yet
our *own*, where else on earth? and reaping stone
from the bush their parents cleared, the sons gave
way and they drank all year, or went strange, or they sat and stared
    outside
as their cars settled back to slag and now what
races toward us on asphalt across the Shield—
by truck, by TV minds and the ore-bearing boxcars—
is torn from the land and all those fruitless lives, it no longer
stays for us, immemorial adversary, but is shipped and divvied abroad.

Take Tom Thomson, painter: he
did his work in the Shield.

Could guide with a blindfold on. Was part of the bush. Often when
   night
came down in a subtle rush and the scorched scrub still
ached for miles from the fires he paddled direct through
the palpable dark, hearing only the push and
drip of the blade for hours and then very suddenly the radiance of the
renewed land broke over his canvas. So. It was his
job. But no two moments land with the same sideswipe
and Thomson, for all his savvy, is very damp and
trundled by submarine currents, pecked by the fish out
somewhere cold in the Shield and the far loons percolate
high in November and he is not painting their cry.

Small things ignite us, and the quirky particulars
flare on all sides.
A cluster of birches, in moonlight;
a jack pine, gnarled and
focusing heaven and earth—
these might fend off void.
Or under the poolside arches the sunlight, skidding on paper
   destroyers,
kindles a dazzle, skewing the sense. Like that. Any
combination of us and time can start the momentary
ignition. If only it were enough.
But it is two thousand years since Christ's corpse rose in a glory,
and now the shiny ascent is not for us, Thomson is
done and we cannot
malinger among the bygone acts of grace.
For many are called but none are chosen now, we are the evidence
for downward momentum, although despite our longing still
restrained within the real, as Thomson's body really did
decay and vying to praise him
we bicker about which grave the carcass fills.

New silences occur in the drone of the square's great spaces.
The light overbalances, shadows
appear, the people walk away.
But massy and knotted and still the Archer continues its space,
which violates our lives, and reminds us, and has no mercy upon us.

For a people which lays its whisky and violent machines
on a land that is primal, and native, which takes that land in greedy
innocence but will not live it, which is not claimed by its own
and it sells that land off even before it has owned it,
traducing the immemorial pacts of men and earth, free and
beyond them, exempt by miracle from the fate of the race—
that people will botch its cities, its greatest squares
will mock its money and stature, and prising wide
a civil space to live in, by the grace of its own invention it will
fill that space with the artifacts of death.

On Queen Street, therefore, in Long Branch, wherever the
people have come upon it, say that the
news is as bad as we thought.
We have spent the bankroll; here, in this place,
it is time to honour the void.

(1968)

if

If it walks like apocalypse. If it
squawks like armageddon.
If stalks the earth like anaphylactic parturition.
If halo jams like septicemic laurels, if
species recuse recuse if mutti clearcut, if
earth remembers how & then for good forgets.
If it glows like neural plague if it grins, if it
walks like apocalypse-

(2007)

holdon

Homeheart, great loanheart,
hang in;
blue planet, hold on.

Are scouts of the aquifer perilous-
ownheart, hang in.
Bog templars. Heroes of tall grass resumption;
geodyssey samurai.

Not fold, great homeheart,
hang in.
Hold hard in the septiclot thromb of extremis.

(2007)

MARGARET ATWOOD (1939–)
The Animals in That Country

In that country the animals
have the faces of people;

the ceremonial
cats possessing the streets

the fox run
politely to earth, the huntsmen
standing around him, fixed
in their tapestry of manners

the bull, embroidered
with blood and given
an elegant death, trumpets, his name
stamped on him, heraldic brand
because

(when he rolled
on the sand, sword in his heart, the teeth
in his blue mouth were human)

he is really a man

even the wolves, holding resonant
conversations in their
forests thickened with legend.

    In this country the animals
    have the faces of
    animals.

    Their eyes
    flash once in car headlights
    and are gone.

    Their deaths are not elegant.

    They have the faces of
    no-one.

(1968)

Sundew

Where I was
in the land-
locked bay
was quiet

The trees
doubled themselves in the water

On half-submerged
branches and floating
trunks, the weeds were growing

Over the canoe-
side, the shadow
around my sinking

head was light

There was no shore,

In the hot air the small
insects were lifted, glowing
for an instant, falling

cinders. The trees drifted.

I didn't want anything.

My tangled head
rested water-
logged among the roots

the brown stones

its hair
green as algae
stirred with the gentle current

The sundew closed
on silence and dead energy
spinning the web of itself

cell by cell in a region
of decay.

After a long time
the leaves opened again slowly

A calm
green sun burned in the swamp
(1968)

Fishing for Eel Totems

I stood on the reed bank
ear tuned to the line, listening
to the signals from the ones who lived
under the blue barrier,

thinking they had no words for things
in the air.

The string jumped,
I hooked a martian/it poured
fluid silver out of the river

its long body whipped on the grass, reciting
all the letters of its alphabet.

Killed, it was a
grey tongue hanged silent in the smokehouse

which we later ate.

After that I could see
for a time in the green country;

I learned that the earliest language
was not our syntax of chained pebbles

but liquid, made
by the first tribes, the fish
people.

(1970)

Fred Wah (1939–)
Don't Cut Me Down

I don't want any of this tree poetry
shit from you. You don't know what a
fuckin tree is. If ya think its only
in yer head yer full a shit. Trees is
trees and the only thing they're good
for is lumber so don't give me any crap
about them bein sumpin else. Fer chrys
sake you think the rest of us don't
know sweet fuck all compared to you.
Well you don't know nuthin till ya go
out there and bust yer back on em.
Settin chockers'd break yer ass so fast
ya wouldn't even wanna look at a
goddamned tree let alone write about
em. Then ya'd know what a tree wuz,
steda yappin about it.

(1972)

David W. McFadden (1940–)
My Grandmother Learns to Drive

There I was standing on the shore of a small lake in the Muskokas
and the sky, the clouds, the waves and the small boats, everything was
composed of tiny patches of coloured light and each patch was a little
being with its own little consciousness, and each patch was swimming
in a unified field of golden light. Even the dreamer was composed of
little patches of light swimming in the same field of golden light, and
my poor old grandmother who was ninety and had never driven a car
came by driving a car and I climbed in and as she drove she drove
slowly into a snowdrift and stalled, she'd been doing pretty well until
then. So we got out of the car and sat in the snow and all around us
the snow was melting into miscellaneous little patches of white and
the earth was becoming warm and rich with new life.

With a finger I started digging little holes absently in the earth and I
touched something soft and round and buried, a young mushroom,
and it must have become aroused by my touch for it slowly began to
grow, pushing up through the soil, and it grew and grew like a penis
slowing becoming erect, and when it had grown to its full height the
earth around it heaved as if with ecstasy and the mushroom shot a
flurry of spores out into the air and I looked at my grandmother and
she smiled.

(1987)

Dead Belugas

Dead belugas washed up on the shore
Of the lower St. Lawrence are often found
With eyes wide open and smiles on their faces.
A mere hundred and fifty exist today
But in Cartier's time there were thousands.
He described them as looking like leaping greyhounds
"White as snow, and without a spot."

Today they are scarred and so horribly deformed
    A single beluga can look like two,
        A living breathing sewage dump,
A trash heap full of plastics and poisons:

An icon of the fate of humanity.
Over three million years the belugas developed
A sophisticated set of navigational skills
And a sensitive range of what we may term
Emotions because we can't understand them.
They travel in formations of intricate patterns,
Rolling over, swimming backwards and upside down,
Turning left, turning right, without breaking rank.
About eighteen hundred were killed each year
During the nineteenth century, until the market
For the whale oil and hides dwindled away.

In the thirties the Canadian government
Offered a bounty of twenty-five dollars
For every beluga tail brought in
Because the belugas were said to be eating
Vast quantities of salmon and ruining the catch.

Turned out they weren't, it was all a mistake.
So by 1940 the bounty was abandoned.
But during the war the small white whales
Were used for aerial bombing practice.
No one can estimate how many were blown

Out of the water with smiles on their faces.
They were once as common as whitecaps it's said
But now there are only a hundred and fifty.

And the hundred and fifty are not in good shape
    I told all this to a thoughtful, inquisitive
        Little girl about eleven years old.
            Maybe when we die, she said,
      Our spirits will swim with the whales in heaven
And we'll discover we're the same as them.

(1995)

Tom Dawe (1940–)
Sandpiper

It hopped
across the pool-streaked sand
as the tide was coming in,
with legs like straws
that would not bend,
and a low, piping call
on the rising wind.

It skipped
along the mussel-beds
as the sun dropped
from the sky,
and faded everywhere
in the surf
with a lonely, twittering cry.

(1992)

Alders

Last night I dreamed
they were bringing the world
back,
verdant tongues, calling out
to sun again;
but we were no longer
a part of it.
There had been great snows,
grey rock, and serrated forms
against a sky.
Millions of what we used to
call years had passed
before that
spear of green
between two stones,
that thrust of arrowhead.
Always apprehensive
of their coming;
we had massacred
in the name of clearing,
we who had whittled
small music sometimes
from the supple bones.

Fearful of advance scout,
of any forerunner
of wilderness,
we had always killed
messengers.

(1992)

Gwendolyn MacEwen (1941–1987)
Dark Pines Under Water

This land like a mirror turns you inward
And you become a forest in a furtive lake;
The dark pines of your mind reach downward,
You dream in the green of your time,
Your memory is a row of sinking pines.

Explorer, you tell yourself this is not what you came for
Although it is good here, and green.
You had meant to move with a kind of largeness,
You had planned a heavy grace, an anguished dream.

But the dark pines of your mind dip deeper
And you are sinking, sinking, sleeper
In an elementary world;
There is something down there and you want it told.

(1969)

Len Gasparini (1941–)

Elegy

*Port Hope: A 52-year-old woman who disappeared from
her home on Sept. 22, was found dead in a tree. Police say
the woman was found fully-clothed in a sitting position up
a tree near the lakefront. The body went unnoticed until
all the leaves fell off.*
                    —*The Toronto Sun*, November 13, 1975

Perhaps she had a covenant with nature, ·
or a death wish that coincided
with the autumnal equinox
of her disappearance. Who knows?
That she chose a tree to die in was peculiar,
as though some primal force in her took root.
But what kind of tree did that woman choose?
How did she climb it?
A druid tree whose leafy branches
almost touched the ground…
And what did the birds do when they saw her body
perched in a tree day after day?
Did they flock to her like a nest?
Did they sing? Or was their singing
silenced by her silence?
Did squirrels bury seeds and nuts
in her pockets?

During the long Ontario autumn nights
she shrank into herself—
a stiff, dry branch
stuck in the wind's throat.
The autumn leaves prepared her shroud.
Along the lakefront her colors were scattered.
When all the leaves fell,
the skeletal tree became her catafalque
in which she sat fully-clothed—
a scarecrow uprooted;

a fugitive from Gothic romance;
a phantom Daphne embraced by branches.

If suicide is a spurious valor,
to die alone in a tree
transcends all knowledge of good and evil.
And what of the tree, with its knot of darkness?
A tree is a tree...
How that beautifully mad, middle-aged dryad
truncated her family tree
is a subject for poets as well as police.

Let the strange circumstances of that woman's death
blossom in the hearts of those who would bury her.
The tree's roots have already dug her grave.

(1978)

JON WHYTE (1941–1992)
Larix Lyallii
for Jean Finley

Its adaptations sequester it in the narrow zone,
    a lonely last high place for trees
    where persistence and resilience
    measure survival, grudge, and fitness on
    bare rock, in thin soil, its competence
    unquestioned (it has no competition);
    it does not scrabble on its knees,
    like krummholz firs, against dessication
but angulates recalcitrant in black Sunday best
    nine months, or, like tormented cocktail
        ladies in grey chiffon
stretches arms in gloves for its expression.

Its young needles may be used for a kind of soup.
    It has "about nine relatives," we read,
    and two in Canada, the Western Larch
and Tamarack, deciduous conifers, which share shape
    with dead spruce at the swamp march
    and on bog edge, like misanthropes,
    their dying unattended, unwept,
    varying true to genotype,
grey ministers in a grove of younger trees,
    bible-black, covering their limbs
        with snow and hope.
The bare branch skeleton is an archetype.

From its fingers' warts in sprays, soft like
    small fountains or needle-ice needles
    of a softness akin to kittens' whiskers
leaves unfurl like chenille. We could make the mistake,
    unless we employed our fingers,
    of thinking them the hard spike
    of fir or pine, the rapiers
    willows bespeak,

but lo, they relent, submitting to late snowfalls
      of the wet June heaviest sort
        and do not break
but, reverberant, apparently kick back.

Their needles are hung so as to filter not obscure
      the sunlight, a green lace mantilla
      worn exotically among anemones
and dogtooth violets, moss campions that persevere
      the wind and sleet, friends in enemies,
      pikas, marmots, ptarmigans that endure
      among lichens the dappling felicities
      that dress the fellfield in grey-green and ochre
making of the alpine slopes a gaiety
      the forty frost-free days, if that,
        before the sere
winds strip needles and petals without care.

This rarest seen of trees in grey bark garbed
      in the Rockies no norther than Hector Lake
      persists; economically of aesthetic purpose only;
was named by David Lyall, a surveyor of the border
      who found it near the home of conies
      making hay on rocks beside it undisturbed.
      In September, a week before the aspens shake
      their gold, sun's equinoctial orb
and deep frost turn the pale and wanly
      green needles an instant gold,
        a gold in blue enrobed,
flung for a day; and in a day they're drab.

(1981)

ERIC ORMSBY (1941–)
Wood Fungus

juts in gray hemispheres like a horse's lip
from tree trunks. The outer edge is crimped
in sandy ripples and resembles surf.
The upper plane of the fungus does not shine
but is studious beige and dun, the hue
of shoe soles or the undersides of pipes.
Jawbone-shaped, inert as moons, neutral
entablatures, they apron bark and pool
rain. Underneath, they're darker, fibrous
and shagged.
              Mountain artists like to etch
delicate patterns on their flat matte skins,
and their tobacco-bright sketch marks look burnt
as tattoos or tribal tangles of scars.
When you grip their surfaces, they bruise.
When you pry them from their chosen oak,
they seem shut fast, like the eyes of sleepers,
or the tensed eyelids of children when they're scared.

(1990)

ANDREW SUKNASKI (1942–)
Soongeedawn*

soongeedawn
the full moon burning tunnels through your soft brain
while you arrive in wood mountain to prey
in silent coulees

soongeedawn
will you ever forgive us for poisoning offspring
of shugmanitou

spring and your bleached spine hangs on a barbed wire
while wind sings through headlights of a charred ford
in the nuisance ground—black ants build an empire
in your ribcage
and three bluebells grow on a hummock
where something struggles
as though trying to send a fist
up through the earth

soongeedawn: fox in dakota

(1976)

Diana Hartog (1942–)
The Great Blue Heron

Bravo! A great blue heron has swooped down. She stalked across the lawn, and is now plucking goldfish from the pool—to swallow whole their delicious struggles.

I prefer to rise early, before my host, and before the cloud hovering low over the lake can disperse. At this hour, from the garden, I can gaze down upon the cloud's white woolly back—and think of England's grazing flocks.

As for the Rockies: the mountains here censor any view but of themselves. I will grant the stars over Canada their tiresome brilliance, but wilderness, wilderness—why so many trees? A miracle, that the heron spied this tonsured patch on which to alight.

And look how she stalks about the garden! Granted, her neck is overlong. She stands on one leg—yet is she mocked as an eccentric? Because she is tall, does one call her grace 'awkward'? It seems that word hasn't yet reached her, of her imminent extinction. '*Oblivion has claimed the Sitwells*'? I agree with you, Osbert, we shall bring suit—much as I would prefer to ignore the grubbing robins with their worms.

Look how she stands, one claw lifted in disdain. O, I wish you could see her. Wind ruffles her pale blue feathers. Always at this hour, as the sun attempts to rise over the thick-headed mountains, a breeze stirs. My papers get blown about. Beside my camp desk, a full-grown *Cranbee-cordata* sways on her stalk. A veritable giantess, with huge flapping leaves—and all from a single cutting, smuggled out through the gate at Kew Gardens in handkerchief.

And now she reigns in this outpost. Turbaned with a single splendiferous bloom, she towers above the lesser flowers as I attempt to scribble, despite the wind, this letter to my dear, dear brothers…

Your loving Edith
6 July 1940

(1992)

Don McKay (1942–)
Field Marks

Distinguished from the twerp,
which he resembles, by his off-speed
concentration: *shh*:
                  bursting with sneakiness
he will tiptoe through our early morning drowse
like the villain in an old cartoon, pick up
binoculars, bird book, dog,
orange, letting the fridge lips close behind him with a kiss.
Everything,
even the station-wagon, will be
delicate with dew—
bindweed, spiderweb, sumac,
Queen Anne's Lace: he slides
among them as a wish, attempting to become
a dog's nose of receptiveness.

Later on he'll come back as the well-known bore
and read his list (Song sparrows: 5
                Brown thrashers: 2
                Black-throated green warblers: 1) omitting
all the secret data hatching on the far side of his mind:

      that birds have sinuses throughout their bodies,
      and that their bones are flutes
      that soaring turkey vultures can detect
                    depression and careless driving
      that every feather is a pen, but living,

      flying

(1983)

Song for the Song of the Varied Thrush

In thin

mountain air, the single note

lives longer, laid along its

uninflected but electric, slightly

ticklish line, a close

vibrato waking up the pause

which follows, then

once more on a lower or a higher pitch and

in this newly minted

interval you realize the wilderness

between one breath

and another.
(1997)

Load

We think this
the fate of mammals—to bear, be born,
be burden, to carry our own bones
as far as we can and know the force that earths us
intimately. Sometimes, while I was reading,
Sam would bestow one large paw on my foot,
as if to support my body
while its mind was absent—mute
commiseration, load to load, a message
like the velvet heaviness which comes
to carry you deliciously
asleep.
            One morning
on the beach at Point Pelee, I met
a White-throated Sparrow so exhausted from the flight
across Lake Erie it just huddled in itself
as I crouched a few yards off.
I was thinking of the muscles in that grey-white breast,
pectoralis major powering each downstroke,
pectoralis minor with its rope-and-pulley tendon
reaching through the shoulder to the
top side of the humerus to haul it up again;
of the sternum with the extra keel it has evolved to
anchor all that effort, of the dark wind
and the white curl on the waves below, the slow dawn
and the thickening shoreline.

            I wanted
very much to stroke it, and recalling
several terrors of my brief
and trivial existence, didn't.

(2000)

Precambrian Shield

Ancient and young, oldest
bone of the planet that was just
last week laid bare by the blunt
sculpting of the ice: it seemed a land designed
to summon mammals—haunched and shouldered,
socketed. Each lake we entered
was a lens, curious and cold
that brought us into focus.
Would I go back to that time,
that chaste and dangerous embrace?
Not unless I was allowed,
as carry-on, some sediment that has since
accumulated, something to impede the
passage of those days that ran through us
like celluloid. Excerpts from the book of loss.
Tendonitis. Second thoughts. Field guides.
Did we even notice
that the red pine sprang directly from the rock
and swayed in the wind like gospel choirs?
Not us. We were muscle loving muscle, drank
straight from the rivers ran the rapids threw
our axes at the trees rode the back of every moose
we caught mid-crossing put our campfires out
by pissing on the flames. We could tell you
how those fuck-ups in *Deliverance*
fucked up: (1) stupid tin canoe (2) couldn't
do the J-stroke (3) wore life jackets (4) didn't
have the wit to be immortal
and ephemeral as we were. Sometimes
in Tom Thomson's paintings you can see
vestigial human figures, brushstrokes
among brushstrokes. Would I go back
to that time, those lakes? Not without my oft-repeated dream
of diving for the body—possibly my own, possibly the lost
anonymous companion's—and surfacing to gulp in air

(the granite ridges watching, the clouds above them vacant
and declarative) and plunging once again into transparent
unintelligible depths.

(2006)

DAPHNE MARLATT (1942–)
  retrieving madrone

take, take the

        arbutus, crazy-woman tree, she said, does
everything at the wrong time, sheds last years' leaves mid-
summer, yellow, out of new green, sheds ochre bark at the
end of summer when

                you'd think she'd hang onto it
                            the way
light catches in the curled edges of her
                    skin, it's only
paper, thin enough to let light, as the words of this world
impinge, turn me out of mine. i throw off words, leave out-
grown images of myself

                crazy-waving-in-air ma-
drone this murmur you make, a stir of bright
leaves hitting home, the sound of *geta*, his
name for the thongs he wears against sharp
things on his path underfoot: a name, a use

overhead, over my head, i listen to slippery
woman, word peeler, leaf weaver, hear the slur
of a different being approach

            leaf   lingua   love-
                    tongue
                        turning me
inside out.
(2001)

SUE WHEELER (1942–)
   Sing a Song of Blackbirds

   So long siskin, goodbye
   junco, towhee and finch.
   The Gang of Eight have hijacked the feeder,
   redwing louts rousting regulars from the bar.
   They shovel for sunflower, splashing millet and wheat
   to mice and the Golden-crowned sparrow.

   The meek retire to the underbrush to wait out
   their inheritance. They know
   this is just a phase April's going through,
   a teenager slamming doors.
                     See him
   requisition the biggest maple
   with its thousand lime-green chandeliers.
   Into this ballroom of bloom and promise
   night comes singing,
   slices of fire on its shoulders.

   (2005)

Michael Ondaatje (1943–)
Breaking Green

Yesterday a Euclid took trees. Bright green
it beat against one till roots tilted
once more, machine in reverse, back ten yards
then forward and tore it off.
The Euclid moved away with it
returned, lifted ground
and levelled the remaining hollow.

And so earth was fresh, dark
a thick smell rising
where the snake lay.
The head grazed ribbon rich
eyes bright as gas.

The Euclid throttled and moved over the snake.
We watched blades dig in skin
and laughed, nothing had happened,
it continued to move bright at our boots.

The machine turned, tilted blade
used it as a spade
jerking onto the snake's back.
It slid away.
      The driver angry then
jumped from the seat and caught the slither
head hooking round to snap his hand
but the snake was being swung already.

It was flying head out fast
as propellers forming green daze
a green gauze through which we saw the man
smile a grimace of pain as his arm tired
snake hurling round and round mouth arched open
till he turned and intercepted
the head with the Euclid blade.

Then he held the neck in his fist
brought his face close
to look at the crashed head
the staring eyes the same
all but the lower teeth
now locked in the skull.

The head was narrower now.
He blocked our looks at it.
The death was his. He
folded the scarless body
and tossed it like a river into the grass.

(1973)

Beaver

*'the Great Spirit was angry with the Beaver, and ordered Weesaukejauk
(The Flatterer) to drive them all from the dry land into the water; and
they became and continued very numerous; but the Great Spirit has been
and now is very angry with them and they are now all to be destroyed'*

Beaver Beaver   slick wet hair
diver to the roots of air

       You appear
eyes washed out, camouflaged.
I've seen your remnants of noise, the
sound of one hand clapping
when I turn and witness blank lake.
You have left—invisible as bullets
you take your dark traffic away from the sun.
If I was beginning again I'd want to be
Beaver, in this wet territory

Plucking his way through slime to nuzzle branch
he shapes forests in the image of his small star brain
(only low flying craft and beasts have seen the chaos plan)
only drunk architects have imagined the bloated structures
the lush corruption of his victims

Industry proposing sloth
maggot introversion
so all will go dark
deep dark black deep till
all his lands and seas shall sing
the humming quiet of the carbon

(1973)

JIM GREEN (1943–)
   Seismic Line

double track drill rig trundles across the tundra
lurches to a standstill   stubby derrick raises
turntable grinds down the steel pipe stem
punching holes in the arctic permafrost

overalled men string out black wire
pregnant tubes are lowered into the earth
cable ends are twisted   charges set
BAROOM   mud and water in the air

all through the night the line snakes on
across swamps   hills   creek beds   and ridges
machines lumber along   men run behind
mother earth erupting   spewing gravel and sand

a white fox slithers from her den
stands on quivering legs   noses the wind
blood wells out around her eyes
drips   from her ear hairs

(1975)

PAULETTE JILES (1943–)
  Blacksnake

A tangle of black calligraphy,
taut as a telephone cord during an important call.

He has the arrogance of Texas oil, the way
his eyes dart little migraines.

His trickling, scaly currents erect on their own coils.

Slimmer and thinner his forepart curves
like a question mark to the hypnotized water—

the clear, beer-bottle-brown lens of these hills
and oaks. A high-power line dips in the pool

                              sip

sip

drops like cheap rhinestones splintering
unwinding like a black umbilicus
his slick glitter is perfectly voiceless and thin.

(1973)

Life in the Wilderness

There is no time to kill and so we don't talk much.
The lakes here have their own systems and currents run

on time, you have to catch them. Like blue pipelines
under water they have some place to go, carrying supplies.

The ship with a fat spritsail bends toward the surface
as if to scoop water, prevailing westerlies winding

through the clear air, which we package and draw.
Everything is whole, unlike home where we were handed our

Eden piecemeal, everything was piecemeal; here, this
country is open to everyone, these great virgin

everythings, the angel with the sword far away and not
a baron in sight. Let's pretend we are inhuman, no one

will know, among these shores like palaces, the cliffs and
towers, on this clean water we walk with our great sails.

We could pretend to be gods if we knew how a god acted,
if we could divine how a god speaks, if we understood

the motivations of gods. At this place the earth's stone
heart shows, like painted Jesus and his picturesque

interior. The red blood of the Benjamins, torn pines.
Let's keep sailing, someone will figure it out. A god

has only one personality, and this is force. One-
dimensional, flat, he is the force on the water.

Geese fly through the sparkling rain.

This is life in the wilderness; hungry.
This is life as a force; uncomplicated.

(1984)

PETER SANGER (1943–)
   Silver Poplar

So is isn't is. It is: a
negative game, apophatic,
turning to rights inside out.

I'd rather watch riddles
of leaves duck when the wind
hits like a flock of, you know

the kind, black on the back,
white as they veer away. I
wish you'd remember their name.

(1991)

Jane Munro (1943–)
Salmonberries

Later, things will get brutish.
I will squat, tug,
swing the mattock, work my fingers
round their knobby taproots,
fall over backward, all
to get the goddamned salmonberries
out of the meadow. But today
I pause to see their delicate green dressing
of April's raw flank—as if a blade had scraped
the scales off winter, then wrapped its ache
in seaweed. Salmonberry leaves
spring from sinewy branches. Each leaf
points toward the sky. Each flower,
a magenta bell, hangs down. A winter wren,
tail tipped up, extends and extends its song.
I turn back to the house thinking
leaves, flowers, bird—
wrapped in neat bundles like sushi.

(2006)

Dennis Cooley (1944–)
how crow brings spring in

                or no not that actually
                they are magicians in capes
                whisk it in from under their arms
                        crepes of sun
                                or egg

        foo yung in black tights acrobats tightly wrapt
        out they strut in those black shorts
                & march crashes
        them onto a trampoline wet with lights

        or lands them feet first
        on the plank of spring

                        & at their feet
                                aahhh the canadians sigh
                green   tumbles up up
                        onto the air over & over
                                somersaulting
                        & everywhere   somewhere
                                it may be
                may maybe
                        vaulting to summer

                under the big top
                in the spotlight
        it runs & drips
                        down the canvas

                                our faces open as kids
                in gum & caramel
                                on a binge
                        stuck all over
        our eyes and our feet

                    we are struck by
            we are stuck on
                        spring
                        imp
    inges
                                crow un
            hinges/spring

    (1996)

SID MARTY (1944–)
   Three Bears

In early September, yellow light
as snow was falling
and he was alone
returning from woodcutting
plans of putting up wood
for a long winter
In the blizzard without warning
he crossed the silvertip's trail
old sow and cubs, and she charged
out of that swirling light
tearing, tearing him

In the snow he woke up later
(this surmised from the signs found)
and she again, feeding nearby
was on him
but seeing no threat
allowed him passage of a kind
under a tree
where he stuffed his sash
a style he wore
into the hole in his side
terrible wound in that cold
and there, he died

2.
In September's fading colours
riding home
three bears, the fatal number
charged the horse which threw him hard
on the downed timber
breaking pelvis and thigh bones
out cold for a time
and coming to, he carved
handholds of sharp stakes
and crawled a mile to his cabin

Piling boxes one on the other
in the intervals of consciousness
he reached the phone
which happened to be working
so they saved him that time

Now he drinks beer in Edson
lives in the old folks home
And they say around the ruin
of that old cabin
there's a bottle of rum he buried
in the roots of an old spruce
But I never could find it

3.
Three weeks passed, and no other voice
but the whiskyjack's mockery around the cabin
I changed my shirt, and rode to Moosehorn Lakes
but the campground was empty

Indian paintbrush flowers
cover the trail
as if rust burst forth in blooms
lulling the senses

I think of Andy Suknaski
baiting a hook with the ochre flower
faithful as a child,
casting it out with a ripple
catching a perfect silver trout
The only fish we caught that day

How we are beguiled

The wind lifts toward the east
to brush these petals
when suddenly, from around a corner
swinging his head from side to side
a Grizzly Bear, silvertip
five, six hundred pounder

coming on so quickly
that motion would be useless

He sounds me, stops at twenty paces
to consider the next move

Speak to this bear
for he may know you,
said a voice
in my frozen senses

So I spoke softly
in his fierce hiatus
a deep and secret language
of love and claws,
a fluency I had only suspected
did make me wonder,
while he reared to his hind legs
in judgement

He swept the air once
with his claws, and hesitated
Dropping to all fours, he grunted
and moving aside
ascended the hill

But I am reminded
I am not at home
here where I live
only at hazard

There is darkness
along the bright petals

(1973)

Big Game

Look how the elk move over that hill

They cut their lives in snow
above Cascade. Higher still, the bighorns go
daring the avalanche slopes

On the road, the skiers jockey
in their fast cars, the sons and daughters
of oil men, Calgarians. They hurry to encounter
ski lifts.

When the game comes down to water
to drink from the clear, blue Bow
in ranges cut by highways

They will die, one after another
beneath the wheels

In the paradise of the middle class
(1981)

JOHN DONLAN (1944–)
High Falls

The north branch of the Muskoka River
airborne, falling
ten metres over its granite dyke
Eehaw! Get *down*!
each sparklet glitters and roars.

Listening;
no clear idea who is addressed;
middling acquainted with myself
lichen-rooted in this Shield
landscape, nature's janitor,

I pick human stuff off the trail:
Molson Canadian bottle-cap maple leaf,
glass blades in wait for animal feet,
double-flanged polyvinylsomething shard
—not the moth wing fallen to needle duff, dissolving.

(1999)

Muskrat
For Ruth and Mark Phillips

The forest gapes with the white scars of split
and shattered tree trunks after the ice storm,
a death-feast for tiniest creatures
bringing lost life to life again

by feeding on it. You feel helpless here
in the face of disaster on a scale unmatched
except by daily human life, that maw
into which the wild vanishes

however carefully you walk. You watch
the muskrat in the lake as if some silent
lesson was being taught all unawares,
as if its steady singlemindedness

in chewing leaves, in tearing small branchlets
from shrubs, in swimming back along the shore
to feed its hungry young, was something else,
some better way that you could live your life.

(1999)

JOHN REIBETANZ (1944–)
The Call
For Barbara Howard and Richard Outram

I.

Was that you? A ripple, arrowing through
the rows of barley, making no more noise
than the wind does when it strokes their tassels.
A call, but in the kind of sign language

that shyness and a mind for a teasing would
conspire to shape, a mute challenge you knew
I'd be too slow to pick up. To follow
across the field at dusk, leap the tangled

masses of deadfall bordering the pines,
and zigzag through the undergrowth without
breaking an ankle or heading into
a tree: that was your specialty, not mine.

II.

I marvel at Nature's reckless spending,
how she throws lives around like small change: each
rabbit the foxes get to, each chipmunk
frozen with tiny feet stretched out, unique

as the dapple of each leaf as leaves drop
by the millions. And you, my elusive
whitetail, the pattern of extravagance
sprouting from your head afresh each summer,

fast-growing branchwork that outpaced the trees
only to be cast off when the snows came:
was your airy leap also a spendthrift's loss,
or a headlong break to throw off gravity?

III.

Living in the country is like standing
under a shining cascade of shed things,

a flotsam of short lives spilling over
the unmoving edge. So I should have guessed,

on skis, doing my level best to catch
what I remembered of your grace of stride,
that the bare stalk tipped over in the field
was no small tree. Though the wolves pared your bones

to match the antler that you hadn't cast,
none of the knobby awkwardness of bones
hampered its branching flow, a silk-gloved hand
tracing one last leap, daring me to follow.

(1996)

Hummingbird

'Where do passions
  find room in so
      diminutive a body?'
          asks
Hector St. John
    de Crèvecoeur in
        Letters from an
            American
Farmer, shocked by
    a finger-long
        power bobbin's
            hot current: wings
spinning themselves
    invisible,
        a needle-mouth
            siphoning half
the body's weight
    each day, a heart's
        thousand stitches
            per minute, and
(most distressing)
    the petit point
        that leaves a limp
            red-threaded bag
where there was once
    a rival bird.
        Passions find room
            by purging the
hummingbird of
    everything not
        passion: no song;
            no orifice
to smell the bloom
    it plunders; legs
        mere filaments.
            Yet, a songbird

might sacrifice
      size, leisure, peace
            for a brief life
                 whose song is flight,
whose heart converts
      sugar to speed
            spinning, spinning
                the sun's gold thread.

(2000)

CHARLES LILLARD (1944–1997)
Little Pass Lake

'I'm looking for a lake'
  —Tom Thomson

Lake in the woods, Little Pass, & hot springs cast
across this beaver country uncut by canoe prow,
we find you pure as an animal's death. Green and lush
    from Packer Ridge

from Kenso Mountain,
  you are imagination's image, captured.
If we must remember
 let it be this
lake's afterlight
  sharpened in mind like
a surveyor's stake for boundaries
for today we are the king of lakes
   —we'll be true to our skins—
but this first view is for Thomson if he can hear…

So, Little Pass, quiet as water sliding from a paddle
we turn toward a highnoon of mountains, westward
and remembering you on the coast, we hope
  you'll forgive these stones
  breaking into your stillness.

(1973)

Peter Van Toorn (1944–)
Mountain Maple

I can't help it if you're under my leaves
when they start skipping around in the breeze
and some wetness on them shakes down on you.
Listen, there's enough wind on this mountain
to send us all skipping, and fire and rain
to blow our noses clean and steam our tears.
Is it my fault you like to lie around
with your head in my lap? I'm too busy
to be looking out for you all the time.
I don't know what I'll be doing this time
tomorrow. Maybe I'll stand here, shifting
from side to side, soaking up dew. Maybe
I'll stand here counting the cracks in my crown,
or sail off, roots and all, in a typhoon.
It all depends on what you think I'll do.
If you think I might drop a fist of keys
on your head, go ahead, and I just might.
You can stay here, or you can go away;
but before you do, try to remember
what you used to do on a scorching day
for some shade. And how did you go about
for a salad without a spot of green?
Oh, yes, let me know, if you ever come
this way again, how you treat your water:
how much you dish out to air in the sun
for the mineral sparkle in the dew,
and how much of it you store up in each root
to go under ground on all winter long
and still come up with syrup in the spring.
And talking about the talking of trees,
what are the birds going to touch down in?
At least my roots pose a problem for you,
so you think twice about axing me down.
I am one of a kind that carry fruit,

feed stoves by the boxful all winter long,
cover the tables with bloom in the spring,
and change with the splash of spring in the fall.
I'm grease on your gums, I'm sweat on your skin;
where my branches are, there are antlers too.
And who is going to do the dancing
that I do—be all arms and legs moving
but standing still, cradlewood for the moon?
On me you scratch and blot your bitter ink.
I make the matches, handles, and boxes
you burn me, cut me, and bury me with.
I am a cross between man and grass, and
grow in the thought of him from the ground up.
Is it for cutting me down for no use,
for letting too many of us go, till
everything's up to the nostrils in snow,
that you sing and cry and write down this thing?

(1984)

Ken Belford (1945–)

I was too poor to want to go camping.
Meaning resists definition but land came to mean
repression and animal slaves, so I migrated from
the rural north to the urban south. Since then,
I don't go to, or through, parks. It's not my territory.
There's too much potential for conflict in them
because the residents hold the place attachments
of imposing men. They build their houses on land
in the city, then they get land vehicles, and then
they return to the land of their birth, the land
of make-believe, the untroubled land of reason.
My land is unknown land, any ground, meadow
or woods. I won't be going back to the river
and I'm growing onward without it. I don't love
those places or groups seeking meaning from
the environment in places with the landscape
preference some call leisure differences. But
education is not the diviner of meaning. This
is about the variables of meaning, about writing
impressions on an affected landscape of place
attachments ripped from white-page phone books.
I wanted to live where there's no work on the land,
where the land had never been plowed.

(2008)

Tom Wayman (1945–)

The Ecology of Place
for Paul Bryant and Benton MacKaye

The place begins with water.
Lake, inlet or river
eddies into a clearing, turns
to planks and houses, businesses.
The forests go elsewhere.

The water moves the earth: supply
for the Interior and wealth
from the bush country.
There is a read-out of names.
Distant law begins to stop
the geography. A mountain is cut
by a noun.

But the place is a stone.
Magnet City. Farmboy and woman arrive,
immigrant. Mills, mines, speculations
become power somewhere as the Magnet turns.

There is a startup of railroad, and thruway.
The air fills; the harbour is
crushed rock; the creek solidifies
below the foodboard plant.
Oolichan, the candle fish,
go nowhere to breed.
But the nights are bright. California arrives.

> Then the City alone
> without the forest
> flows back looking for the child,
> free of beginning things, of logic.
> It wants to create again
> wilderness, but the trails are marked
> *for power toboggans, no hunting.*
> It desires a countryside

but the cows stand in feedlots of
urine and dung, eating grain.
Hens turn endlessly in the tiers
rotating like huge trademarks of the corporations.

The City dreams of a balance.
Of finding land under its feet.
Of exchanging commodities that are not on fire.
But it is the dollar and oil who stay awake all night
to draw up the Plan. Fish offshore
begin to cough.

I walk into the street.

(1973)

The Man Who Logged the West Ridge

The man who logged the West Ridge,
unlike the person who owns it,
has his home on the Valley floor.
The money this man got
for taking away the West Ridge's trees
paid a crew, made payments on a truck
and a skidder, reduced a mortgage, bought food
and a new outboard
and was mailed off to the owner.

So the fir and larch and pine
of the Ridge, its deer and coyote,
snails and hummingbirds,
were dollars for a brief time,
then were gone from our Valley.
Fair enough. While the logging was in progress
the man stood on the new road along the slope
to shout at a pickup full of people from below
over the howls of the saws
and the surging diesels:
I don't have to talk to you.
I am leaving a few trees. I don't have to do that.
Bug me, and I'll level this place completely.

Once the West Ridge was empty,
the owner put the land up for sale.
Remaining that close to the sky
is slash, and the churned soil,
heaps of cable and plastic oil containers
and a magazine of photographs
of young women's breasts and vaginas
that got passed around one lunchhour
and looked at, while everyone ate their sandwiches
resting against some logs. Nobody wanted to keep
the publication, not even the one who brought it,
so its pages lie on the earth near a torn-out stump,
the paper shrivelling into rain.

And the man who logged the Ridge
is finished with it, although he and the rest of us
constantly traverse its lowest levels
where the lane winds between our houses
and fields
toward the highway. Yet the Ridge
is not finished with the Valley
—its shadow continues to slip down its creekbeds
every afternoon
darkening the land as far as the river
while the other side still receives the sun.
That shadow, once of a forest,
now is born from an absence, from money,
from eight weeks' work.
We live each day shadowed by the Ridge,
neighbours of the man who cut it down.

(1994)

ROBERT BRINGHURST (1946–)
Anecdote of the Squid

The squid is in fact
a carnivorous pocket
containing a pen, which serves
the squid as his skeleton.

The squid is a raised finger or
an opposed thumb. The squid's quill
is his long, scrupulous nail, which
is invisible.

The squid is a short-beaked
bird who has eaten
his single wing, or impaled
himself on his feather.

The squid, however,
despite his Cadurcian
wineskin and four hundred cups,
does not entertain.

The squid, with his eight
arms and his two
brushes and his sepia,
does not draw.

The squid knows too that the use
of pen and ink is neither recording
impressions nor signing his name
to forms and petitions.

But the squid may be said,
for instance, to transcribe
his silence into the space
between seafloor and wave,

or to invoke an unspoken
word, whose muscular
non-pronunciation the squid
alone is known to have mastered.

The squid carries his ink
in a sack, not a bottle.
With it the squid makes
artifacts.

These are mistakable for
portraiture, or
for self-portraiture, or,
to the eyes of the squid-eating whale,

for the squid, who in the meanwhile grows
transparent and withdraws,
leaving behind him his
coagulating shadows.

(1975)

Rubus Ursinus: A Prayer for the Blackberry Harvest

Reaching through thorns,
milking the black
udders with stung
wrists. Sister and
mother and un-
named stranger, say:
whose is this dark
blood on my hands?

(1986)

Gloria, Credo, Sanctus et Oreamnos Deorum

1.

Knowing, not owning,
Praise of what is,
not of what flatters us
into mere pleasure.

Earth speaking earth,
singing water and air,
audible everywhere
there is no one to listen.

2.

Knowing, not owning:
being, not having,
the rags and the blisters
of knowledge we have:

touching the known
and not owning it. Holding
and held by the known,
and released and releasing,

becoming unknowing.
Touching and being
unknowing and knowing,
known and unknown.

3.

Sharpening, honing
piece of knowledge,
pieces of earth,
and unearthing the knowledge

and planting the knowledge
again. Question
and answer together
inhabit the ground.

This is our offering:
hunger, not anger,
wonder, not terror,
desire, not greed.

Knowing, not owning
the touch of another,
the other's reluctance,
the incense of fear;

the smell of the horses
in darkness, the thread
of the story, the thread
of the thread of the story;

arrowhead, bowstring,
snare; the breath
going out, the breath
going all the way out

and half-turning
and waiting there, listening.
Yes. Breath
that is lifted and carried

and entered and left.
Through the doorway of flesh,
the barely invisible
footprints of air.

4.
Killing and eating
the four-footed gods
and the winged and the rooted,
the footless and one-footed

gods: making flesh
of their flesh, thought
from their thought in the form
of the traces they leave,

words from their voices,
music and jewellery
out of their bones,
dreams from their dances,

begging forgiveness,
begging continuance,
begging continuance and forgiveness
from the stones.

(1995)

SHARON THESEN (1946–)
Axe Murderer

Look out!
Run!

Here he comes
dragging his axe.

He drags it because
he is so evil & stupid
he cannot hold it up

Unlike the whistling woodcutter
who lives in the little log house.

Chop chop, chop chop
goes the axe.

Eek! and O my God!
say the trees and the women.

All this goes on
in the forest.

So you can relax.

(1999)

Scenes from the Missing Picture

Funny, I hadn't even noticed it was gone.
Then Alice was over—she'd come on her bike,
shaking her blond hair out from the helmet,
pulling the material we'd contracted for
out of her messenger bag. "Here it is," she
said, placing the envelope on the cluttered
kitchen counter—cluttered as only the life
of a flame-haired divorcée could be—kids,
booze, boyfriends, you name it, social workers

Nosing around, late car payments—I lit up
a Parliament (Alice doesn't smoke) and said,
"So, how's it going, kid?" I thought we'd
catch up a bit before getting to the heart
of the matter. Alice didn't want a Cuba Libre
either, she wanted to get back to her apartment
and start working on her new film noir. In
the film she stars as a scuba diver and detective
called Nora Maple. In murky Vancouver inlets

At the edge of night she gets into her wetsuit,
puts on her mask after spitting into the visor, attaches
the hose and jumps feet first off an idling speedboat.
Cement blocks the size of Italians,
rusted out cars, octopi, cat-clawed sofas all
heaving around in the weedy current—it was some scene
down there all right. Your average tourist snapping
the sunset that flamed over the greasy pink surface
could have no idea what lies beneath.

As a bit of a connoisseur of psychoanalysis
I could relate to Alice's project. I realized
that the unconscious in this post-Freudian
context was a discredited concept, that our best hope
would be to overturn the stack of superego, ego, id,
and put desire back on top—top and centre,

the smartest poodle in the dog and pony show,
both paws raised and a cute little hat on,
the horse bounding round and round the ring.

Alice agreed. She drank a glass of water
and looked around. "Hey," she said. "What happened
to the painting that used to be over there?" She indicated
a large empty space with a nail hole at the top.
I squinted my eyes and puzzled at the wall. We
both remembered at once: "The Great Outdoors"!
In the painting, a man in a canoe paddles away from the
viewer. Large mountains tipped with pinkish peaks
loom around the lone canoeist, lost among loons.

Could someone have purloined "The Great Outdoors"
while I was busy spanking some executive or trying to get
one of the kids to bed? Some thief with gloves on?
Maybe the man in the canoe was a self-portrait
of the thief bidding farewell to the viewer
as he skipped out of the country with a bag of emeralds
worth millions on the black market of blond-seduction,
blond-amelioration, blond-appeasement.

The emeralds matched her eyes. Her nails matched the skies.
Her skirt matched her stilettos and her slip matched her
thong. She was in short a real siren. She'd never be trying
to make ends meet in a lousy condo on the East Side.
Her chinchilla coat she'd lay aside on an armchair at the Wedgewood
and four waiters would be there pronto with order pads
at the ready. It was obvious "The Great Outdoors" was part
of a world of crime and deception of gasping proportions.
Who knew what terrible deals were being made at knifepoint

On an idling speedboat anchored in Horseshoe Bay? "The
Great Outdoors" was just a pawn in a much larger grab for
hydro and hegemony, and it wasn't just about forests.
It was water, it was oil, it was natural gas, it was moose
heads over filmstar fireplaces in Wyoming. Whole rivers
could be diverted to squeeze themselves over dams

so teenagers could download porn off the net. As Alice
and I sat there contemplating the theft of "The Great Outdoors"
we felt like question and exclamation marks respectively.

With a sign bordering on panic, then sadness, then acceptance,
then closure, Alice put her head back in her helmet and
prepared to get back on her bike. One of the kids was crying
so I had to go anyway. Later that evening, looking at the blank wall
and wondering where "The Great Outdoors" had gone, I
glanced at the clutter on the counter and noticed a book
by Nora Maple called *The Mirror Murders*. Was it the clue
to the mystery? I'll bet Nora sees things on a regular basis
that would give H. P. Lovecraft the creeps. Meanwhile

Disposing of "The Great Outdoors" would be no piece of cake.
I felt kind of sorry for the art thief with that
in the back seat trying to be inconspicuous. In the rear
view mirror the canoeist held his paddle on the opposite
side, and the pinkish glow in the sky was that of morn
not eventide. A brownish tinge on shore was proving to be
a rogue moose in heat. "The Great Outdoors" was becoming
a case only Nora Maple could solve.

The phone was already ringing at Alice's house as the
sheepish thief wiped his brow, too frightened now
even to glance into the back seat where "The Great Outdoors"
stood propped, shining, immense, and fragrant—or
was that smell the bright green fir-shaped
pine-scented Magic Tree air freshener
hovering over the dashboard?

(2006)

Leona Gom (1946–)
North of Town

The fist of this town opens,
cracking its fingers north
across pine and spruce and muskeg.

    this is the symbol
        falling on the land
    this is the road
        fitting around itself
        the forest

Culverts knuckle under
        its wrinkle-pleated skin;
ditches fall away like dead cells,
        coagulate with old rain.

The road points into the wilderness,
to this final break with metaphor:
    what would be fingertip
    becomes tree,
    the road becomes path,
    the path does not leave
    the incomparable forest

(1980)

David Zieroth (1946–)
Coyote Pup Meets the Crazy People in Kootenay National Park

Brian brought him in
dumped in the back of his warden's truck and we watched him
die, a gasp at a time
spaced so far apart we knew he was
gone but suggested this or that anyway,
his breath hooked on a bone in his lungs,
his brown sides heaving for the sky
and we all felt for him in our different ways
which are the differences between men.
And twice Larry said, "Poor little fellow."
And Brian: "I could give him a shot of 'nectine
or a bullet but all I've got
is the .270 and that's
too big." So we hung on
till Ian pushed down on his ribs:
"Not much there." And still we
wanted him to run like the wind for the bush.
"Is that it?" I asked, hearing his
last lunge at the air, which it was, anyone
could tell he was gone,
off in a new direction
heading out somewhere else and leaving all
or nothing behind in those damn yellow eyes
staring out at me, out into a darkening world
where four men shuffled and laughed,
went in for coffee.

Inside with the rest of the crazy people
sitting down for coffee,
making words do all the work, talking shop, talking
park in the jargon of the civil servant man,
we know what chairs to sit in
we listen to the whirl of tongues
and the talk goes wildlife and telex and
choppers   it goes numbers and man-years and

stats it goes nuts for
fifteen minutes
and behind the words sometimes we hear
the anger and sometimes we hear the pettiness
and then the hurt. And someone tries to tell me
what this park really needs
what this park is really like, but I know already
it's like a dead coyote pup
lying out in the back of a warden's truck
waiting for the plastic bag we're
going to stuff him in and then we're going to
shove him in the freezer along with
the lamb that got it from the logging truck
along with a half dozen favourite
birds wiped out by cars, specimens now
and we'll save you that way, fella,
we'll cut off your head and throw it
up on the roof and wait till the bugs
clean you up and someday your skull will be
passed around
hand to human hand
and not one of them will be
afraid of you not one of them will let himself know
how the last gasp was also like a sigh
how it was the wrong way to die in the back of
a warden's truck   looking at steel
watched by humans   handled and pitied and
down on your side in the muck
a pup seven months out of the den.

Coffee's over   we turn from our chairs
notice the blue sky outside
the cold sweet air that comes from the breath
of the animals and we hurry to our places
the crazy people and me, we gotta get back to our
paper work.

(1981)

A. F. MORITZ (1947–)
The Ravine

To this shelf of rock so many movements
carry the things that wear the names.
Messengers, no things in themselves:
the different kinds of distance—to rocks,
to the ailanthus clump;
the kinds of heat that rise from the glowing
banks, warping the slope of weeds,
and are changed to coolness among
bearded syllables of a word
that day by day flows over.
The wind gives sudden bows
to each spire of grass,
to each its own style of address:
gifts of the air
pouring into the hollow
and down on the green spaces of river
shining in the gaps.
The purple thistles bob,
poplars choosing not to decide
sway and snatch their leaves
continually from silver into green.
A hushed noise rests all around,
choired in the glowing distances,
one locust and one bird
melding nameless music, the sounds
married in scent that also
has no name: a scent
shaken by the wind, lifted by noon
to this shelf of rock.
Here the first man returns
to his nude and mute survey,
to the voids of his speech
in which he perishes, worn out
by ghosts who offer themselves
and always unanswered escape.

(1981)

JOHN STEFFLER (1947–)
from *The Grey Islands*

black spongy paths,
caribou trails, cut
deep in the wiry scrub,
wander up on the island's plateau,
fade on the rock outcrops

pick up again in the brush,
drop, skirting bogs,
fan into squishy hoof-holes
black soup
stranding you hopping tussock to tussock

then gather again with the rising ground,
thin tracks cleaving mounded moss,
juniper, blueberries, crowberries, heath,
knee-high billions of matted micro-leaves
sharp in blue light tiny fruit trembling

 •

five tons of fish slippery as
pumpkin seeds on the longliner's deck,
I lift my foot high and wade
into them, feeling their bodies press
my sinking legs, stepping
on eyes and bellies, things
I usually treat so carefully.

two splitting tables ready to go,
Cyril gives me a knife and shows
how to slit the throats just
back of the gills then run the
blade down the belly seam to the tail.

I do this, passing the opened fish
to Ross who tries to twist their
heads off on the table's edge

the way Cyril tells him to. but
some of these fish having
necks thick as a wrist, Ross
struggles and Cyril shows him again
using his weight, using the table's
edge, until he gets it down pat.

taking the fish last, Cyril
moves his knife twice, down
one side of the spine and back with
a quick jerk, stripping the spine away
like a chain of ice,
his blade never touching the meat,
laid flat now, the white
triangular ware, the Newfoundland trade,
and he skids that into a barrel
for Pete to scrub.

the table's old wood gets
plush with blood then ridged
in grey scum and Pete sloshes
a bucket of water under our hands
and the scuppers gradually clog and we
move knee-deep in fish and blood
a thick pool washing heads and entrails
under us and blood drips from our jackets
spatters our faces and dries and
spatters our faces again, and I squeeze
my gloved hands and the fat and blood
pour out of them like gravy
and all around the air is flashing
white gulls, shrill with their crazy
hunger, wheeling, diving to
fight for the floating guts.

all this life being
hacked apart, us letting
blood out of its envelopes,
the world suddenly seems to be all

alive, blood running inside
of us and outside of us, inside
our hands and over them, with little
between the two, a cover of skin
keeping me in or out I'm not
sure which, but some sharp
bones have gone into my hands
and some of the running blood is mine.

(1985)

The Green Insect

I had a green insect, a kind that had never before been seen,
descendant of an ancient nation, regal, rigid in ritual.

It would sun itself on my windowsill, stretching its legs one by one,
  its hinged joints, its swivel joints, its claws,
unfolding and folding its Swiss army knife implements.
It was ready for a landing on the moon.

Around my page it marched itself like a colour guard.
It halted, and its segments fell into place, jolting all down the line.

It uncased its wings, which glistened the way sometimes very old
  things glisten: tortoiseshell fans, black veils, lantern glass.

It was a plant with a will, an independent plant, an early invention
  wiser than what we've arrived at now.
It was a brain coiled in amulets for whom nature is all hieroglyphs.

People gawked, and a woman pointed a camera, and I hesitated,
  but—I did—I held the insect up by its long back legs like a
  badge, like my accomplishment,
and the air flashed, and the insect twisted and fought, breaking its
  legs in my fingertips, and hung

lunging, fettered with stems of grass,
and I laid it gently down on a clean page,
but it wanted no convalescence,
it ripped up reality, it flung away time and space,
I couldn't believe the strength it had,

it unwound its history, ran out its spring in kicks and rage, denied
  itself, denied me and my ownership, fizzed, shrank, took off in
  wave after wave of murder,
  and left nothing but this page faintly stained with green.

(1998)

JOHN PASS (1947–)
Kleanza Creek

How will we get up Kleanza Creek
who deserve it least, road-dozy, teeth afloat
on litres of coffee? We gotta stop somewhere

and this is it, exquisite twist
of water from the miniature gorge, a sheen
of pool behind the boulder, a riffle across

this pristine gravel
back-filled and levelled for picnic tables, grass—
the facilities operator even now sweeping
the parking area.

Its beauty is a pang, a duty
we get free. "Fish me," it burbles.
"Take the trail." But ours is a serious

recreation, the camping with kids denouement:
motel-hopping home. Re-load the camera
and back of that, let poetry do it.

Poetry goes where no-one follows anyway…

me and that utterly mythical beast, the reader
dreaming a way up Kleanza Creek
for our arcane two-step…

last-ditch landscape sleazes wheedling
"Show us, you'll be famous, really."
Open the cliff's cleft, the spigot

in the bedrock. Let's taste the salt-
lick in the alpine meadow

from the highway, the *open road*
before the delusion swung
off at every exit shopping

the next (some chalk-blue pot-hole
of the disappearing pick-up, the cast-off
gear, some well-bucket for the soul)

scoops me weeks later on a lake on "lack of…"
a cutthroat sudden on my line, a catch, a whine

in my voice at, "what grinds me
down is the lack of…"

get the trout in the boat and come
back to it: gracious, humbling

in-your-face reflection…"attention."

(2000)

ANNE COMPTON (1947–)
Trees in Summer

Talk to me about trees at night.

How they move up the hill, or so it seems, in rows.
Their rainy heads full of wind: Red Maple, Sugar Maple, Elm.
The one at the window, a deeper darkness rising over the roof.

We sleep above. The day below on benches. Afternoons in summer,
a restless hammock. It's the nights we've waited winters for.

I've turned my bed around—did you notice—head to head
with all that rustling. A clairvoyance, I fall into. Call it sleep.

The ocean loosens something in us. We step out and for a moment,
anything's possible. There are pools in backyards, artfully fenced
frauds. Keeping the wind off.

Desire speaks the numeration of air. We have no words for this.
Only these lesser sounds.

Trees hold the story of flight in their branches. Birds have told
how we could be free. I want an end to this: Mornings

that disappoint with newspapers, phone calls. Called down.

In daylight, we are small beneath the branching,
awkward and off balance where roots curve ground.
The square root of bliss beneath our feet.

Talk to me in an idiom intimate as a binomial. Give
a sign. I'm this close and waiting. Some are here a century.

(2005)

June Bugs

Like prom queens, or brides, they have their season.
Nightly for a month, thudding the pane for lamplight, night light,
any light at all. By midnight it's all over. Their brief lives,
so many scuffed pumps discarded on the floor.

Ten (thousand) Foolish Virgins who never figured out flame.

Any entomologist will tell you, the June bug's an evolutionary freak.
Plump bodies, brittle and lacquered, they fly about as fallibly as hens
and with as much racket. Brownish beetles of the cockchafer group,
they crash the future. Fig-eaters out of Eden
clinging to hope and drapery.

(2005)

CRISPIN ELSTED (1947–)
  Swan Written

I watch it have no colour.
As it moves I see it
make the lake seem to.
I move farther back to see it seem

not smaller but larger and more marked
among rubbled ducks. I see it
move rushes toward me inhale banks.
I see it is inclined to nest through true reeds.

It is white there.
Swimming it has no colour
but a white bearing, an inclination
a leaning toward. It is about to occur.

This injures only in comparing.
I have been waiting not to hurt.

It has a white shield now.
It may argue the sun for me
many such days as this.

I know no finishing of it.

Now it is all moving.

(1996)

LORNA CROZIER (1948–)
Carrots

Carrots are fucking
the earth. A permanent
erection, they push deeper
into the damp and dark.
All summer long
they try so hard to please.
Was it good for you,
was it good?

Perhaps because the earth won't answer
they keep on trying.
While you stroll through the garden
thinking *carrot cake,*
carrots and onions in beef stew,
carrot pudding with caramel sauce,
they are fucking their brains out
in the hottest part of the afternoon.

(1985)

A Prophet in His Own Country

The gopher on his hind legs
is taut with holiness and fright.
Miniature and beardless,
he could be stoned or flooded out,
burnt alive in stubble fields,
martyr to children for a penny a tail.

How can you not believe an animal
who goes down headfirst
into darkness, into the ceaseless
pull of gravity beneath him?
What faith that takes!

I come to him with questions
because I love his ears, how perfectly
they fit, how flat they lie against his head.
They hear the inner and the outer
worlds: what rain says
underground. The stone's praise
for the sparrow's ankle bone.

Little earth-otter, little dusty Lazarus,
he vanishes, he rises. He won't tell us
what he's seen.

(2002)

Kristjana Gunnars (1948–)
Thorleifur Joakimsson, Daybook III

october 7, 1876: more rain
since august, whole days
of rain from the north

september mild, first nightfrost
october, otherwise
easy with cicadas

in the brush, fast moving
wind in the dry rushes
loud rattle of song

of the four-winged cicada
the nonjumping, large, black
seen the eggs in twigs

dead, broken on the ground
seen them feed brown
on roots, crawl treetrunks
easy

to harvest early mornings
pluck away the wings
bring them in, a sack full
for stew, sometimes whole

days I've eaten boiled

cicada from the dry brush
have to stay alive, have to

sing the easy songs, the ones
that flow like rivers, easy

on the memory

(1980)

BRIAN HENDERSON (1948–)
Theory of the Family

Thicket, anguished
insect music, the lonesome
call of the phoebe, its little ladder
leaving you in mid air.

Here as far from anywhere as I thought
you could get: wire fences
at stream mouths.
For lamprey, our father explained.
Then we learned the gruesome details.

Later, at dusk, everything
ours, everything human:
the canvas awning, the Coleman stove, the scattered
rosette of knives on the picnic table, the
two-tone green Buick under the cedars, our fears
smeared, becomes fluid.

Through the skin of night, the great
rasped punctures of stars.

(2000)

Mortals

They unfurl luxurious reds like lovers
one after another all the way up
each green stick, pouring their lives into a flight
sucked from sun and bog. The cardinal
flowers ignite the verges of the swamp,
but it makes no difference.
Among the fine white spray of water
parsnip in the green glade, they shine,
they shed their lit darkness
back into the dark.

And the heron floods miraculously into the top
of the willow like a great dark wave cresting
and enters the invisible, the underglimmer
of undertow among branching shoals
of silver-green fish.

(2000)

ROBYN SARAH (1949–)
Nature Walk

In the long grass of a country graveyard, my children find a bird's-egg, intact, china blue, so perfectly small they gasp to see it. How did it fall without breaking?

Another year they find a dead cicada in a weed-choked city yard; their father preserves it in an empty spice-bottle. Wings like lace kites; faint smell of cardamom.

In his drawer, rummaging for matches, I come across a curious brown knobbled thing, hard as a pebble but wrinkled, I take it for peyote and quiz him, a bit surprised. He laughs, it is the stump, he says, of our son's umbilical cord, he saved it when it fell off.

On the mountain these Sundays, we pick seed-pods of milkweed, we break open the spiky husks of horse-chestnut to extract the gleaming kernels, we gather berries of mountain-ash, pieces of bark and leaves we don't recognize. We fill our pockets with them. But my daughter finds a thorn-bush with thorns as long as her thumb, thin black daggers, razor-straight. She breaks off a twig of these, who will carry it for her so she doesn't hurt herself? It is this above all she wants to bring home.

(1987)

Tim Lilburn (1950–)
Ghost Song

Pretty soon…next spring.
    —Wovoka, ghost Messiah

Buffalo under the earth raise up a hundred-mile-wide dance.
Blood ribbons from their noses.
Their humps are bright rattles of wounds.
Hairy feet rustle the dark's tall grasses; green dust rains endlessly.
The buffalo are under the earth, they are under the earth, a people.
They dream towards afternoons of sad rivers, the hill's flute lines;
Soft roots full of breath go out from their mouths
Into the mouths of the astounded dead.
The buffalo dance. They dance up the medicine of everything being
    alive.
They wear bright shirts that bleep like radio transmitters.
They dance, thunder on their backs, as the turtle carries the world.
Under the earth they move, the buffalo, hillocking, mounting one
    another,
                        deaf from the compulsive guns.

One third of a man's soul quivers into rock, another goes up
To meet lightning.
A third flies all night into the body of a woman.
The buffalo kick up in tall dark under sod; in their humps, thunder's
White roots.
Yes they carry wampum for the New Earth, tail sections of veering
    aircraft, Sitting Bull's
Trick pony, Custer's baby hair forked in a stick.
They have with them the dead, laugh tracks of broken situation
    comedies,
                        meadowlarks, doorless refrigerators
To build their careful villages in the Mountains.
The dead are jumpy.
Each death has its own body, given it by the Lord. This is a
                        killer horse from Alberta foothills.
The buffalo calm them, standing by one, silently, for decades.
They will come back.   Soon, all, in the spring.

Earth, the green sleep, will roar up a great wave of itself, sweet,
    glittering
With fossils and wild turnip, and eat the white cities.
Crazy Horse's bulletproof silence will kill-dance on the mounded
    banks.
They will'come back the egoless herds and their Lakota.

(1989)

Contemplation Is Mourning

You lie down in the deer's bed.
It is bright with the undersides of grass revealed by her weight during the
length of her sleep. No one comes here; grass hums
because the body's touched it. Aspen leaves below you sour like horses
after a run. There are snowberries, fescue.
This is the edge of the known world and the beginning of philosophy.

Looking takes you so far on a leash of delight, then removes it and says
the price of admission to further is your name. Either the desert
                                                    and winter
of what the deer is in herself or a palace life disturbed by itches and
    sounds
felt through the gigantic walls. Choose.

Light comes through pale trees as mind sometimes kisses the body.
The hills are the bones of hills.

The deer cannot be known. She is the Atlantic, she is Egypt, she is
the night where her names go missing, to walk into her oddness is
                        to feel severed, sick, darkened, ashamed.

Her body is a border crossing, a wall and a perfume and past this
she is infinite. And it is terrible to enter this.

You lie down in the deer's bed, in the green martyrion, the place where
language buries itself, waiting place, weem.
You will wait. You will lean into the darkness of her absent
body. You will be shaved and narrowed by the barren strangeness of the
deer, the wastes of her oddness. Snow is coming. Light is cool,
nearly drinkable; from grass protrudes the hard, lost
smell of last year's melted snow.

(1994)

from *To the River*

13

The river lives in shadow-pools of tall stones.
It is immortal and long haired, its fingernails grow.
Small feathers of impulse kiss its stalk, it
lives in these colourless leaps from itself, it tends a small
                                garden of bells.

Slop-bellied, radiant, left-slumped river, the thrown world,
holds a pale green stone fire in its arms always;
it is oiled with inertia, wolf-
coloured, laying small pubis mounds of clay.
The light-ghosted cottonwood, the one
near the unfolding water, the light idling in the cottonwood,
suddenly stands up, stands up, palms raised at sunset, stands up.
I don't know anything.
A towering generosity in things being where they are.
Far along, north, spruce coming into aspen, half a mile in
from the river, an antler in grass leaking in barely lit grass.

(1999)

AGNES WALSH (1950–)
   Angel's Cove

A cove nearly abandoned,
but there's haymakers cutting,
arching into the wind and sky.

The hills roll down,
down onto black rocks that stop the sea.
The waves swell up, leap like geysers:
liquid fireworks.

We're expecting a full moon any minute.
I lie down on the soft worn rock,
let the water push over me,
feel love moving around the beach:

he, standing on the highest rock,
 throwing up his arms into the fury;
she, bending forward gathering fuel,
heaving bleached timber, eyeing the sky.

The hills never move. The grass stands
straight for the scythers' swoosh.
My body shifts to fit
the rounded places in the rock.

I press my cheek into the smooth hardness,
feel the world through the rock,
feel love circling me, the centuries under me.

(1996)

BRIAN BRETT (1950–)
Small Joys on the Farm

Winter came weird this year, as it always does—
cool and wet—rain after rain, the ponds flooding,
the sheep limping on rotten hooves.

Then the cold snapped its brittle fingers
and a sheet of ice shielded the ponds
for a week before the rain came again,
leaving a deceptive film of water on the slick surface.

I was sitting by the window drinking red wine
in the afternoon, depressed, lost in my life,
losing money on a farm, thinking above the large
destruction my race has engraved into the earth,
when the flock of mallards whistled through the rock maples.

I was alone, except for the animals, the sheep and the horse,
the audience of winter crows dotted like black crescent moons
on the green pastures that were wearing me down.

Then the mallards hit the secret ice like a circus pouring
onto a stage, skulls driving into the earthen bank,
tangles of feathers, collisions, and sliding webbed feet;
a duck braking with its beak, leaving a white crease
like the track of a lost arrow leading to the shore as
15 mallards attempted to regather the honour of a flock.

Even the crows rushed to the shoreline
to witness the relics of this indignity
while the last ducks waddled, graceless,
off the ice like miniature Charlie Chaplins.

And for a slender moment in the furrow of time,
on a farm in nowhere, everyone stopped to rejoice and wonder,
horse and sheep and mallards and man and crows.

Yes, the ecology retains its own madness, attended or unattended by
  us—
this planet overflowing with
odd carcasses skating on hidden ice.

(1998)

Blue Heron Moon

Alright,
long have I known your cry
in the dusky half-light
between sleep and dawn,
winging low;
you, yes you,
spawn of the pterodactyl
with the throaty voice and piercing beak.
Awkward flyer.
Stilt walker.
Frog-eater.
Fish stalker.
Solitary contemplator of horizons.

I saw you whirling snakes
over your head like a baton tosser.
I saw you spearing the bellies
of fish too fat to eat.
I saw you taking the grace of the sun
on a bleached morning,
wings shaking in the ecstatic glow.
I saw you step swiftly aside
when the eagle ripped
your prey from the long hunt.

Giant bird,
awkward ballerina
the lonely one,
old man of the water,
old woman of the sea caves,
born old in the nest, eager to be alone,
staring at the moon as if you owned it.
They say that nature makes a harmony;
well, I don't believe it. I have seen your ghost
in my dreams and sometimes in my nightmares—

the endless snake sliding down your throat,
that hilarious windup into flight—bird
with a voice like an indignant bullfrog
that's been stepped on.

The precious god of patience,
the one who waits
even as your world is whittled down—
the ponds broken into landfill and subdivisions,
lakes roaring with jet skiers,
the ocean polluted and empty.
First child of the dinosaurs
where will you go now?
Old one.
In the rain
you resemble
an ancient Taoist sage on a bad hair day,
a bipedal billy goat fixated on an enemy tin can,
a skinny Englishman without his umbrella—
the bony, hard edges of wisdom
that come from days of staring at water;
a shade of blue
like the sky before the sun arrives;
you resemble
all the memories I had of a world
when that world was wild.

(1998)

Don Domanski (1950–)
Owl

the timberline is all driftwood
floating in from the millennium
the bogs search for pleasures
that only a mother could provide

I'm a few feathers and a clock face
the presence of clasped hands in the tree
of a fist succeeding in the democratic air

each of my wings is a district that knows of no other
I'm carried along by the suspension of disbelief
holy   holy   holy
it's silent and dark and the shadows are rising
the spirits of bears lift the trees
mice follow me into the air.

(1998)

from "All Our Wonder Unavenged"

1.

particles of evening warm themselves in the afternoon sun
pieces of solitude gather slowly   one under each gingko leaf

I sit on a rock of saddlebacked granite
                  I sit in a world of abundance
a handful of bees goes down to the river   two handfuls return
you deadhead the dog rose and two stray curs appear

you deadhead a memory and two more appear
long and deeper and more alive than the last

I remember my mother seated at the kitchen window
her cat's-eye glasses staring out into the night
trying to find divinity and divinity's reasons

my mother believed God moved sparrows around day after day
as a teenager I believed sparrows moved God around
all the inexhaustible crutches He leaned upon
all the underweights of silence to find His way

now the only god I believe in are the sparrows themselves
                  unaltered by my belief
their wings contain hollow bones where a pantheon could pass through
and they do   hundreds pass through at every moment
this is how they fly   by allowing passage to earth's beliefs
the little deities of the big thunder and the rain that falls.

(2007)

MARY DALTON (1950–)
Pitcher Plant; Bog Pluto

That mudsucker:
Its bloodshot slimy
Bowls of green
Lurked in the mash,
Waited for youngsters—
To carry them down
Down to the soft dark
Smothering, the fathomless
Underbelly of the bog.

(2003)

Stingers

Where sheep huddle
Where goats piss
Where outhouses crumble—
Slash them, dig them,
Burn them—it doesn't
Matter a rat's ass
How you set out to
Put a stop to their gallop.
Those green bastards'll
Come back to laugh at your puny murders,
Come back to put a little sting in your day.

(2003)

HARRY THURSTON (1950–)
Dragging Bottom

A chain link hand, a titantic dustpan
stirs a turmoil of sediment in its wake,
furrows the seafloor. A ploughshare
that keeps on going beyond land's end
over endless wet horizons, leaving
the sea bottom cross-hatched as a griststone.
A horn blows, the capstan sings, a maul is swung,
the drag belches the benthos onto the deck.
Life so lowly, it most resembles globs of oil
but for the holes at either end, mouth or anus
(who knows?) that filters water endlessly as thoughts.
Eels excitable as neon, animals turned inside out,
with skin rough as stucco.
And this magnificent fish, big and flat as a coffee table,
wide wings spread for undersea flight—landed here.
A man, sore and numbed, hefts the biggest stone he can
to crush the skull of this monarch of the deep,
then kicks the brained fish through the scuppers
to sink. This is our shame, repeated again and again.
What we cannot sell, we kill or leave to die.
It is only these, a treasure chest
of calcium dollars, we stoop to gather.
Curved knives flash between hard halves, lift,
the top springing open like a locket
to reveal a cameo of viscera.
A flick of the wrist feeds the ever-vigilant hags
that plane and parry, shearing water.
The horn blows, men take cover, the deck
raises like a drawbridge, dumps everything,
half-alive or dead, back into the sea.
This is our shame, repeated again and again,
until there is nothing but stones and broken shells to spend.

(2000)

CHRISTOPHER DEWDNEY (1951–)
August

August occupies 50 million miles
a function of the radius
                    extended
to find me here in October
a full 125 million miles from August
with its leaves still green (entirely on some trees).

January is a gleaming highlight on the other side
of a gold-platinum alloy ring.

Occupying some position unrecognizable
on the space-time grid.
Plotable, determinate, flexible
under certain relativities.
As the velvet meniscus
enfolds August, a tiny stage winks
deep in the theatre night.

August's survivors are Acheta assimilis (field cricket)
still chirping, a wasp (indeterminate), Danaus plexippus
(Monarch butterfly), Pieris rapae (cabbage butterfly) &
a Colias philodice (sulfur), here on the twenty second
of October.

(1975)

Out of Control: The Quarry

It is a warm grey afternoon in August. You are in the country, in a deserted quarry of light grey devonian limestone in Southern Ontario. A powdery luminescence oscillates between the rock & sky. You feel sure that you could recognize these clouds (with their limestone texture) out of random cloud-photographs from all over the world.

You then lean over and pick up a flat piece of layered stone. It is a rough triangle about one foot across. Prying at the stone you find the layers come apart easily in large flat pieces. Pale grey moths are pressed between the layers of stone. Freed, they flutter up like pieces of ash caught in a dust-devil. You are splashed by the other children but move not.

(1975)

SUSAN MUSGRAVE (1951–)
I Took a Wire Cage into the Woods

I took a wire cage into the woods
in which to sit and watch the animals.
They gathered round me as I'd hoped they would
and sat, expressionless, with closed eyes,
warming themselves in the sun.

Their bodies were beautiful, unlike mine;
their bodies were solitary, never lonely.
They must have sat for hours in one place
as if to reassure me all was understood.

Their patience was exhausting. All night
I watched till dark and light were
blotted out and whole seasons passed.
I did not leave that cage again but lay
under the cool influence of the stars,
awake and dreaming.

My dreams were always the same.
Always in my own image those animals rose
out of the dust, animals with human faces
whose eyes were open, sorrowful.

Their bodies were broken.
No longer content to sit and stare
at one such as this, confined by choice
within the shadows of a spectral cage,
they paced as those condemned and wept,
while I, the guilty one, was saved.

(1985)

JOHN B. LEE (1951–)
The Day I Found Four Score of Starlings Dead in the Franklin

The day I found four score of starlings
dead in the Franklin
the living room smelled
like a pigeon coop.
We'd been away for the summer
and they'd flown
down the flue
and been trapped there
beating their black wings blacker against creosote
then finally falling to form a heap
the bottom birds crushed and stiff, long dead
each one flat like a crushed corsage.
The top birds
some still warm, still full of what it meant to fly
to hold the sky
beneath them like a nest.

And afterwards I climbed the house
to fix a wire grill
above the hole
while the starlings circled anxiously
as if I were sealing off
their last passage of escape.
As if the chimney were a tunnel
they'd dug
to get out of the world.

(1993)

PETER CHRISTENSEN (1951–)
Keeping Fear Away

At the site
ribbons flutter
tell tales of wind of men
who have surveyed the valley

I am a jughound
planting the geophones
to record blast vibrations

Sometimes   between   shots
I toss a stick of geogell
          into the air
Shoot it
          c r a c k the morning
Blow up rocks and trees
          for fun

          Near a field
I watch
          Doug
blow the ass off a gopher
halfway down its hole
cap wire trailing behind
A raven picks up
          the bread
wrapped around a blasting cap
flies for a hundred feet
Up   into his sky
And then   the electric touch
black feathers
          floating down
to the shouts and yahoos
on the ground

I help the powder monkey
shove geogell   into the mountain
Make it vibrate
        under our feet
the blast
        comes back
        comes back

(1981)

ROO BORSON (1952–)
Upset, Unable to Sleep, I Go for a Walk and Stumble Upon Some Geese

Bright dime
cut in two, one half
in the sky, the other fallen on the pond,
but no one will bother to pick it up,
the moon will never be whole again.
Up and down the grassy hillocks
they follow one another, walking
in groups under the grey glow.
I haven't even startled them, this is no hour
for a human. Together here they act
differently, like themselves,
warm-blooded, clumsy, bitching
at one another in a common language.
I wish I were asleep. They are large and warm.
I'd like to hold one of them,
hold, be held.

(1985)

The Trees

Their lives are longer, slower than ours.
They drink more deeply, slowly,
are warmed, do not shiver at dusk.
The heart unwinding makes a small noise.
Who would hear it?
Yet the trees attend,
perhaps to us, perhaps to nothing,
fragrance maybe, not of
flowering, but leaves and bark.
Trees. Dusk. Hand-coloured photographs
of the world before we were born.
Not sweet, but as water is,
sweet to a mouth long closed on itself.
Befriend them.

(1989)

Snake

"A gardener's snake," the city employee told me,
a snake no bigger than a shoelace
(himself a gardener)—holding it curled
once around the thumb and once
around the fingers of a hand—
a mitten of a snake
on possibly the last day of summer warmth.

The snake was avidly licking at the air,
its tongue like a Tibetan banner
or a young eel
of black silk—

We stood a little uneasily,
on the common path before winter,
the air around us golden,
like a temple wall.

If to record is to love the world,
let this be an entry.

(1996)

JULIE BERRY (1952–)
daisy cole's woods

in daisy cole's woods
jan points out the wilted leaves of wild leeks
pokes at trilliums with a stick
they're almost done she says
we look at the flowers
their solemn froth pink-turning
i think of the blown-up words
taped to my walls
hanging from windows
how the light shines through the stanzas
things i know fight for a place in my throat
thistles are edible when peeled
plantain's good for burns
burdock tea

at the edge
harrowed fields rise like waves
everywhere dirt is higher
than we are
we turn back into the woods
jan says be careful of your boots
be careful of your shoes
your books
your words
everything can be eaten she says
i step carefully through the maidenhair fern
or is it meadow rue i ask
who cares what it's called says jan
a hillside of young ashes swallows her legs
foxtail's good for scrubbing pots i advise
seconds before she disappears

(1995)

Daniel David Moses (1952–)
A Spider Song

I wait for black ferns and pines
to fill up with light after rain

and almost all my breath is gone
spinning across the cold. Oh on

the lake that breath joins up with mist
and grows so delicate and long

the moon turns round on legs and cuts
all uttering from the tongue.

(1980)

CORNELIA HOOGLAND (1952–)
The Orcas, Great Story

Duffy's nose over the rim of canoe,
sunshine, strong current against us,
sea lion lollygagging, watching us.
We're working the current (east
point off Saturna) when
orcas behind
sea lion beside
(we think is a goner)
three orcas pass, pass the lion,
ignore us, ignore it
then more and in every direction
all sizes, babies, giants, dorsals,
whole backs gliding through the water,
breathing noises,
breeches, four, one within forty feet.
The dog's eyes saucer.
The whale slaps its back
down hard   *almighty splash*,
the dog pitches   *down Duff*   the canoe
more excitement   strong paddling
large areas of welled-up water
turn the canoe then *snap*
the paddle breaks. *Okay* I say
shore! now! which we do.
Watch the whales   let
the current bring us thrill
another dimension let
the things of the sea inside us
love what they love.

(2001)

BARRY DEMPSTER (1952–)
  Wild, Wild

Wild, how trees claw at one another,
rocks buried half-alive, spiders spitting
mid-air. We are not to confuse these wilds
with human pathology. Nor to let literature
weep pathetic. Wild is numb, is brainless.
Where nothing ever happens twice.

This tree is a wooden cell; it knocks
in the wind and grows. This rock is a mineral
deposit. And the spider, the most alive
we'd say (like us), is a dark enzyme
oozing in the so-called light. A man may walk
through these wilds, or he may not.
If a poet, he will probably want to tell:
the same weeping willow again and again.

Numb is somehow tender to the touch—moss,
bark, breeze. A beautiful brainless rock,
the act of sitting an act of love.
Each soft spider dashing the wrist
brings one thrill of skin alive.

Wild, how trees touch back, rocks
muscle into open hands, spiders land.
A man sits confused in the forest,
pathetically talking to himself.
Everything feels and can't forget.

All men are pathological. Weeping,
they bring the adjectives down.
Always another man, half-awake, dangling
in the air. This is man's makeup,
the literature of all kinds.
The same man tough as trees, deep
as rock, spitting dreams. *Wild*,
he says. Wild.

(1990)

Monty Reid (1952–)
83H 2 9 78

two rocks doves
mate on top of
the low level

bridge
the male's wings
stretched out

an indifferent
balance
as though there

was no noise
no voice beyond
this level

the two
rock doves
on a bridge

suspended
with its traffic
in the valley

Dave Spalding
made this note

(1985)

BRIAN BARTLETT (1953–)
If I Knew the Names of Everything

If I knew the names of everything
the depths of this canyon would rise
to the surface, these forests swallow
their own shadows.
       If I'd sniffed and kicked
every spot on earth, I wouldn't be holding
this torn map up in clear light, brushing
my eyes over rivers I'll never cross.

       Fun to bump into
a different species or two
a year, but praised be the biggest zoo
for being
small,
       just a neck—or toe—of the Woods.
Praised be the anonymous fish, the bird
free from all human eyes, the undiscovered
insect biting the rarest antelope's ear.

My boots at my side, I'm waiting
for the Maligne Canyon to turn
malign. Swollen by heat, my feet bathe in water
fallen from white peaks where bighorn
feed, cold climbing from my legs to my skull.

       If I'd spotted and tagged
every species, if I'd stared down
every sub-species, if every Sudanese
savannah, Arctic pingo, or Pacific reef
were home and native, I'd burn this map.

Flecked with heraldic gold,
       what winged thing has landed
           on my drying foot?

(1993)

from "Talking to the Birds"

2. to a northern gannet

Fog like cold sweat coated every inch of the ferry,
swathed and hid the ocean ten feet out. Downstairs
indoors, passengers snacked, napped,
fought the warriors and demons of video games.

For those of us circling the deck
the first hour of the crossing didn't yield
one bird, one mewl or wayward cry. Grand Manan
could've been a mile off, or a thousand.
If allowed extravagance, I'd say
the waves peaked and toppled like the waves
        in the story of the seven days
when "everything according to its kind"
was born. Then, you:
        flying, unmistakable, goose-sized,
your butter-yellow head the one contrast
to all that pallor. Where everything else was wispy
and smudged, you were suddenness, otherness
completeness,
eyes and beak and wingbeat.

Just as quickly, you slipped back behind
the gathering of spectres. When I pushed closer
against the cold iron railing
        you were back with me,
then vanished again, like a feeling that keeps coming
and going on the verge of sleep.
For a minute you were the first bird, or the last.

(2002)

JOAN CRATE (1953–)
The Year of the Coyote

Oh their terrible stealth!
Babes have been snatched from campgrounds
while parents gathered firewood,
cooked dinner, slept on either side
wild roses bordering carpets of dream.
These days wherever you look, coyotes
lope a lullaby across the horizon,
teeth clipping clean as needles through cloth.
        Oh, their red velvet thirst!

We don't allow our kids out the door
without a dog anymore, keep a .22 handy.
Even mid-day, I take the truck to Hilda's.
Her husband stares out the window
at wheat spilling over the prairie,
wishes to hell it were legal to kill
coyotes, shoot them mid-stride.
        How their howls snarl up the combines!
Grain, never priced lower since 1917, overflows
bins, wails through rust holes.

Post Office closed down, we straggle
at Gray's Hardware, talk about bankruptcies,
auctions, dogs killed by coyotes.
A few mate with them, steal home
on a leash of moonlight and treason,
                        wait.

Sometimes I still dream of you,
of you no longer knowing your own children
playing at the edge of twilight. I try
to call them, try and try, but their names
stick to my tongue, consonants, vowels stillborn
in the gorge of distant hills.
I wake up to coyotes ripping open the dark.
You gone.
The howl remains.

Driving home, Hilda talks
faster and faster down the stuttering gravel road,
says she wants another child
but her husband avoids her. All night long
she hears the pad of his feet down the hallway.
At dawn he slinks to the barn to sleep with the chickens.
                                        I nod,
in the rear view mirror, catch a shape
skirting the truck.

(2001)

Ross Leckie (1953–)
The Natural Moose

This forest is coextensive with the mind's
expanse of spruce and pine and snow. Through it,
the moose meander mechanically in uncanny
circular tracks, following the map of their antlers'
tedious pointing. And here they come again
in an eternal return through space already occupied
by their previous going, until—you stop dead
to see one by the side of the road—it has entered
your map of asphalt disappearing over the hills.
What is your name and what are you called,
it seems to say, and how did you bring me here.
The crown of thorns lacerates your passing.
Is there an 'acrid odor'? Is it 'original response'?
But the night is as cold as white china and the air
is a dinner plate with a fine-edge crack. The moose
disappears back into its habit, and one night
as you stand at the sink washing dishes the phantom
moose vanishes, so you drop the plate. It lands on an edge
and circles back on itself; it doesn't break, the spruce
arched in the dark, and the pine thinking itself alone.

(1997)

John Terpstra (1953–)
Varieties: *Acer negundo*

Also known as Manitoba maple, ash-leaf maple, box elder, or,
less respectfully, garbage tree. Ubiquitous. Is not always allowed to con-
sider itself truly a tree, as opposed to a weed, and is therefore unsure of
its place. This lack of certainty is apparent already in its leaves, which
have no single, distinct shape, but appear in several variations on a
theme taken from both the ash and other, more decidedly, maples.

In the more boreal regions of the country the Manitoba maple's
hardiness has led to its being lofted to the level of an ornamental, and it
may often be found lining city streets. Around here, however, they grow
wherever there is no one tending the soil: in vacant lots, along railways,
or between the fence and the alley.

Thousands of their little apostles twitter down to earth each
year in a persistent attempt to convert the entire deciduous zone. Most
are hoed down as young shoots in early spring by the gardeners, and
this may be why the ones who do attain some form of maturity often
have a surprised if not furtive look about them. Rather than grow
directly up, they shoot off at various angles to the ground, as if they
had taken a running start at treehood but could never have anticipated
their present stature and feel ill-equipped to deal with it.

Full-grown, the Manitoba maple presents a case of the one that
got away, or an act of charity.

(1990)

Marlene Cookshaw (1953–)
Fox

Until last fall I'd never seen a fox, and then,
from a moving train, on a foreign track.

And, more than that, the fox was dead, tossed
to a ditch that trailed the outskirts of the city, end

of my marriage, though I didn't know that yet.
Its muzzle rested on its back. With the prescience

of the stricken, it had turned its head
to watch death overtake it. A year later, two days

before my forty-seventh birthday, another fox
trots past.   Fox! I think, and can't

sift out the meaning of its shape. Nothing flickers
with a red that true. And self-possessed: its walk

no more than twenty feet away so nonchalant
that all my programs threaten default, threaten

dance. Fox! Its unexpected breach of this world's
reasoned work. This far, no farther. Its

ordinary calm demeanour, keep-to-the-trail,
bomb-in-a-baby-carriage fur. Oh, farther, please.

Dear Ruth, I've seen a fox. Dear Mary-Rose, A riot
of such dignity just passed. I want more now,

the jay's note, eclipsing seasoned
thought, more than I know, more than

one man in my bed, whisky before noon,
the saxophone's bright veering

into trees. Yes, black-stockinged. Yes,
the tail: a streak of cedar, eucalyptus, sage.

And when the moon appears, it has a fox's voice.
Its pawprints burn the snow. Sprung

from measuring the first half of a life, it speaks
with gravity, the common weight that swings us.

It says, I've hidden, offered this side, that. And
sometimes too I'm buried in a blackness. Well,

here I am full upon you. Fall on your back. Or topple
me. What's wanted doesn't matter, nor even who

desires. Nor reason, much. Just fox.

(2005)

ALLAN COOPER (1954–)
The Seed of the Blue Spruce

The prickly porcupine-like cone which has fallen from the
Christmas wreath has opened in the kitchen warmth. This cone is a
house with many doorways, penetrated by the light of early spring.
The season of its celebrations is over; if it is to salvage anything at all,
it must give up the gift of seed and put its trust in common soil.

One delicate seed falls out of the cone onto the table. This
could be a mosquito's wing, if you didn't look at it closely. Held up to
the light, it has the colour of split wood, or honey. There is the promise
of an entire forest inside it.

This is the seed of the blue spruce tree, the colour of some
wild dancing god. It is the darkness of Krishna dancing with abandon
around Radha, attentive as a bee to the first honey beading on the
white clover. How wild that dance is, like the understanding between
two people who know their purpose together at last. It is also the dance
Thoreau felt when he and a raindrop drew near to one another. A man
opens his eyes to a simple Christmas wreath and feels the circular
energy of the planet moving inside his own chest.

(2001)

ERIN MOURÉ (1955–)
Vision of a Woman Hit by a Bird

The flutter in my blood after the bird hit, as if
I would fall too,
head-on
into my throat, a soft body shaking its wings
& fallen
past me, the shock of it, its fury

at my chest unseen,
as if the bird had nested in me, that quickly.

Always now I am the woman hit by a bird.
I stand without emblem & defer
to my companions, their maleness & femininity,
their dress is a strangeness without purity;
I can't show them
my memory of the path under the trees
where I ran & was hit by the bird,
its brown eye, sincerely,
the blurred flight too late to stop
hitting my neck, then diving unhurt past me

Its mark is on my skin, a thin scrawl
invisible to medicine,
the bird's look in me, a hole,
sensible
Now I see the world thru my chest without asking,
as if I had the bird's eyes & bone flotation,
the earth's axis tipped,
spun away from the humans with their doctors' faces

The bird's stain I bandage on me,
heroically,
not like an emblem,
as if it were still the size & weight of a bird,
transubstantial,

its body on my throat with a flutter,
inexcusable surely,
my temperature at long last,
my melting point

(1985)

Tropic Line

The northern pike, blinded, its mouth open in the hook's pull
upward from the water, reverse gravity
My brother's hand holding the pike's body,
long & more muscled than his arm,
lifting it:

My brother is in the jacket too small for his age,
its green quilt unraveling
around him, unweaving his body into the cold March
air, the snow receded but not gone,
the river's effluent opening

Our hands nearly solid with cold, gloveless,
immobile
Out on the river ice, hearing it explode
beneath us like a rifle
Deep noise of the hemisphere, turning toward the sun

What we would do, to go out with the narrow rods
like saplings, fiberglass, the crude reels,
cheapest ever made,
we would hike behind the river houses, the winter unchanged
Sun risen just past the Tropic of Cancer

To rub our hands & feel ice crack inside the fingers,
not like rifles,
like meat slightly frozen
Billy still holding up the pike, stubborn,
bright fish dripping water

Fish we hurt in the sole motion our hands were capable
before we threw it back
into water that would freeze us if we fell
Not knowing how the pike had come where we were fishing,
crazed & lonely, searching its prey

How it saw our pattern of light on the river surface,
our shadows & colours, the last it saw
Blind with cold we blinded it with ice shards,
& returned it, & ourselves, our arms & hands raised
like rifles, triumphant
The sun at our backs too cold to kill us,
pushing north over the tropic line

(1985)

JAN ZWICKY (1955–)
Lancey Meadows

Needing cloth to dry themselves, and food, they came out into the
ocean and over wide expanses, away toward Wineland, up into the
uninhabited country. Evil can take away luck, so that one dies early
                    — Runic inscription, Ringerike, Norway

Late in May, the strait is filled with ice.
Across it, fifty miles away, a patch of sunlight
scrapes the edge of the plateau. You see the axe
glance off and sink itself in bone two fields away
before you hear a sound: that silence
is the coast of Labrador.

For a year or two, they must have faced it dry-eyed
every morning. And in the spring
the wind would still have chased itself
along the flanks of their sod huts.
It would have been at night that empty heartbeat
opened in them, billion-year-old granite
weeping up into their pillows, lightless,
groping for its name.

(1998)

Bee Music

Keepers of the secret
sound of sunlight, no job
too small, this
is the cheerful
earless tuning of the music
of the spheres: O
lunchpail Pythagoreans,
who'd have guessed
the crystal nocturne
of the cosmos was first
scored for miniature
fun-fur kazoos?
Deaf as tiny
Beethovens, you bend
the goldenrod
beneath your weight.
In your toolbox, Euclid
and the sextant of your
sunstone eye.
Ah, little nectar-
mules, you
scholars of the azimuth! Ah,
perfumed geometers
of the fields!

(2004)

Aspen in the Wind

Little tree, tree of slopes and coulees
and wolf-willow scrub, tree of seven
months of winter and a two-week spring,
of childhood and the endless

sky of loss, I've come
for the light in your leaves,
those brief mosaics of starched silk, the rill
and sifting of the August air against

the speechless blue, for this light like light
off water gurgling past the snowbank in the first
real thaw, for shade, for the rest
of weightlessness, I've come

to close my eyes
under the bright wind of summer,
the light-in-water of the wind in your leaves,
the starched silk of their rushing, that quilt

of sorrow and light.
What is the light for
but to lie down in? What is sorrow for
but to lie down in.

(2004)

Armand Garnet Ruffo (1955–)
Bear Death

Familiar with bear death
I have seen him served as an offering
hot on a plate, supper for the successful.
Penis bone scraped clean
and drying in the sun. Caged
corpse braided in tassels
and bells, lying like a rug.
Head stuffed.

Squat on a log dreaming slick ants
thick as people or thick people slick
as ants was the first time he was shot.
Right between the eyes.
It was raining a smell
of earth and water.

If I say today he's bent and lumbering
over your city street believe me.
The faces he sees are smudged against glass.
Enticed by flesh's soft currency, he is expected
to eat heartily, lick his lips
and join the crowd.
He tries to keep his head, take only
the choice bits, give
only the odd unfamiliar
       growl.

(1994)

Kebsquasheshing

The Kebsquasheshing floats through my back door,
carrying my youth, the fishing rod I dropped overboard
fifteen years ago, carrying the pike and their pike dreams
of barbless lures, fat worms and clean water.

Today I tear into *The Globe and Mail* searching
for an article explaining why the transformer blew
spewing hundreds of gallons of PCBs
into the water. Discover there is no explanation.

Ontario Hydro blameless. No harm done.
And still we drink and the water continues
past us, past the newspaper, up and out to the Arctic.
Where big fish eat small fish and dream clean.

(1994)

MARILYN DUMONT (1955–)
Liquid Prairie

I miss the North Saskatchewan that runs through
those trees that shoot up black and grand
from its cool hips,

I miss those spruce that
defy the flatness,
gloat at the pressing palm sky, the
loaded rifle earth and
grow anyway.

I sit on this thin coast
but haven't yet been on that belly of water

they call the ocean.

(1996)

Anne Simpson (1956–)
  Deer on a Beach

Once in Africa I heard voices wailing, then turned a bend
in a muddy track and saw the wagon full of women,

faces greased with white, like a chorus from a Greek tragedy,
reminders—strophe and antistrophe—of what was lost.

Yesterday, when the beach was blindfolded with snow,
I found parts of a deer. My daughter wouldn't look

at the elegant hoof (which I lifted with the tip
of my boot) or the half-ellipse of jawbone. She hung back,

afraid, while I examined the hide, and the way it seemed
to be cut, slashed from the body. I could see the lining

of red, like an opera cloak. The head was gone, and the antlers,
but I didn't think about this until further up the beach,

where I saw the two forelegs, stuck in a drift
of snow feathered with animal hair. Grief has no words,

only a trailing off into things remembered
inaccurately. Months ago we'd seen a doe a half-mile away,

sleek and young, in the sparse woods above the beach, her flanks
heaving gently. We left the beach—where the ocean had thrust

glassy fragments of ice into the soft strip of land—and climbed
the steps to a little deck. Below us, the remnants of the deer,

cast here and there, did not keep us from looking further out
to where the frozen sea, in folds and dips and pans, spread white,

unmoving. But something had changed, as if a lock in the cold air
had clicked open with a key. The ice was cracking, abruptly;

we shuffled up the next slippery flight of steps,
and through the woods. We saw crisscrossed tracks

of deer and dog, and perhaps snowshoe hare, though human
prints obscured them in places. I thought of the deer's small, cloven

hoof, and its fur, threaded brown and gold. Trophies not taken.
    Nothing
was left but tidbits for the crows: such food, stinking of violence,

comes from our world, not the next. Death gets into it
one way or another, a voice that follows wherever we go.

(2000)

Diana Brebner (1956–2001)
from "The Sparrow Drawer" Part III

It is time for us to be leaving; somehow we find
ourselves before one final display. It is the same

forest, rearranged by seasons, and including
the ducks, herons, owls, and hawks, that are

familiar to *The Forest*, as they call the example of
hardwood forest that is local, and ours. And then,

beneath the glass cases, my eldest daughter finds
two drawers. Above them a simple label reads:

Would you like to know more about birds? How
many times did I bring that other child to this

place? We never found those boxes. And they
are not hidden, merely unexpected. The first

lights up as we pull it out. Eggs. Large and
small. Blue, green, mottled beige, brown. Great

white goose eggs, the hummingbird's egg glowing
a white pearl, all in rows, labeled, an old child's collection.

And the second drawer opens quietly, and as easily
as the first, lights up, displays its contents.

This is the sparrow drawer, No-one has gone to any
trouble to make this look pretty. Dead sparrows

lie in an uneven row, their bodies in disarray,
frozen on snow, which is also synthetic batting,

with black plastic arrowheads stuck in strategic
areas to accentuate their differences. The caption

tells us: all sparrows look alike to the untrained
eye. They are difficult to tell apart in the field.

Chipping Sparrow. Savannah Sparrow. Lincoln's Sparrow.
Song Sparrow. Swamp Sparrow. And alone, beneath

the line of identical bodies, a Pine Siskin, just
to show us how even one species can be mistaken for

another. And what have I seen hovering in a field?
I could swear it was the child I have lost. Love

I have learned the hard way; how many hovering boys
in schoolyards look just like him. Of course, I don't

want to see this, or the dead birds, and I close
the drawer. But my girls will not leave it alone.

They open it. I close it. They cry. So, we open it
again. We say the names of the different sparrows.

I tell them that any creature, once named, cannot
be forgotten. This, I believe. You see, there are

no numbers there, only names. The Pine Siskin trembles
at the bottom of the drawer, as we roll it shut.

(1990)

JULIE BRUCK (1957–)
  Notice to Cut Tree

This week in the country, I've run
on dirt roads, where select trees
have numbers posted on their trunks,
and the small print urges interested parties
to a meeting on each tree's future.
I've grown attached to tree twenty-seven,
want to stay, discuss it with the tree warden.

How quickly we make the strange familiar,
the places we're known in, remote.
The town meeting on the poster took place
a month ago, and I have one night left here.
This afternoon, I open the doors
to the slanting light, the field mouse
I woke to on my pillow, resolute skunk,
snazzy as a spectator shoe, who pitched and reeled
along the road to a Richard Thompson tune,
until I jumped into the ditch, and let him pass.

This afternoon, I sit on the front step,
offer my arm to the mosquito, my ankle
to the swollen black fly; the mice can come
and make their beds here—and to the wind,
which needs nothing from me, I say, *tree, tree.*

(1999)

Harold Rhenisch (1958–)
Hymn for Herbicide

Consider for a moment the water strider
that skips across the surface of the water

    held up by the tension

    held up by the love of water

for its own kind

    So do we throw the plastic jugs of Roundup
    in the backs of our pickups

along with the broken bits of PVC pipe
and the blow torches

    and the rusted clippers!

because there's couchgrass under the trees
It's got them by the trunks

    Because there in that black oil and dioxin
    you are hiding

At one kiss of your lips

    the grass turns brown and withers

We are two of a kind
we've got to stick together

    Do not leave us alone
    in this desert of mock orange and cactus

Stay with us
cling to our faces like a cloud of dust
fill our lungs

    We're just 12-year-old kids
    out discing the fields in April

  thrilled to be so dirty and so tired

Fill our lungs with dust
grind the enamel off our teeth
it's nothing

You are great

  You are the mercury fillings

dissolving into the bloodstream

  of the 32-year-old nursing mother

and the iodine sprayed on the bunchgrass

  for mile on mile on mile

above the moon-grey waters
of the Columbia river

  draining out to the Pacific!
(1994)

The Hidden One
Hedley

The ravens write with their claws in the snow.
I walk through the junk: I can't read a thing.
The king stands proudly on an old mattress.

He has found a piece of rusted steel
and is using it for a voice. His calls
echo off the smoke-blackened cliffs. His band
call to him like politicians: self-effacing and loud.

They have a big secret: they have found a small
clot of self-consciousness in a tomato sauce tin—
it is enough for the lot of them.

But I am not a politician. I turn
amid the filth to look at the king
once more. His wings are two metres broad.

He glides slowly over the writing;
my footsteps lead illegibly through it,
breaking the sentences apart. The king screams.

Landing, he scratches a new sentence in the snow.
He looks like something that he found here—
or something he lost. He stands motionless,
a black period, and stares at me. I stare back.

In the clear light between us, above
the filthy soil, quivers the consciousness,
which we both at the same time
gently and wonderingly touch.

It doesn't make a sound.

(1998)

Elise Partridge (1958–)
Plague

Heal-all, yarrow, alum-root,
sweet annie, angelica, hazel shoots;
swinging in foxgloves' purple bells
secrets to make a sick heart well—
at the eastern farm we waded flowers
and herbs renowned for healing power.
Lemon verbena, spearmint beds,
feverfew blooms nodded heads
as I strolled into the waving wood.
Dim, plicking, laundromat-humid;
mosquitoes—motes blown into flight—
almost casually swirling to bite.
Two pinks caught my eye. I bent down.
Caterpillars were going to town
on a faltering stem, bodies slung
underneath, like sloths'. The feet clung;
the heads chewed. Four gnashed a meal
under a spray of Solomon's-seal
whose white drops quivered. Paired prongs,
the front legs worked like icemen's tongs
curving to stab. Rear-guard pylons,
flat-soled, gray, dutiful cousins,
helped shiver along the elegant back,
blue-and-red pustules edged with black.
Veering into a sunny aisle
—magenta balm, white chamomile—
I saw dozens more, heads like helmets
bobbing over lambs-ears' velvet.
Medicinal ferns were brewed for tea
to soothe sore throats, cure pleurisy—
their two-inch, humping, whiskered lines
writhed over the naturalists' signs.
They sprawled under spindly buds
of red-root, used to strengthen the blood;

a jewelweed's freckled orange scoops
hung by gnawed leaves, spicebushes drooped—
whirling, peering, now I could see
worms glued to boles on every tree.
Plicks I'd thought were rain in my ears
sounded like cuts of tiny shears—
their migrant, hungry, sticking strips
made, as I stood there, sawtoothed rips
in thousands more seedlings. Soon
they'd each find twigs and start to spin;
one moonrise not too far from this,
fresh from a cracking chrysalis,
their tawny, fluttering selves would come
tilting to this wild geranium,
alight on fewer, finer legs
and discharge arsenals of eggs.

(2002)

Laura Lush (1959–)
Winter

So this is winter—
and what remains of the world

now that autumn has left us,
gone underground with the

once luminous grasses and the husks
and seeds of all the left-behinds.

This is the cold season.
Learn to endure it.

Winter teaches us to love the long
liturgies of ice, the sudden stopping of water

before the black flock of birds
lifts blindly off the pond.

(2002)

RUSSELL THORNTON (1959–)
Creek Trout

Silver, dark-spotted, each spot with a pale halo,
its sides striped with a rainbow band,

a flawless swimmer, it knows its way perfectly
through the water, as if its smooth, quick body

could feel the length of the creek—
from the source in the mountains to the inlet-meeting mouth.

To see the trout, to gaze after it
as the doors of the water open before it,

as the innumerable chambers of the creek open before it,
each chamber flowing through the other,

each a new exultation, a new feeling of the touch of the creek,
a new entering and entering,

is to look through water
in which the trout is a rider of a single journeying pulse,

a piece of the voluptuous refuse of the first stars,
a darting purple-silver ray,

and imagine looking through the trout
as through a living lens into what the trout knows—

through flesh wholly a vivid eye,
blind sight seeing light before it shines—

before the trout as soon disappears
behind the final door of the water,

shimmering, shadowy traces, connecting up all its traces
somewhere on the other side of the world.

(2000)

Heron

In the deep-cut, swerving ravine
the hour before dawn. Creek more spirit than water
pouring white down the bouldery creek path
at arm's length toward me and past.
                            Out of the grey dark
a heron rises, a grey lopsided bundle,
a tent suddenly assembling itself and, in a split-instant,
collapsing and assembling itself again in mid-air.
There it is, opening its near-creek-spanning wings,
trailing its long thin legs, carrying its neck
in an S-shape, head held back: silent heron
flying away farther up the ravine.
                            Is it the same heron
I saw once before—the sensitive-still, slender,
blue-grey mystery alone in front of me in bright daylight?
I watched it until the houses, people, streets and cars
faded into the fringes of the light,
faded, and reappeared along with this same creek
spilling out of a pipe and flowing for a block
through old backyards and into another pipe?
and then saw the still one gone. The entire creek unbroken
could be the heron's home, these waters
of the snowmelt and rain that gather and surge
and twist their way down to the sea.
                            The heron
alights somewhere, disappears, and lifts again
as I come around a turn—and I see it again. And now
I see it at the shallow creek-edge, in an eddy
where the current swings out around a boulder and is lost—
all calm attention standing there, searching
through the creek waters' sunless rays.
                            It finds a fish—
the fish swims quick into the poised long bill.
The heron lifts, the dark tasting itself, the ravine
flying through the ravine—living sign,
secret heron of the beginning, morning bird.

(2003)

ERIC COLE (1959–)
Blackpoll Warbler

If winter scared him down to Argentina,
this half-ounce migrant champion hid it well.
Drab flitter combing leaves…slipped in
and out of shadows from hawks' eyes.
Brushed off the Andes to beef up in Brazil,
on a surfeit of bugs voraciously beaked.
When the season turns inside him like a maggot,
his plumage rises to the fulcrum of his urge.
A cut above Colombia's corrupted jungle,
he dashes on Panama, up the troubled isthmus,
skirting The Gulf, possessed in night skies,
that stride The Great Lakes, homing to the boreal.
When he thumps into my window, dies in my hand,
he's hours short of summer's expanse of black spruce.

(2005)

KEN HOWE (1960–)
Notes on the Urban Squirrel

"I think this squirrel was out cruising for victims
and spotted Fred and Deborah on the road..."
— Patricia Cornwell: All That Remains

1. From the heart of the cone of shadow
the voice spoke its
staccato denunciations, enunciating
my failings, berating,
raining, like spruce needles
upon the ubiquitousness of impropriety.
Squirrel morality is reductive but most vociferous.

2. Urban squirrels are certainly not rats with fuzzy tails. Rats are
nocturnal social omnivorous with distinctive hairstyling and the best
legal advice. Contrast also the squirrel's sense of high moral purpose
with the rat's corrupt politicking—infecting the body politic with
young offensiveness and single motherness. Both rat and squirrel
can admittedly carry bubonic plague, though no one much wants it
anymore.

3. Squirrels encircle my sandwich, a rogue's gallery chain gang
            posturing in ratty punk haircuts.
Suddenly one pulls up in an out-of-province Oldsmobile,
            screwdriver in hand—he's snickering "they can't touch us
            boys, remember the sciurine offender's act, and besides,
            we're ALL underage."
One of them had his paws on my boot—"spare crumbs?" he jeers,
            and there's no mistaking the menace in his voice, "or
            wouldja rather I give ya some BUBONIC PLAGUE?"
Jeez behind every bush there's a squirrel, gnawing rat-a-tat-tat at
            what looks like a pineal gland, the social fabric, and like
            as not collecting benefits from YOUR tax dollars as well.
            (Come on, write to your M.P.—get the bastards before
            they get you.)

4. No new model of squirrel has been introduced in North America since the old "stop-action" squirrels pioneered by Hollywood B-movies in the fifties. Since the public seems accustomed to these older models further refinements will probably concentrate on the technologies of production.

5. The squirrel explicated.
The squirrel vociferated.
The squirrel insisted.
"Be little." Said the squirrel.
"Be troth." Said the squirrel.
"Be labour." Said the squirrel.
"Be reft." Said the squirrel.

Squirrels eat eggs
And burros eat eggs
And little roe feed orcas
A kid'll feed orcas too
in the zoo.

6. The squirrel incarnates accumulated residue of human temporal consciousness scanning the future. Discontinuously it gnaws on discarded pine cones, apple cores, beernuts, stop-action clicking its way across gaps in our reasoning toward a hidden stash organized in patterns too complex for its own tiny brain.

(2001)

BRUCE TAYLOR (1960–)
Stovewood

The last place I wanted to be was cutting stovewood
with my dad and his giant friend
in late fall under a scoured aluminum sky.
Not dressed for the weather I'd lean on the Dodge,
surly fists jabbed in my jeans pockets
while the old man turned primitive,
gripping a tartan thermos full of scotch and coffee,
steam nuzzling his chin,
his work gloves armoured with frost,
biting down on a hank of wind and peering
north at the geese, or whatever,
a yessiree look in his eyes, and the giant friend
throttling a hatchet, hands heavy as car parts,
thumping a dopey rhythm on the truck fender
a you bet look in his eyes
as if he knew something about some things
alright, about this place, for example,
the maple and elms
poking black over a skin of ice like
skeletons of dead fire, frozen in attitudes
of frantic gesticulation
and that nothing could surprise
him, like if a woodpecker landed on his nose
he'd snicker and brush it away, adjusting his cap
"You have to watch those little bastards." Like if a bear
chomped off his leg, "Well it's a tough old world."
Like he could be standing anywhere,
on Mt. Everest, or the South Pole, in the rain forests
of Thailand, Borneo or British Columbia,
surrounded by mushrooms big as sofa cushions,
black vipers slithering with orangutans in their bellies
and he'd be right there in the darkest, most terrifying
manifestation of nature ever and anywhere in the history
of everything, squinting at some unmentionable outgrowth
of tropical weeds, saying, "Well I've thought

about trimming them back a few
yards, but what's the use? In a year
they'll be bad as before." And for some reason I wished
I was anywhere other than there, scrounging for wood
in the ditch off a meager road cut right
and straight and with no second thoughts
through the misery and rage of nature,
I wished I was anywhere
else and of a different species.

(1989)

Eric Miller (1961–)
Song of the Vulgar Starling

Was werde ich durch mein Tier werden, mein Erbstück?
"What will become of me through my animal—my legacy?"
        —Kafka

O, ein Engel geht vorbei!
"Oh, an angel is passing!"
        —Wings of Desire

1.
Ach, Starling, what can I sing for you you haven't sung for yourself
already? When after rainfall moss and lichen glow on the pine-bark like
chlorophyllian sunrise and the formal Robins step and stop
in their courtly lawn dance like lovers at the wedding at the end
of a comedy you stomp along with your yellow schnozz screwing
around in the mud
like a legion of littermen with their pointed sticks
stabbing at every accident that provoked kids' tears and at once
became classified as garbage.

And in the spring your grey offspring bleat with the voices of dictator
sheep in the mongrel scrub by metropolitan culverts, drowning out
the dwindling Yellow Warblers and even hysterical Redwing hens,
outnumbering the clacking Grackles; and soon your kids moult
from stocks-and-bonds grey to the greasy suit that makes their shifty
eyes impossible
to scrutinize.

2.
And look, I can't even write a tight lipped gun-wielding *Moritat* cuz
though you nest in the neon of strip-joints and pace by the leaking
losers whose life-blood is the splashy red solvent
of drugs pooling like cold coffee on asphalt
you manage a sort of gentility, oblivion, as if a crack-willow mansion
by the water-striders' limpid sunfish-swum rink were the same as a vent
above the split-seamed rubby's back
alley. No, I can't sentimentalize the calamitous after-hours

of streetcorners asserting, *Here is one bad bird who knows all the moves,*
cuz face it, you can't tell an industrial from a national
park but raise your family undeterred and incorrigible, *aequo animo*
like the Stoic philosopher, *secundum Naturam*—and that's
anywhere.

So you scud over beaverponds, flap above drums of chemical sludge,
Caelum non animum mutant reads your frayed passport,
and I can't help wondering about you, let go by white guys,
their heirloom in the air of North America, ubiquitous as highways,
with your silly tune in the skies of Miami, Moosonee, and like
the damn Europeans you're a poignant plugugly lump of *je me souviens-*
hélas! Où sont les oiseaux...? Guilty you are and guilty you'll be,
driving the autochthonous Red-headed Woodpecker from his tree,
though Hölderlin heard you as Apollo's sibilous spirits
screaming in his ears while lightning tore his eyes open,
though tubercular Sterne found you enraged, chanting
encaged *I can't get out* and
now you're universally sprung—tell me, Everybird, who
can escape your freedom?

And Pliny spoke of you, Starling, Sir *Sturnus*, without detectable distaste,
nec occultantur, "nor are they hidden" (that's for sure!) but as for me I
might say, *Fuck it*, I might say *Fuck it*,
I don't want this inheritance, no thank you, Europe flapping around
    like a
low-grade Fury and in the sky always squealing and jumping
into every available hole
and killing and evicting and singing miserably bad.
But I confess it, O Starling, you sang to me in my cradle
(over the Song Sparrow, over the Cardinal and the Flicker)—
the first sounds I heard were surely cars and Starlings
and then the chimes from the unbelievable church, child as I am
of the guys from Europe with their guns, rum, and chains
and then their for-sale signs and the world a baking parking lot.

3.
Yet in the weeping willow my friend, *Salix babylonica*, willow by which
one might well sprawl and lament, you are a figure for pure idiosyncrasy

in your twinkling green coat that takes a sheen diffidently
like the bottle glass exploded at the punks' law-breaking whoop-up
in the municipal park last night. You woozy musician
with your buttercup-yellow beak! You're a heartbroken guy
vulnerable reluctantly to the pleasure of the sun who whistles a tune
to himself and plays with fresh leaves of grass in his lips
and the chlorophyll stains the skin of his elbow and his tongue—
if he could remember the words that go with the tune
he'd understand his pain better, *vielleicht, peut-être?*

Ach, Starling, anyway Charles Darwin would say, *Well Friend wait
long enough
and you'll become something else.* There's infinite hope
for something
somewhat like us. Starling, let's remember
the Galapagos. Let's wait around, eh? Let's wait, sing and change.

(1999)

ELIZABETH PHILIPS (1962–)
Tales from the Green Revolution

"The use of these new high-yielding Rice and also Wheat varieties ... has given rise to what is called the 'Green Revolution.'"
— Anthony Huxley, *Green Inheritance.*

You walk home from work through snow flecked with grey ash, along streets spilling with cars. Stopped at a corner you watch a man beat on the hood of his stalled car with both fists, his face crimson, his figure wreathed in exhaust from passing vehicles. His car blocks the walkway and you step quickly around it. Living here, on the prairie that is no longer prairie, demands exacting acts of the imagination. You believe the city doesn't count, under the asphalt the land waits to renew itself with russian thistle and pigweed and scarlet globe mallow. You have learned that these are the plants that succeed after the ground has been stripped bare by catastrophe.

You wish to remain true to the prairie. Imagining the buildings gone, you see mile upon mile of blue grama and buffalo grass. You know the names of plants, though you couldn't find them in a field. Wood anemone, gum weed, valerian. You even know their uses—to cure headache, to purify the blood, to ease digestion. Crossing the last jammed intersection before the tree-lined streets of your neighbour-hood, you work hard to conjure the blue-white fields beyond the city, the silent tracts of bush, where your fancy hears only the language of trees in the wind, maple, trembling aspen, and spruce.

In the evenings your mind lies fallow. You meditate on the snow-light that hangs between dull overcast and the crested white drifts. Awake late into the night, you lie in bed with the window open a crack, and a restful calm leaks in. You can feel the living presence of the land. You imagine the grass beneath the snow, crumpled under the sleeping weight of the city. Soon you too are asleep, the night covers you in a green darkness and you dream the wet smell of spring, pungent as sweat. You rush down to the river where you stand swaying, out of breath, your body hot as blood, your flesh pulsing. You watch the trees bud, and the buds unfold into leaves the size of your hands.

(1990)

Joseph A. Dandurand (1964–)
Feeding the Hungry

blue jays nest beside my legs.
flying to eat winter bugs juicy with nectar.
black birds squawk at me and my day.
telling me that I should've stayed in bed.

spring.
day.
mid-afternoon.
quiet.
no one about.
just me and the island.
no one drunk on the side of the road,
not even me,
not even my spirit.

blue jays eat big worms.
choking on their hunger.
chewing too quickly.
throwing up the day.
the day.
quiet.
no one dead.
everyone alive.
even the old ones in the trees.
they squawk at the warm wind.

blowing dust into the eyes of birds:
blue and black.
tired and hungered by the length of the winter months.
skinny birds nest in swamp waters,
their wings too weak to fly.
they stand and stare at the owl as she dives for unsuspecting mice.
the cracking of their skulls echoes around this island.
this island where everyone is alive.
this island where spirits eat you.
you can hear their songs pounding in the trees.

can you hear them?

quiet.
owl dives.
cracking bones.
drum.
whispers of the old ones.
something touches my arm.
I open my eyes.
it was my spirit.

someone forgot to feed him.

(1998)

Sue Goyette (1964–)
Vigil

The last river nymph is dying of thirst. She is surrounded
by farmers and can only swallow the lake a teaspoon at a time.

One of the farmers plays a drum quietly for her
the way he's heard rain on his roof. Another brings his guitar.

The sixth string, he explains, is the earth, the deep bass
of elegy that reverberates into morning like a mirage.

Another farmer lights five candles and places them high above
her bed. *Hyades*, he says, the rising stars that mark the beginning

of the season of rain. One farmer has fallen in love with her
and has lost everything to stay by her side. *Les poissons*,

les poissons is just one of the songs he's composed in her honour.
He whispers small poems about water striders and lily pads,

and in the moments when his shyness ebbs, he kisses her,
thinking *delta*, thinking *cove, creek, lagoon.*

She has asked for smooth stones to hold, she has asked for reeds,
she sometimes forgets where she is and speaks pickerel,

speaks trout, and they stand around her like she's still a pond
and nod like they understand. One has named his first born

after her. *Naiad*, he announced to his wife, to the midwife,
and plunged the baby into a basin of water. They have gathered

all the coin they can spare and have sent one of their daughters
to a far-away school to learn the art of describing the different
movements

of water and eagerly wait her return to teach them rivulet,
teach them current. They tell the nymph all of this,

wishing their words into ladles she can use to dip
and drink from, and are deeply saddened when she begins to resemble

a drying well. She has a gift for each of them, she manages to say,
and when they can lean forward, her last breaths are those of a stream,

roiling and rushing at root and rock. Only after she departs
do they realize how refreshed they feel, how quenched.

(2004)

Tim Bowling (1964–)
On the Disappearance of Two Million Sockeye Salmon

Tonight
the river is black as the pupil of a Spanish murderer.
Guilty men skulk along the dyke carrying burlap sacks
of mewling kittens while their children sleep. Gill-
netters named for long-dead women rub moss from broken
wharves while the poplars stand like quill-pens
saturated with a wordless ink.
A full moon floats above but can't be seen.
It has taken its light home. It has swallowed
its own tears, like an oft-beaten child
who finally gives up on love.

Tonight
the river is black as the pupil of a Spanish murderer
drifting through a moonless town with a knife in his grin.
The tossed sacks throb like hearts as they sink.
The ghosts of all women weep for their names
though so many lives will never be written
in the distant valleys of our longing.

Now a blue heron settles on the grass-tombed weighs
of an abandoned boatworks
and carefully counts each breath
that leaves its frail body.
There aren't enough.
There can never be
enough.

Far from here, the dawn,
like a rusty freighter,
drags its heavy chains across the sea.

(1995)

Late August at the Mouth of the Fraser River

The wind pulls the full blackberries gently
from their stems, the way a woman
removes her earrings after a dinner-party,
sighing as her tongue forgets the wine
and her cheek her host's kiss. Nearby
in the boatless harbour, a muskrat swims
from darkness to moonlight, silk sliding
down the white flesh of a thigh, and on
the farther shore a pregnant doe steps out
of the woods to listen to the two red watches
ticking at two different speeds
between her tissue-paper ribs.

Silt from the mountains is filling the channel,
the slow current is making tails out of heads
on a coin dropped by one of Galiano's sailors,
and auburn is packing its only good suit
to go off on a journey through a million leaves.
The moment calls for us, but we're staying here
to allow the world its own sweet company, to
let the berries drop on the grass, the musk-
rat reach home, and the deer time her pause
by the water. Stay quiet a while. Listen
to the ticking womb. Be in the world
while absent from it, like the sun,
the dead, the panting fawn.

(2000)

MICHAEL CRUMMEY (1965–)
  Cod (1)

Some days the nets came up so full
there was enough cod to swamp the boats
and part of the catch came in with other crews
once they'd filled their own dories to the gunnels,
the silver-grey bodies of the fish rippling
like the surface of a lake
the weight of them around their legs
like stepping thigh-deep into water

Most of the work was splitting and curing
the thin gutting knife slivered up the belly
and everything pulled clear with the sound bone
liver into the oil barrel
the thick tongue cut from the throat
and the splayed fish ready for salting then
set out on a flake to dry

This until one in the morning sometimes
a river of cod across the cutting table
in the yellow swirl of kerosene lamps
and everyone up by three or four
to get back out to the nets with the light

There was no talk of sleep when
the cod were running strong,
a few good weeks could make a season;
if they dreamt at all
in those three brief hours a night
they dreamt of the fish
the cold sweet weight of them,
fin and tail flickering in their heads
like light on the water

(1996)

Cod (2)

August.
    My father has sent the crew
home early for the second year in a row
the cod so scarce he can do
the work himself and still have time
to sit in the evenings
time to think about the flour and molasses
the netting, the coils of rope and twine
the tea and sugar and salt he took
on credit in the spring

Every night he dreams of them plentiful
the size of the fish years ago
big around as your thigh,
the thick shiver of their bodies
coming up in the cod traps

He turned seventeen this February past
his father has been dead two short seasons;
alone at the water's edge he sits
mending a useless net and smoking,
already two hundred dollars in debt
to the merchants

There are no cod in the whole frigging ocean

(1996)

Michael Redhill (1966–)
True Story

You got your big lakes and you got your small lakes.
From space it looks like a buckshot stopsign.
Some of 'em are knee-deep all the way across
(like your Nipissing)
and these ones breed your giant insatiable pike.
A friend of mine let his golden
jump around in the water, way up see,
and the dog could swim, but then suddenly
it vanishes. "Ranger!" we're yelling,
"Ranger"! But Ranger doesn't answer.
Pike attack. Honest.
Now you listen to me:
Don't walk across Lake Nipissing—
run. Run like hell because they got pike in that lake.

(1993)

Barbara Klar (1966–)
Blue Gramma

Priestess of the grasses.
Crescent flower: quarter moon,
mouse's comb, fetus
of the blue bear
hanging. In the dusk
the autumn Blackfoot count.
When the blue gramma grass
has only one flower it will be
a mild winter. Does it mean
the sow will bear single children,
loners, hermits, onlybears, their tracks
and their mothers to talk to?

(2008)

Barbara Nickel (1966–)
Athabasca Falls, 8:40 a.m.

We're here,
early for a change. Still, we didn't beat the rush
already spilled
from minivans, buses, and rental cars into
the rainbow mist below. Be careful not to stray past
the railings; some have,
the brochure says, and died.

Behold—
our cameras, efficient and tiny!
We can pose
endlessly, waste not, delete
all closed eyes, goofiness, bird-shat-on clothes,
and view, endlessly, ourselves
viewing the view, with screens
designed to perfectly capture

this morning—
white beast roaring, unseen away.

(2007)

KAREN SOLIE (1966–)
Sturgeon

Jackfish and walleye circle like clouds as he strains
the silt floor of his pool, a lost lure in his lip,
Five of Diamonds, River Runt, Lake Ike,
or a simple spoon, feeding
a slow disease of rust through his body's quiet armour.
Kin to caviar, he's an oily mudfish. Inedible.
Indelible. Ancient grunt of sea
in a warm prairie river, prehistory a third eye in his head.
He rests, and time passes as water and sand
through the long throat of him, in a hiss, as thoughts
of food. We take our guilts
to his valley and dump them in,
give him quicksilver to corrode his fins, weed killer,
gas oil mix, wrap him in poison arms.
Our bottom feeder,
sin-eater.

On an afternoon mean as a hook we hauled him
up to his nightmare of us and laughed
at his ugliness, soft sucker mouth opening,
closing on air that must have felt like ground glass,
left him to die with disdain
for what we could not consume.
And when he began to heave and thrash over yards of rock
to the water's edge and, unbelievably, in,
we couldn't hold him though we were teenaged
and bigger than everything. Could not contain
the old current he had for a mind, its pull,
and his body a muscle called river, called spawn.

(2001)

Pastoral

I hold a short softwood stick some worm took to
and runnelled with its mouth parts, ambling
as it ate. Note how its carvings imitate
furlings of the mildly impressive waterfall
still at it, chewing the valley. And these again
in whorls of amber gunk oozing from a pine.
Worm-addled stick, river, sap, my fingerprints, all of it
points in patterns on a complex plane: A Julia
Set. We even sound the same, a surge of air
and fluids, though I beaver myself up
with cigarettes and booze and jut from the cliffside
like a mine disaster. You should see what I cough
from my lungs at night. Gasses and dust
of one stupid thing after another. I'm here to relax

even as noxious weeds overrun the parkland:
mugwort, foxtail, stinkweed, goatsbeard, dropped
from hindquarters of foreign Airstreams jackknifing
in the townsite. I look for beauty and find it,
floored by lichen's radial grace and the incisive liquor
of juniper. Upending rocks, parting creeping spruce,
I exclaim each time: *Aha!*
An indigenous squirrel regards me squarely
from a branch. Cougars are culling local pets,
elk calve with murder in their eyes, and it's the worst
tick season in 40 years. The whole valley
is out for blood, for itself. As, of course, am I.

(2005)

Randy Lundy (1967–)
  The Great Sand Hills

It was easy to believe as the century was closing
that the world was ending. But now you know
the millennium has turned and nothing has changed.

At the edge of these hills, red ants biting your legs,
mosquitoes biting you everywhere else. These and
the dragonflies and the damselflies a blue hovering.
The hum of their wings an amber-coloured song.

Since the ranchers have quit grazing their cattle here
juniper, sagebrush, and fescue have insinuated themselves
into the bald dunes. Nothing has ended.

Not even the mice, whose delicate bones you gather
as if they are relics, and perhaps they are. A hawk
has left these offerings, but you don't know
how to respond.

The hawk has fed, his belly distended like the waxing moon;
he has entered sleep and the beetle has left its hieroglyphic trail
and disappeared beneath the surface of the sun-bleached sand.
The hawk has fed

but his hunger has not ended; it has subsided with the wind
its last sigh hanging like the low but rising moon.

(2004)

KAREN CONNELLY (1969–)
The Moment

Back of the orchards
opens the deep ravine,
the wildness at the edge of order.
Bears down there, they say, and coyotes
barking below the bone-pale cliffs.
Crumbling hoodoo faces stare
into the dark ruckus of trees.

For a while I searched
for a path into that adventure,
then gave up, seduced instead
by winter apples.

Mid-December, the trees are without leaves
but a few yellow apples cling
and glow like sunlit gems.
They are better than the apples
of high-season leaf and green.
They are the rare, uneaten apples
of the world. They did not fall
and fill the shallows of the field
like red and ochre pebbles in the silt-beds
of certain rivers. They are not
the apples picked and tumbled
into the great wooden crates.
They are not bought
and sold apples, these,
but gift apples.

The chill flesh and juice
sting my teeth.
The globe turns in my fingers
until I have swallowed it whole.

The entire field smells
of cold apples. And, at the edge

of the ravine, pungent sage finds
its way into my apple-filled
pockets, my mouth.
Sage, Russian thistle, sere grass.
The land keeps her heart
close to desert while her body
rolls down luxuriant
to the raw-silver lake.

At the place where
the orchard stumbles and falls
into the ravine,
a deer appears.
First as noise among the brush,
and now as a white nose floating
through the poplar branches.

Then up, openly,
into the naked orchard,
a young mule buck.
There are no apples left down there.
He eats the dry scraps of autumn.

When the wind turns
he pauses, lifting his head into the air
of my scent. He poises himself
near the ledge of his body,
ready to bolt.
His eyes scout back
and forth along the cliffs,
trying to see the smell of me.

I crouch in the sage,
gazing down,
holding my breath,
knowing it cannot last:
soon he will strike
the drum in the ground
with his hoof and

bound down the ravine
like the stag in an old painting,
unhuntable, unholdable,
leaping forever
into the great trees.

For a moment we stare directly
into the black gleam
of each other's eyes.

Then he is gone.

(2000)

ALISON CALDER (1969–)
The Animals Dream

"What do geese dream of?
Of maize"
  —Sigmund Freud

Inside his salty shelter the badger smells himself,
the entombed pharaoh reading hieroglyphic dreams.
Outside the snow piles up, fumbles at his door
but cannot move the stones.
The pharaoh sleeps.
The river under Faucette's field drips slowly,
when will the cup be filled and tip
to wash him with its waters?
He yearns towards the grubs, seductive
as the call from any Cairo market stall.
Their heat defies the barometric drop. He is beguiled.
But now, through dark, roots grow, ribs surround
his sleeping form. He groans, blunt-snouted,
noses at the webs that wrap him close,
his opiate stupor turning blue sky
to litmus red of poppies. He digs
his heavy head beneath his paws, cries out
for mother with her bursting teats.
And now the river's dry, the ferryman
returns him to the shore. He curls into his claws,
growls once to hear his voice. *I am*, he thinks,
I am, I am. And then he sleeps again.

(2007)

Stephanie Bolster (1969–)
Many Have Written Poems about Blackberries

But few have gotten at the multiplicity of them, how each berry
composes itself of many dark notes, spherical,
swollen, fragile as a world. A blackberry is the colour of a painful
bruise on the upper arm, some internal organ
as yet unnamed. It is shaped to fit
the tip of the tongue, to be a thimble, a dunce cap
for a small mouse. Sometimes it is home to a secret green worm
seeking safety and the power of surprise. Sometimes it plunks
into a river and takes on water.
Fishes nibble it.

The bushes themselves ramble like a grandmother's sentences,
giving birth to their own sharpness. Picking the berries
must be a tactful conversation
of gloved hands. Otherwise your fingers will bleed
the berries' purple tongue; otherwise thorns
will pierce your own blank skin. Best to be on the safe side,
the outside of the bush. Inside might lurk
nests of yellow jackets; rabid bats; other,
larger hands on the same search.

The flavour is its own reward, like kissing the whole world
at once, rivers, willows, bugs and all, until your swollen
lips tingle. It's like waking up
to discover the language you used to speak
is gibberish, and you have never really
loved. But this does not matter because you have
married this fruit, mellifluous, brutal, and ripe.

(1999)

RACHEL ROSE (1970–)
Raccoons in Garbage

Some nights, I've nearly
caught them.

This afternoon, interrupted
by a ceramic pot knocked off the deck,
I put aside my books
and saw them, a team of three
beneath the porch, attacking the green-black sacks
with their neat hands.

Out came the small stained napkins
used to catch my monthly blood
and the blood of packaged meat.
Out came the grapefruit rinds, disposable diapers,
coffee grounds, nylons with runs,
eggshells in a small stack,
hollow monument to Wednesday's
omelette.

The stooges snickered
behind their bandit masks as they sorted
the offal from the meal. I forgot to be annoyed,
so curious I finally abandoned my body,
all but the observant eye
I seek but never find in meditation.

As soon as I recognized its scent,
whatever it was,
being or *not-being*,
lifted its sharp nose,
sensed a trap, slipped under the fence
and was gone: one dark shape
shadowing the others.

Alone with the remnants,
the sheerest glimpse of grace,
throbbing, wild as any beast,
I knelt to sweep away the feast.

(2005)

KEN BABSTOCK (1970–)
To Lichen

Something's remains refused
by death, learning to spread; clustered, buckling
    in thin grit. Cling
    and be low, be

sparse as moments of wholeness, treasured
and severe. Scrapings off rock's
inner ear that's heard epochs
    in sound wave striating a sheer
face—

        Cliff snot, brittle
crispness that stays, stays somehow
cloud-coloured, orangish, starved
    green: Dickensian waif-cousin to
    moss, to plush bedding. Oh, granite trying

to be snow, you sleepless, sleep-
proof, trod on and sniffed
    at reverie—

        Stretch.

(1999)

Bear 10

Between next year's Lexus and someone
cooing at conditioner
he rakes his massive back along low spruce boughs.

How many pounds of Alaska berries in a day?
Smell it: dark, fecal
timbits steaming on flattened fireweed; the puffy,

antique dust-scent of pawed stump; dripping
cedar and glacier water
he laps at then glares into your living room, a barrel

of head rusted to distaste at what you've done
with the furniture. Harsh
light over the recliner and you *like* Kandinsky?

He's on a treadmill of alpine scenery from the west
half of the park to the Cariboo
range, this area filled in with a red matching the "on" indicator

blipping from his collar. Mike's picked up his transmission—
always Mike, or Walt—and they
know for a fact he's crashing this ridge unspooling into

the wherever beyond the framed glass of the chopper's cockpit.
—Seles in straight sets—
He's shoveling steelhead out of the frigid shallows,

mopping up a tributary of the Fraser that blackens him
to his throat. Hooks a nose
into a down-valley draft from offscreen. Single male

in a how many square kilometre tract? 10 likes his space.
—Everybody in khaki, Valvoline, Once
you pop you can't stop—but Mike has landed the bird

safely and shows us the overpass built for 10 and
they don't know if he's used it
but it appears well-engineered so why not. Could be

he's lumbering around the dank lee of the bookshelf
waiting to cross over in private,
chewing into the root-mat, a backhoe with breath, rolling

blowdown for the white nodes of grubs, hefting
his tonnage upright, wobbling
like a toddler for days through the wild grid looking

for nightfall and a back to embrace that won't break.

(2001)

PHILIP KEVIN PAUL (1971–)
ĆIAAĆU

The way night goes west, followed by
deer, the carriers of dawn.

They shy-step
behind their leader into the meadow
from the bush-stifled hills, as though
from someone's private thought
into plain sight, as though to console
the crying of the Old People in me:
a century of wailing finally coming to tears.

No Hunting in the Place of Deer.

The deer lower their heads into the mist
one by one
and then all at once—raise them.

With a snort and two sharp stomps
their leader hurries them through
the meadow, back into dark woods
and down their great-grandfather's path
toward spring ocean, spring tide.

Maybe everything has gone as planned,
by *some* plan, but I still want to know
why no one said a word when someone
fenced off the Place of Deer, and what
the Old People ate when the spring came
and they weren't allowed to hunt.

Just one word.

ĆIAAĆU, name of the spring hunt.

ĆIAAĆU, name of the sick deer and
the tide that leaves salt to cure them.

ĆIȺȺĆU, the one word waiting
behind a salal blind to erupt
from its own eternity of silence
and run down the hill.

(2003)

GEORGE MURRAY (1971–)
Memories of the Snake

My father has always been afraid of snakes,
their muscular bodies lying close
to the earth, how they can taste the planet

from currents of air across thin tongues.
He despises their lidless eyes that see
things his do not, their chiselled heads

working as basins for mysteries dirt has known
since well before him—
a fear he has been mute with

through almost every year I've known him.
Yet once when I was a child, I remember
walking with him through a thicket

where I found a tiny serpent overturned
deep in the bush, its pale underbelly exposed
to the sun, its dry tongue lolled

across the path beneath us, sense memories
soaked back into the soil.
This is how secrets are kept so long, I thought

and, hooking it over a stick
so its body draped limp over the fulcrum
of twig, I held it up to him at arm's length,

unaware of the reaction to come—
his recoiling head, skinned eyes, bared teeth,
body twisting away as though tearing itself

off at the top.
                Get it the hell away! he yelled,
throw it back where it came from! (What I recall

first when I remember that day is the scent
of the thicket, a lilac bush nearby.)
But it's dead, I replied, *it can't hurt you—*

It could once, he spit, sniffing out my lie,
and that's enough for me.

(2001)

SUE SINCLAIR (1972–)
The Least Terns

'What interested me most…was the manner in which the birds
had decorated their nests…Here and there along the beach, the
'leasties' had picked up flat bits of sea shell about the size of a
finger nail, and with these bits they had lined their nest, setting
the flat pieces in flat, like parts of a mosaic.'   —Henry Beston

When the sky finally falls
only the tiniest tern will remember
what holiness is: a flower
in mosaic at the bottom
of his nest. As storm after storm
rages he flies through the eye
of the needle
into a seamless place with a cracked

scalloped shell in his beak, drops it
into the nest, a shallow bowl
of mussel shells, moon shells, clam shells
chalky pieces softened
by water, like the look
on your face when you wake up and discover
you are at home.

The tern's eggs lie bare
on the shore, this open cradle full
of open cradles. Sand rips
the air. You'd think the eggs
would be blown away, smashed
when everything around them seems
to have cracked, but they,
in these wild days
before sleep, know something
of life on a shelterless beach

and keep themselves
quietly to themselves.

(2001)

S. D. JOHNSON (1973–)
  Two Magpies

Two magpies
on the river's edge,—
              one carcass of seagull.

      They're like nuns
thrown out of the convent,—
heartling chortily.

The river drags its memory over stones,
                        haling away from them
something of their time: —

      I want to lie here like this forever, or at least
until a quiet overtakes me,—and grass
grows up through my mind.

The gull is meat,—its mother
is oblivion.

The sisters nod and nod, the gull
is good food.

They're tearing it
into pieces of heaven.

(2000)

Adam Dickinson (1974–)
Great Chain of Being

Linnaeus connected the world through teeth,
beaks, and bills.
This was the point where one thing entered another:
minerals the appetite, voice
the open air.
Ornament entered function.
And so it was that the vernacular languages of Europe were insufficient.
Only Latin or Greek;
other tongues were dark and crowded.

Chokeberry seeds must first pass through the intestines of black bears.
In abundant seasons, a sow comes upon the patch on the open edge of
a riverbank. While chewing, something provokes her to turn suddenly
upstream and brace herself against a rock. This small amount of
anxiety stimulates enough acid in the stomach to break down the hard
shell of the berry seeds.

The mouth is the symbol for a corner.
Phoenicians built the alphabet out of joints,
sounds whose shapes in the throat and lips
were translated into sticks
piled or bent on the page.
Small fires grew.
People stood at windows to watch,
arms outstretched.
For the Greeks this was epsilon;
for the Romans the letter E.

Cough then glottal stop,
heartbeat then iamb,
marshland then coal
then greenhouse.
All bells are held at the top,
just as all plants are tied to the sun, just
as language, despite its vacuums and cinder blocks
hangs above heads,
rings in the ears.

Sometimes in Canadian forests small pale plants stick up in clusters
from the ground with flowers that hang from their tops like bells.
These are pine-saps, ghost plants, or corpse flowers. No Kingdom will
accept them (neither plant nor fungus) because they are vascular
organisms that do not need the sun: plants with no chlorophyll,
mushrooms with rudimentary leaves. Aboriginals pick eyebright for
the eyes; European settlers, convulsion weed for the nerves.

Linnaeus read the atlas wrong
and gave plants in the high Andes
names derived from the arid New Mexican plains.
Nature doesn't jump.
Kingdoms are carefully spaced ladders
against the sides of burning buildings.
One rung at a time,
women and children are the first to descend.
If the final goal of creation is us,
then why for the index of berries in a small pamphlet
did Linnaeus write: "too sour"; "black and unpleasant"?

Unlike most birds, he said, swallows do not migrate during the winter
months to warmer southern latitudes. Instead they gather in the late
fall at the margin of cold lakes and estuaries. Here they plunge them-
selves over the edge of the ice and pile on the bottom like hibernating
frogs. If you come upon a lake full of swallows and break the ice in the
parts that are darkest, the birds will appear in their masses, cold, asleep,
and half-dead. If you fish one out and warm it with your hands, it flies
away too soon. Every hole beneath it mistaken for an opening.

Homo sapiens was a draft.
So was *Homo diurnus*.
Both were crossed out and reinserted.
Well before Darwin, Linnaeus put us in with apes;
the only difference he could see
was in the canine teeth.

Whatever is, is right.
This is not an order but a riddle,
not a single thought, but many.

(2006)

Zachariah Wells (1976–)
Duck, Duck, Goose

The A340 ate up the runway and blasted off
Over the bay just as a skein of Canadas
Lifted—straight into the wake

Of the great tin goose. Before they could pattern
Themselves, choreograph that famous V,
They were flattened, flapping

Hard against the downdraft uselessly,
Thudding the tarmac in salvos
Of down, blood and down.

Iqaluit

(2004)

MARK CALLANAN (1979–)
 Barn Swallows

But who owns it?
The barn I mean.
It's hard to say, but probably
an old man with a limp,
one eye to tell the time of day
and one to watch
the swallows in their flight,
their brief glide
down from the loft
to the hay-strewn floor.
Someone just like that.

The swallows sing
of blindness and other afflictions,
slit their own throats
on the stalks of wheat
then speed towards
their nests to sleep.
The swallows.
Who owns them? Probably
no one. Probably no
one but the wind.
Something as simple as that.

(2003)

Biographical Notes
on the Authors

Milton Acorn (1923–1986) was born in Charlottetown and lived in Montreal, Toronto, and Vancouver before returning to Prince Edward Island in 1981. *The Island Means Minago* (1975) won the Governor General's Award. His other books include *Jackpine Sonnets*, *I've Tasted My Blood: Poems 1956–1968*, and *More Poems for People*.

Adam Allan (1757–1823) was born in Dumfries, Scotland, and immigrated to New Brunswick. He published *The New Gentle Shepherd*, which contained "A Description of the Great Falls, of the River St. John, in the Province of New Brunswick."

Patrick Anderson (1915–1979) was born in England, studied at Oxford University and Columbia University, and moved to Montreal in 1940. He taught at McGill University and then left Canada in 1950 to teach in Malaysia and Britain. He returned to Canada in 1971. He wrote many non-fiction books and several collections of poetry, including *Return to Canada: Selected Poems*.

Margaret Atwood (1939–) was born in Ottawa and raised in various places in Ontario. She studied at the University of Toronto, Radcliffe College, and Harvard University. She currently lives in Toronto. She has won the Governor General's Award for both fiction and poetry, and she is a winner of the Booker Prize. Her most recent poetry collection is *The Door*.

Margaret Avison (1918–2007) was born in Galt, Ontario, and raised in Regina and Calgary. She worked as a librarian, editor, and social worker in Toronto where she lived for most of her life. She received Governor General's Awards for *Winter Sun* (1960) and *No Time* (1990). She was awarded the Griffin Poetry Prize for *Concrete and Wild Carrot* (2003).

Ken Babstock (1970–) was born in Newfoundland and Labrador and grew up in Pembroke, Ontario. He now lives in Toronto where he is the poetry editor for the House of Anansi Press. His collections of poetry include *Mean, Days into Flatspin,* and *Airstream Land Yacht.*

Brian Bartlett (1953–) was born in St. Stephen, New Brunswick, and grew up in Fredericton. He now lives in Halifax where he teaches at Saint Mary's University. His selected poems are published in *Wanting the Day: Selected Poems.* His newest book is *The Watchmaker's Table.* He edited *Don McKay: Essays on His Works* and *Earthly Pages: The Poetry of Don Domanski.*

Ken Belford (1945–) was born to a farming family in DeBolt, Alberta, and now lives in Prince George, British Columbia. For many years he lived in the unroaded wilderness area of the headwaters of the Nass River. His most recent books are *ecologue* (2005) and *lan(d)guage* (2008).

Julie Berry (1952–) was born in St. Thomas, Ontario, where she continues to live and work. Her first book, *worn thresholds,* was reprinted in 2006.

Earle Birney (1904–1995) was raised near Calgary and in Banff, Alberta. He taught for many years at the University of British Columbia. *David and Other Poems* (1942) and *Now Is Time* (1945) both won Governor General's Awards. His *Collected Poems* were published in 1975, and since then various new and selected collections have appeared, most recently *One Muddy Hand.*

bill bissett (1939–) was born in Halifax, lived in Vancouver and London, Ontario, and now lives in Toronto. He is a visual artist as well as a poet. His most recent publications are a CD called *deth interrupts th dansing/a strangr space* and a collection of poetry, *ths is erth thees ar peopul.* Other works include *inkorrect thots, th influenza uv logik,* and *Nobody owns th earth.*

E. D. Blodgett (1935–) was born in Philadelphia, Pennsylvania, and studied at Amherst College, the University of Minnesota, and Rutgers University. He taught English and comparative literature at the University of Alberta for twenty-four years. *Da Capo* is a volume of selected poems from his first five books. *Apostrophes: Woman at a Piano* (1996) won the Governor General's Award.

Peter Blue Cloud (Aroniawenrate) (1935–) was born to the Turtle Clan of the Mohawk tribe on the Caughnawaga Reserve in Kahnawake, Quebec, where he now lives. He has written fiction and non-fiction, as well as poetry. Many of his poems are collected in *Clans of Many Nations: Selected Poems, 1969–1994.*

Stephanie Bolster (1969–) was raised in Burnaby, British Columbia, and now teaches at Concordia University. Her first book, *White Stone: The Alice Poems* (1998), won the Governor General's Award. She has also published *Two Bowls of Milk* and *Pavilion*. Her next collection of poetry is forthcoming in spring 2009.

Roo Borson (1952–) was born in Berkeley, California, and now lives in Toronto. Some of her earlier poems are collected in *Night Walk: Selected Poems*. *Short Journey Upriver Toward Oishida* won both the Governor General's Award and the Griffin Poetry Prize. She collaborated with Kim Maltman and Andy Patton to write *Introduction to the Introduction to Wang Wei*.

Tim Bowling (1964–) was born and raised on the west coast of British Columbia and now lives in Edmonton. He has published seven collections of poetry (most recently, *Fathom*), three novels (most recently, *The Bone Sharps*), and a work of non-fiction, *The Lost Coast: Salmon, Memory and the Death of Wild Culture*.

Diana Brebner (1956–2001) was born in Kingston, Ontario, and grew up near Montreal. She lived in Ottawa until her early death from cancer. Her works include *Radiant Life Forms*, *The Golden Lotus*, and *Flora & Fauna*. The most recent collection of her work, *The Ishtar Gate: Last and Selected Poems*, was edited by **Stephanie Bolster**.

Brian Brett (1950–) was born in Vancouver, studied literature at Simon Fraser University, and lives on a farm on Salt Spring Island, British Columbia. His most recent book is a memoir, *Trauma Farm: An unNatural History of Small Farming from Babylon to Globalization* and a book of poetry, *Wind River Elegies*.

Elizabeth Brewster (1922–) was born in Chipman, New Brunswick, and was educated at the Universities of New Brunswick, Toronto, and Indiana. She has lived in Saskatoon since 1972. She has published more than twenty books of fiction and poetry. Her collected poetry, *The Collected Poems of Elizabeth Brewster*, is published by Oberon Press.

Robert Bringhurst (1946–) was born in Los Angeles and raised in Montana, Utah, Wyoming, Alberta, and British Columbia. He now lives on Quadra Island, British Columbia. He is a poet, essayist, linguist, and typographer. His most recent book is *Everywhere Being Is Dancing: Twenty Pieces of Thinking*, a collection of essays. Selections of his poetry were published in *The Calling: Selected Poems 1970–1995*.

Charles Bruce (1906–1971) was born in Port Shoreman, Nova Scotia, and attended Mount Allison University. He worked for the Halifax *Chronicle* and then joined the Canadian Press (CP), eventually serving as CP's general superintendent from 1945 until his retirement in 1963. He received the Governor General's Award for his book of poetry *The Mulgrave Road* (1951).

Julie Bruck (1957–) was born in Montreal and now lives in San Francisco where she teaches and writes. Her two books of poetry are *The End of Travel* and *The Woman Downstairs*. A third manuscript, *The Mandrill's Gaze*, is under way.

Adam Hood Burwell (1790–1849) was born near Fort Erie, Upper Canada (now Ontario), and raised on his family's farm. He was a minister of the Church of England, spending his last years in Kingston, Ontario. Some of his work appeared under the pseudonym "Erieus."

Alison Calder (1969–) was born in England and raised in Saskatoon. She studied at the University of Western Ontario. She currently lives in Winnipeg and teaches at the University of Manitoba. She is the editor of *Desire Never Leaves: The Poetry of Tim Lilburn*. Her first collection of poetry is *Wolf Tree*.

Mark Callanan (1979–) was born in St. John's. He studied at Memorial University of Newfoundland and lived and worked in Leeds, England, for two years. He now lives in St. John's. His collections of poetry are *Scarecrow* and *Turk's Gut Wolf.*

Wilfred Campbell (1860–1918) was born in Newmarket, Canada West (now Ontario), and studied at the University of Toronto and at a school in Massachusetts. In the early 1890s, he began to work in the Ottawa civil service, eventually working in the National Archives. He published several volumes of verse, including *Lake Lyrics and Other Poems* (1889).

Bliss Carman (1861–1929) was born in Fredericton and lived in New England for most of his life. He was an editor and writer who published more than fifty volumes of poetry, including *Low Tide on Grand Pré, Behind the Arras: A Book of the Unseen, Songs of the Sea Children*, and *The Kinship of Nature*.

Thomas Cary (1751–1823) was born in Bristol, England, and his early life is largely unknown except that he worked for the East India Company until his arrival in Quebec. By 1775 he was living near Montreal and working as a merchant and government employee. He was a journalist and operated a lending library and bookstore in Montreal.

Peter Christensen (1951–) was born in Red Deer, Alberta, and raised on a parkland farm. He lived for many years near Radium Hot Springs, British Columbia, where he worked at various times as a guide, park ranger, rancher, and consultant. He now lives in Terrace, British Columbia. His books of poetry include *Hail Storm*, *Rig Talk*, *To Die Ascending*, and *Winter Range*.

Fred Cogswell (1917–2004) was born in East Centreville, New Brunswick, and lived most of his life in Fredericton. He was the editor of *The Fiddlehead* from 1952 to 1966, the publisher of Fiddlehead Poetry Books from 1960 to 1980, and a professor at the University of New Brunswick from 1952 to 1983. He published thirty-three books of poetry from 1954 to 2000.

Eric Cole (1959–) was born in Dublin, Ireland. He studied zoology and English and then worked at the Dublin Zoo. In 1992, he moved to Canada and began to work at the Toronto Zoo where he is the animal care supervisor of the African Savanna. He now lives in Whitby, Ontario. His first book of poetry is *Man & Beast*.

Anne Compton (1947–) was born in Bangor, Prince Edward Island, and was raised on PEI. She teaches at the University of New Brunswick. She edited *The Edge of Home*, selected poems of **Milton Acorn**. Her books of poetry include *Opening the Island* and *Processional* (2005), which won the Governor General's Award.

Karen Connelly (1969–) was born and raised in Calgary and has lived for extended periods of time in Thailand, Greece, Spain, and France. She currently lives in Toronto. She has published travel writing, including *Touch the Dragon: A Thai Journal*; a novel, *The Lizard Cage*; and several books of poetry, including *The Border Surrounds Us*.

Marlene Cookshaw (1953–) was born and raised in southern Alberta. She now lives on Pender Island, British Columbia. A long-time editor of *The Malahat Review*, she is the author of several collections of poetry, including *Double Somersaults*, *Shameless*, and *Lunar Drift*.

Dennis Cooley (1944–) was born and raised in southeast Saskatchewan and has taught for many years at St. John's College at the University of Manitoba. He lives in Winnipeg. He has been involved in many aspects of publishing, editing, and teaching. His latest publications include *By Word of Mouth* (2007) and *correction line* (forthcoming 2008).

Allan Cooper (1954–) was born in Moncton, New Brunswick, and studied at Mount Allison University under the late **John Thompson** and Herbert Burke.

He now lives in Alma, New Brunswick, where he is a musician and the publisher of Owl's Head Press. He has published twelve books of poetry, most recently *Singing the Flowers Open, Gabriel's Wing,* and *The Alma Elegies.*

Stanley Cooperman (1929–1979) was born and raised in New York City. For the last years of his life he taught at Simon Fraser University. In his lifetime, he published four books of poetry. A selection of his work was posthumously published in *Greco's Last Book.*

Joan Crate (1953–) was born in Yellowknife and grew up in Vancouver. She now lives in Calgary and teaches creative writing, children's literature, and First Nations literature at Red Deer College in Red Deer, Alberta. She is the author of a novel and two books of poetry, *Pale as Real Ladies: Poems for Pauline Johnson* and *Foreign Homes.*

Isabella Valancy Crawford (1850–1887) was born in Dublin, Ireland. Her family immigrated to Canada in 1857, eventually settling in Peterborough, Ontario. She lived in Toronto from 1883 until her death. She published one book of poetry in her lifetime, *Old Spookses' Pass, Malcolm's Katie and Other Poems* (1884). Her *Collected Poems* was published posthumously in 1905.

Lorna Crozier (1948–) was born in Swift Current, Saskatchewan. She now teaches at the University of Victoria. She has published several collections of poetry and won the Governor General's Award for *Inventing the Hawk* (1992). Her most recent book is a selected edition, *The Blue Hour of the Day.*

Michael Crummey (1965–) was born in Buchans, Newfoundland and Labrador, and lived for a time in Labrador. He studied at Memorial University of Newfoundland and at Queen's University. He now lives in St. John's. He has published half a dozen books, including *Hard Light* and *Salvage* (both poetry) and two novels, *River Thieves* and *The Wreckage.*

Mary Dalton (1950–) was born in Lake View, Conception Bay, Newfoundland, and grew up in Harbour Main, Conception Bay. She now lives in St. John's where she teaches at Memorial University of Newfoundland. Her collections of poetry include *The Time of Icicles, Allowing the Light, Merrybegot,* and *Red Ledger.*

Joseph A. Dandurand (1964–) is from the Kwantlen Indian (Xalatsep) First Nation in British Columbia. He studied at Algonquin College and the University of Ottawa. He is a playwright as well as a poet. His poetry books include *Upside Down Raven, I Touched the Coyote's Tongue; burning for the dead and scratching for the poor;* and *looking into the eyes of my forgotten dreams.*

Tom Dawe (1940–) was born and raised around the Conception Bay area in Newfoundland. He studied at Memorial University of Newfoundland where he worked for many years. He has published several books of poetry, including *In Hardy Country*, as well as folklore and children's literature.

Barry Dempster (1952–) was born and raised in Scarborough, Ontario, and lives just north of Toronto. He was educated in child psychology. He is a fiction writer and an author of children's books and several books of poetry, including *The Words Wanting Out: Poems Selected and New* and, most recently, *The Burning Alphabet*.

Christopher Dewdney (1951–) was born and raised in London, Ontario. He now lives in Toronto. He writes both non-fiction and poetry. His poetry collections include *Predators of the Adoration: Selected Poems, 1972–1982*, *The Radiant Inventory*, *Demon Pond*, and *The Natural History*, as well as his multi-volume poetic project *A Natural History of Southwestern Ontario*.

Adam Dickinson (1974–) was born in Bracebridge, Ontario, and studied at the University of Alberta. He currently teaches at Brock University. He is the author of *Cartography and Walking* and *Kingdom, Phylum*.

Don Domanski (1950–) was born and raised on Cape Breton Island, Nova Scotia. He currently lives in Halifax. His collection *All Our Wonder Unavenged* (2007) won the Governor General's Award. His other books include *The Cape Breton Book of the Dead*, *Heaven*, *Wolf-Ladder*, *Stations of the Left Hand*, and *Parish of the Psychic Moon*.

John Donlan (1944–) was born and raised in the Muskoka region of Ontario. He now divides his time between a home on a lake near Kingston, Ontario, and Vancouver where he is a reference librarian at the Vancouver Public Library. His collections of poetry are *Domestic Economy*, *Baysville*, *Green Man*, and *Spirit Engine*.

Marilyn Dumont (1955–) was born in northeastern Alberta. She lives in Edmonton and teaches at Athabasca University. Her books include *A Really Good Brown Girl*, *green girl dreams Mountains*, and *that tongued belonging*. She is working on a manuscript that explores Métis history, politics, and identity through her ancestral figure, Gabriel Dumont.

Crispin Elsted (1947–) was born in Vancouver and studied at the University of British Columbia. He lived for a time in England and then moved to Mission, British Columbia, where he still lives. He is a typographer, jazz musician, compositor, translator, essayist, actor, and director. His commercially published book of poetry is *Climate and the Affections: Poems 1970–1995*.

R. G. Everson (1903–1992) was born on a small farm in Oshawa, Ontario, and lived in a log cabin in the Muskoka Woods near Huntsville, Ontario, for six years in the 1930s. He received a law degree and became the president of a Montreal public relations firm. Many of his poems are collected in *Everson at Eighty.*

Robert Finch (1900–1995) was born in Freeport, Long Island, New York, and was educated at the University of Toronto and the Sorbonne in Paris. He was a professor of French at the University of Toronto and received two Governor General's Awards for poetry, first for *Poems* (1946) and then for *Acis in Oxford* (1961).

Joan Finnigan (1925–2007) was born in Ottawa and educated at Carleton University and Queen's University. She lived in and around Ottawa and Kingston for most of her life. Of her twenty-six published works, several were collections of poetry, including *Living Together, The Watershed Collection, Wintering Over,* and *Second Wind, Second Sight.*

Len Gasparini (1941–) was born in Windsor, Ontario, and now lives in Toronto. He writes fiction and children's books, as well as poetry. Many of his poems are collected in *The Broken World: Poems 1967–1998.*

Chief Dan George (1899–1981) or Teswahno (Dan Slaholt in English) was born in the Sleil Waututh First Nation on the Burrard Indian Reserve in British Columbia. He was involved in television and film, appearing in several Hollywood films. His poems were published in *My Heart Soars* (1974), and a second volume, *My Spirit Soars*, was published posthumously in 1982.

John Glassco (1909–1981) was born in Montreal. At the age of twenty, he moved to France, and then returned to Canada in 1932 and settled in the eastern townships of Quebec. His *Selected Poems* (1971) won a Governor General's Award. He is most well-known for the memoir of his youth in France, *Memoirs of Montparnasse.*

Leona Gom (1946–) was born in the north Peace River country of Alberta to homesteader parents. She now lives in White Rock, British Columbia. She has published six books of poetry and seven novels. Her *Collected Poems* was published by Sono Nis in 1991. Her most recent novel is *Hating Gladys.*

Sue Goyette (1964–) was born in Sherbrooke, Quebec, and grew up in Montreal. She now lives in Halifax and teaches at Dalhousie University. Her books of poetry are *The True Names of Birds* and *Undone*. She has also published a novel, *Lures.*

Jim Green (1943–) is a poet, storyteller, writer, broadcaster, and entertainer. He was born in High River, Alberta, and grew up around Pincher Creek, Alberta, where he learned to hunt, trap, and fish. For the past forty years he has lived in the Northwest Territories. His books include *Beyond Here* and *North Book*.

Kristjana Gunnars (1948–) was born in Rejkjavik, Iceland. Her family immigrated to the United States, and she came to Canada in 1969. She has taught at the University of Alberta and now lives in Sechelt, British Columbia. She is well-known for her prose works, including *The Prowler* and *Zero Hour*. Her most recent poetry books are *Carnival of Longing* and *Exiles Among You*.

Susan Francis Harrison (1859–1935), also known by the pseudonym "Seranus," was born in Toronto and educated in Montreal and Toronto. She lived in Toronto for most of her life. She was a composer, song writer, and music critic, and was interested in French-Canadian folklore. Her poems are collected in *Pine, Rose and Fleur de Lys* and *Later Poems and New Villanelles*.

Diana Hartog (1942–) spent her early life in the Sierra Nevada Mountains in California and now divides her time between California and New Denver, British Columbia. She writes non-fiction, novels, and poetry. Her poetry books are *Ink Monkey*, *Polite to Bees*, *Candy from Strangers*, and *Matinee Light*.

D. E. Hatt (1869–1942) wrote several books of poems related to forestry and British Columbia life, including *Okanagan*, *Outdoor Verse*, and *Sitka Spruce: Songs of the Queen Charlotte Islands*. The latter is about the airplane spruce loggers with whom he worked in 1918 on the Haida Gwaii/Queen Charlotte Islands.

Brian Henderson (1948–) was born in Kitchener, Ontario, and lives there today. He is the author of nine collections of poetry, the most recent of which is *Nerve Language* (2007). He was a founding editor of *Rune* for its decade of existence. He is working on a book of poetry exploring the interrelations of water and landscape.

Cornelia Hoogland (1952–) was born in the Fraser Valley of British Columbia and grew up there and in Victoria. She has also lived in Calgary and Vancouver and currently divides her time between Vancouver Island and London, Ontario, where she teaches at the University of Western Ontario. Her most recent book of poetry is *Cuba Journal*.

Ken Howe (1960–) was born in Edmonton and moved with his family to Beaverlodge, Alberta, when he was nine years old. He went to university in Edmonton and lived in Regina where he played the horn in the symphony. He now lives in Quebec City where he has a job as a translator. His books include *Household Hints for the End of Time* and *Cruise Control*.

Paulette Jiles (1943–) was born in Salem, Missouri, and studied at the University of Missouri. She immigrated to Canada in 1969. She currently lives in San Antonio, Texas. Her books include *Celestial Navigation: Poems* (1984), which won the Governor General's Award, *Waterloo Express*, *The Jesse James Poems*, and two novels: *Enemy Women* and *Stormy Weather*.

Rita Joe (1932–2007) was born in Whycocomaugh, Cape Breton Island, Nova Scotia. She lived most of her life in the First Nations community of Eskasoni, Nova Scotia. Her autobiography, *Song of Rita Joe: Autobiography of a Mi'kmaq Poet*, tells her story of Mi'kmaw experience. Her four books of poems are *Poems of Rita Joe*, *Song of Eskasoni*, *Lnu and Indians We're Called*, and *We Are the Dreamers*.

Pauline Johnson (Tekahionwake) (1861–1913) was born on the Six Nations Reserve near Brantford, Ontario. She travelled extensively across Canada, the United States, and Britain until 1909 when she retired to Vancouver. During her lifetime, she published her poetry in *The White Wampum*. Her posthumously published collection of poetry, *Flint and Feather*, is still in print.

S. D. Johnson (1973–) was born in Craik, Saskatchewan, and grew up in Eastend in the Cypress Hills area of the province. Her books include *Pale Grace* and *Hymns to Phenomena*.

George Johnston (1913–2004) was born in Hamilton, Ontario, and was educated at the University of Toronto. He taught Old and Middle English and Old Norse at Carleton University for many years and translated Danish, Norwegian, Faeroese, and Icelandic literature. His poetry is collected in *Endeared by Dark*.

D. G. Jones (1929–) was born in Bancroft, Ontario, and educated at Queen's University and McGill University. He lives in North Hatley, Quebec. He taught for many years at L'Université de Sherbrooke. He has won the Governor General's Award for *Under the Thunder the Flowers Light Up the Earth* (1977) and for translation in 1993.

Lionel Kearns (1937–) was born in Nelson, British Columbia. He studied at the University of London, worked in Trinidad, and now lives in Vancouver where he taught at Simon Fraser University. Some of his poetry is collected in *Ignoring the Bomb: New and Selected Poems*.

Adam Kidd (1802–1831) was born in Tullynagee, Ireland. He arrived in Canada between 1818 and 1824. His best-known work is the long poem *The Huron Chief*. He died in Quebec City of tuberculosis shortly after writing the poem.

William Kirby (1817–1906) was born in Kingston-upon-Hull, England, and immigrated with his family to Cincinnati, Ohio, in 1832. In 1839, he settled in Niagara-on-the-Lake, Ontario, where he lived for the remainder of his life. His most well-known work is the novel *The Golden Dog*. His *The U.E: A Tale of Upper Canada* is a long poem in twelve cantos.

Barbara Klar (1966–) was born in Saskatoon and now lives in an old farmhouse northwest of Saskatoon. She has worked as a tree planter, bush cook, editor, mentor, and freelance writer for both print and radio. Her latest collection is *Cypress*, and her other books are *The Blue Field* and *The Night You Called Me a Shadow*.

A. M. Klein (1909–1972) was born in Ukraine and raised in Montreal. He practised law in Montreal. He won the Governor General's Award for *The Rocking Chair and Other Poems* (1949). *A. M. Klein: Complete Poems* is a scholarly edition of his poetry published by the University of Toronto Press.

Ann Cuthbert Knight (1788–1860) was born near Aberdeen, Scotland, and came to Canada, first in 1811 and then permanently in 1815. Her books include *A Year in Canada and Other Poems* and *Home, a poem*. She founded a ladies' school in Montreal and published three school books.

Raymond Knister (1899–1932) was born near Lake St. Clair, Ontario. He lived in Chicago, Illinois; Toronto; several small Ontario towns; and Montreal. He published novels and short stories during his lifetime, but his poems were published in book form only after his death. **Dorothy Livesay** edited his *Collected Poems* in 1949.

Joy Kogawa (1935–) was born in Vancouver but during the internment of Japanese-Canadians, she and her family moved to Slocan, British Columbia, and then Coaldale, Alberta. Her most well-known work is her novel *Obasan*. Her poetry includes *The Splintered Moon, A Choice of Dreams, Jericho Road, Woman in the Woods*, and *A Song for Lilith*.

Robert Kroetsch (1927–) was born in Heisler, Alberta, and grew up on his family's farm. He taught at the State University of New York and the University of Manitoba. He lives in Winnipeg. He is a novelist and critic, as well as a poet. Many of his most well-known poems are collected in *Completed Field Notes: The Long Poems of Robert Kroetsch*.

Edward A. Lacey (1937–1995) was born in Lindsay, Ontario, and studied at the University of Toronto and the University of Texas. Most of his adult life was spent travelling. His collections of poetry include *The Forms of Loss*, *Path of Snow: Poems 1951–73*, *Later: Poems 1973–1978*, and *Third World: Travel Poems by E. A. Lacey*.

Archibald Lampman (1861–1899) was born near Chatham, Ontario, and grew up in the Rice Lake district of Ontario. He briefly taught high school and then became a civil servant in Ottawa where he worked until his death. *The Poems of Archibald Lampman* was published by **Duncan Campbell Scott** in the year following Lampman's death.

M. Travis Lane (1934–) was born in San Antonio, Texas. She studied at Vassar College and Cornell University and immigrated to Fredericton in 1960. She taught at the University of New Brunswick and lives in Fredericton. She has published over ten books of poetry, including *Temporary Shelter*, *Night Physics*, *Keeping Afloat*, and *Touch Earth*.

Patrick Lane (1939–) was born in Nelson, British Columbia, and grew up in Vernon, British Columbia. He has lived in many parts of Canada and now lives near Victoria. His *Poems, New and Selected* (1978) won the Governor General's Award. He has published a memoir and more than twenty books of poetry, most recently *Last Water Song* and *Go Leaving Strange*.

Irving Layton (1912–2006) was born near Bucharest, Romania, and immigrated with his parents to Montreal. He spent much of his life in Montreal, but he also taught at York University. He published more than twenty volumes of work, including *A Red Carpet for the Sun* (1959), which won the Governor General's Award.

Ross Leckie (1953–) was born in Lachine, Quebec. He has degrees from McGill University, Concordia University, and the University of Toronto. He now lives in Fredericton where he teaches at the University of New Brunswick and is the poetry editor for Goose Lane Editions. He has published three books of poetry: *A Slow Light*, *The Authority of Roses*, and *Gravity's Plumb Line*.

Dennis Lee (1939–) was born in and still lives in Toronto. His *Civil Elegies and Other Poems* (1972) won the Governor General's Award. Many of his early poems are collected in *Nightwatch: New and Selected Poems 1968–1996*. He is well-known for his children's books *Alligator Pie* and *Garbage Delight*. His most recent poetry books are *Un* and *Yesno*.

John B. Lee (1951–) was born and raised on a farm near Highgate in southern Ontario and lived for many years in Brantford, Ontario. He now lives in Port

Dover, Ontario. He has written numerous books of poetry. Some of his poetry is collected in *The Half-Way Tree: Poems Selected and New*. He has also written memoirs, most recently *Left Hand Horses*.

Douglas LePan (1914–1998) was born in Toronto and educated at the University of Toronto and University of Oxford. He taught at Harvard University and Queen's University before returning to Toronto to teach at the University of Toronto. LePan's second volume of poetry *The Net and the Sword* (1953) won the Governor General's Award, as did his novel *The Deserter* (1964).

Kenneth Leslie (1892–1974) was born in Pictou, Nova Scotia, and studied at the University of Dalhousie, the University of Nebraska, and Harvard University. He moved to New York City to work as a journalist for *Protestant Digest*. He later returned to Halifax. He was awarded the Governor General's Award for *By Stubborn Stars* (1938).

Tim Lilburn (1950–) was born in Regina and now teaches at the University of Victoria. He is the author of eight books of poetry, most recently *Orphic Politics*. *Kill-site* (2003) won the Governor General's Award. Lilburn has edited two essay collections on poetics, *Poetry and Knowing* and *Thinking and Singing: Poetry and the Practice of Philosophy*.

Charles Lillard (1944–1997) was born in Long Beach, California, and spent much of his childhood on the waters off the southeast coast of Alaska. He studied at the University of British Columbia and was a logger, fisher, and chronicler of the West Coast, as well as a poet. Many of his poems are collected in *Shadow Weather: Poems Selected and New*.

Dorothy Livesay (1909–1996) was born in Winnipeg and moved to Toronto in 1920. She taught in Africa and at a number of Canadian universities. She lived on Galiano Island, British Columbia, and in Victoria. She won the Governor General's Award for *Day And Night* (1944) and again for *Poems for People* (1947).

Douglas Lochhead (1922–) was born in Guelph, Ontario, grew up in Fredericton and Ottawa, and now lives in Sackville, New Brunswick. He studied at McGill University and the University of Toronto. For many years he was the director of Canadian studies at Mount Allison University. He has published two dozen books of poetry. His most recent selection of poems is *Weathers*.

Pat Lowther (1935–1975) was born North Vancouver, British Columbia, and lived most of her life in and around Vancouver. During her lifetime she published three books, and just before she was murdered, a new collection of poems, *A Stone Diary*, had been accepted for publication. Many of her poems are collected in *Time Capsule: New and Selected Poems*.

Malcolm Lowry (1909–1957) was born in Birkenhead, Cheshire, England. He lived in many places during his lifetime, including Vancouver. He died in Sussex, England. He is famous for his works of fiction, especially *Under the Volcano*. **Earle Birney** edited a collection of his poetry in 1962. *The Collected Poetry of Malcolm Lowry* was published in 1992.

Randy Lundy (1967–) is a member of the Barren Lands (Cree) First Nation. He was born in Thompson, Manitoba, and grew up in Hudson Bay, Saskatchewan. He studied at the University of Saskatchewan and now lives in Regina where he teaches at First Nations University. His books are *Under the Night Sun* and *The Gift of the Hawk*.

Laura Lush (1959–) was born in Brantford, Ontario, and studied at York University and the University of Calgary. She teaches in the School of Continuing Studies at the University of Toronto. Her books of poetry include *Hometown*, *Fault Line*, and *The First Day of Winter*. She also has a collection of short stories, *Going to the Zoo*.

Gwendolyn MacEwen (1941–1987) was born and lived much of her life in Toronto. She published fifteen collections of poetry, as well as fiction and drama. Both *The Shadow-Maker* (1969) and *Afterworlds* (1987) won Governor General's Awards. Exile Editions has published her collected works, *The Poetry of Gwendolyn MacEwen*, in two volumes.

L. A. Mackay (1901–1982) was born in Hensall, Ontario, and studied at the University of Toronto, then at Balliol College, University of Oxford. He taught classics at several Canadian universities before settling at the University of California at Berkeley. His English poetry was collected in *The Ill-Tempered Lover and Other Poems*, and he wrote many plays and Latin poems.

Charles Mair (1838–1927) was born in Lanark, Upper Canada (now Ontario). He went to the Red River Settlement area (now Manitoba) where, during the Red River Rebellion, he was sentenced to death by Louis Riel. He escaped and lived in Toronto. Afterwards he lived in various parts of Ontario and western Canada, and eventually retired to Fort Steele, British Columbia.

Eli Mandel (1922–1992) was born in Estevan, Saskatchewan, and studied at the University of Saskatchewan and the University of Toronto. He taught at the University of Alberta and York University. He wrote ten books of poetry. His poems are collected in *The Other Harmony: The Collected Poems of Eli Mandel*.

Daphne Marlatt (1942–) was born in Melbourne, Australia, and immigrated to Canada. She studied at the University of Indiana and lived in Wisconsin and California before returning to Vancouver where she now lives. She has written several books of poetry, including *Steveston*, *This Tremor Love Is*, and *The Given*. Her novels include *Ana Historic* and *Taken*.

Anne Marriott (1913–1997) was born in Victoria. Her long poem *The Wind, Our Enemy*, about the prairie drought during the Depression years, is her most well-known poem. She won the Governor General's Award for her chapbook *Calling Adventurers!* (1941). Her other books include *Sandstone and Other Poems* and *The Circular Coast*.

George Martin (1822–1900) was born in Ireland and immigrated to Canada in 1832. He moved to Montreal in 1835, a city he lived in for most of his life. He was a novelist and photographer as well as a poet. His only book of poetry was *Marguerite, and Other Poems*.

Sid Marty (1944–) was born in England and raised in Medicine Hat, Alberta. He spent several years as a park warden and ranger in Yoho, Jasper, and Banff National Parks. He now lives near Pincher Creek, Alberta. His poetry books include *Headwaters*, *Sky Humour*, and *Nobody Danced with Miss Rodeo*. He is also a musician and non-fiction writer.

David W. McFadden (1940–) was born and raised in Hamilton, Ontario, and now lives in Toronto. He has written over a dozen books, including such prose works as *A Trip Around Lake Ontario*. His poetry books include *Gypsy Guitar* and *There'll Be Another*. Many of his poems can be found in the recently published *Why Are You So Sad? Selected Poems*.

Don McKay (1942–) was born in Owen Sound, Ontario. He has lived in Ontario, New Brunswick, and British Columbia, and he now lives in Newfoundland. He is the author of *Vis à Vis: Field Notes on Poetry & Wilderness*, and both *Night Field* (1991) and *Another Gravity* (2000) won Governor General's Awards. He has also won the Griffin Poetry Prize for *Strike/Slip* (2007).

Alexander McLachlan (1818–1896) was born in Strathclyde, Scotland, and lived in Glasgow, Scotland, before immigrating to Upper Canada (now Ontario) in 1840. He published six collections of poetry, including the long poem *The Emigrant*.

Kenneth McRobbie (1929–) was born in England and immigrated to Canada in 1954. He taught history for many years at the University of Manitoba. He now lives in Vancouver. He is a well-known translator of Hungarian poetry.

His poetry books include *Eyes Without a Face*, *What Is on Fire Is Happening*, and *First Ghost to Canada*.

Eric Miller (1961–) was born and raised in Toronto and has lived in Virginia, New Brunswick, Nova Scotia, Alberta, and British Columbia. He is the author of three books of poetry, *Song for the Vulgar Starling*, *In the Scaffolding*, and *The Day in Moss*, and a collection of essays, *The Reservoir*. He teaches at the University of Victoria.

A. F. Moritz (1947–) was born in Niles, Ohio. In 1974, he came to Toronto where he still lives and teaches at the University of Toronto. He has translated poems from French and Spanish and written more than ten books of poetry, most recently *The Sentinel*.

Daniel David Moses (1952–) is from the Six Nations Reserve near Brantford, Ontario, and teaches in the Department of Drama at Queen's University. He has edited *An Anthology of Canadian Native Literature in English*. His books of poetry include *Sixteen Jesuses*, *Delicate Bodies*, and *The White Line*. He is also a well-known playwright.

Erin Mouré (1955–) was born and grew up in Calgary. She has lived in Vancouver and has been in Montreal since 1985. Her book of poetry *Furious* (1988) won the Governor General's Award. She has translated poetry from French, Galician, Spanish, and Portuguese. Her most recent book of poetry is *O Cidadán*.

Jane Munro (1943–) grew up and lived for many years in Vancouver. She now lives on the west coast of Vancouver Island. Her books are *Point No Point*, *Grief Notes & Animal Dreams*, *The Trees Just Moved into a Season of Other Shapes*, and *Daughters*.

George Murray (1971–) was born in Toronto and raised in rural Ontario. He has also lived in New York City and rural Italy, and now lives in St. John's. He is the author of four books of poetry, including *The Cottage Builder's Letter*, *The Hunter*, and *The Rush to Here*.

Rona Murray (1924–2003) was born in London, England, and spent her childhood in India. She came to Canada in 1932. For many years she lived in Metchosin, British Columbia. Her works of poetry include *The Enchanted Adder*, *The Power of the Dog*, *Ootischenie*, *Journey*, *Adam and Eve in Middle Age*, and *The Lost Garden*.

Susan Musgrave (1951–) was raised on Vancouver Island. She divides her time between Vancouver Island and Haida Gwaii/Queen Charlotte Islands. Her earlier poems are collected in *What the Small Day Cannot Hold: Collected Poems 1970–1985*. *When the World is Not Our Home: Selected Poems 1985–2000* is forthcoming from Thistledown Press in 2009.

John Newlove (1938–2003) was born and raised in Saskatchewan. He began publishing while in Vancouver in the 1960s. He won the Governor General's Award for his book *Lies* (1972). The most recent selection of his poetry has been published by Chaudiere Press: *A Long Continual Argument: The Selected Poems of John Newlove*.

Barbara Nickel (1966–) was born in Saskatoon and raised in Rosthern, Saskatchewan. After living in Vancouver and St. John's she now lives in Yarrow, British Columbia. Her collections of poetry are *The Gladys Elegies* and *Domain*. She is also the author of books for children.

Alden Nowlan (1933–1983) was born in Windsor, Nova Scotia, and spent much of his life in New Brunswick. He was a journalist, novelist, and playwright. His collection *Bread, Wine and Salt* (1967) won the Governor General's Award. There have been several selected editions of his poetic work, most recently the House of Anansi's *Alden Nowlan: Selected Poems*.

Standish O'Grady (1793–1846) was born in Ireland and immigrated to Quebec in 1836. He settled on a farm on the banks of the St. Lawrence River near Sorel, Quebec. He relocated to Toronto in 1842. His one printed work is a long poem entitled *The Emigrant: A Poem in Four Cantos* (1841).

Michael Ondaatje (1943–) was born in Colombo, Ceylon (Sri Lanka), and moved to England in 1954, then Canada in 1962. He lives in Toronto. He has won the Governor General's Award five times, twice for poetry (*The Collected Works of Billy the Kid* [1970] and *There's a Trick with a Knife I'm Learning to Do* [1979]) and three times for fiction. He won the Booker Prize for *The English Patient*.

Eric Ormsby (1941–) was born in Atlanta, Georgia. For many years he lived in Montreal where he taught at the Institute of Islamic Studies at McGill University before moving to London, England, in 2005. He has published six collections of poetry, including *For a Modest God*, *Araby*, and *Time's Covenant*.

Martha Ostenso (1900–1963) was born in Norway and immigrated to South Dakota, eventually living in Brandon, Manitoba. She worked as a teacher and journalist in Manitoba until she moved to New York. She died in Seattle, Washington. Her novel *Wild Geese* is her most well-known Canadian work. She published over fifteen books, including her poetry collection *In a Far Land*.

Richard Outram (1930–2005) was born in Oshawa, Ontario, and studied at the University of Toronto. He lived in Toronto where he worked for the Canadian Broadcasting Corporation. He wrote ten commercially published collections of poetry, including *Hiram and Jenny* and *Mogul Recollected.*

P. K. Page (1916–) was born in England, grew up in Alberta, and has lived in many parts of the world. She now lives in Victoria. She received the Governor General's Award for *The Metal and the Flower* (1954). *The Hidden Room: Collected Poems* was published by The Porcupine's Quill.

Elise Partridge (1958–) was born in Philadelphia, Pennsylvania, and has lived in Cambridge, England; Boston, Massachusetts; and Vancouver, British Columbia, where she now works as a teacher and editor. Her two books of poetry are *Fielder's Choice* and *Chameleon Hours.*

John Pass (1947–) was born in Sheffield, England, but has lived in Canada since 1953. He teaches at Capilano College in North Vancouver, British Columbia, and lives in Madeira Park, British Columbia. He has published twelve books of poetry, including *Stumbling in the Bloom* (2006), which won the Governor General's Award.

Philip Kevin Paul (1971–) is a member of WSÁ,NEC (Sencoten) First Nation from the Saanich Peninsula on Vancouver Island. He has taught at the University of Victoria and lives in Brentwood Bay, British Columbia. His poetry collections are *Taking the Names Down from the Hill* and *Little Hunger.*

Elizabeth Philips (1962–) was born in Winnipeg and raised in Gimli, Manitoba. She now lives in Saskatoon. She has taught creative writing and is the former editor of the literary magazine *Grain*. She is the author of four collections of poetry, including *Beyond My Keeping, A Blue with Blood in It*, and *Torch River.*

Marjorie Pickthall (1883–1922) was born in England and immigrated to Toronto in 1889. She lived in England between 1912 and 1920, returning to Canada and settling on Vancouver Island. Besides poetry, she wrote hundreds of short stories and several novels. Her *Collected Poems* was published in 1936.

Gregory J. Power (1909–1997) was born in Dunville, Placentia Bay, Newfoundland. He was an athlete until he contracted tuberculosis. He had a long career in journalism and politics, including being the Minister of Finance and the Minister of Highways in the Newfoundland and Labrador government. Many of his poems are collected in *The Power of the Pen: Writings of Gregory J. Power.*

E. J. Pratt (1882–1964) was born and raised in Western Bay, Newfoundland. After living in various towns in Newfoundland and Ontario, he began to teach at the University of Toronto. He received the Governor General's Award three times, including for his two long poems *Brébeuf and His Brethren* (1940) and *Towards the Last Spike* (1952).

Al Purdy (1918–2000) was born in Wooler, Ontario, and lived in many places across Canada, eventually dividing his time between Ameliasburg, Ontario, and North Saanich, British Columbia. He received the Governor General's Award for *The Cariboo Horses* (1965). His most recent collected works is *Beyond Remembering: The Collected Poems of Al Purdy* (2000).

James Reaney (1926–2008) was born in Easthope, Ontario, and taught at the University of Manitoba and the University of Western Ontario. He lived in London, Ontario, from 1960. Three of his works of poetry received the Governor General's Award: *The Red Heart* (1949), *A Suit of Nettles* (1958), and *Twelve Letters to a Small Town* (1962).

Michael Redhill (1966–) was born in Baltimore, Maryland, and raised in Toronto where he now lives. He is an editor, a novelist, and a playwright as well as a poet. His poetry books include *Lake Nora Arms, Light-crossing, Asphodel, Temporary Captives*, and *Music for Silence.*

John Reibetanz (1944–) was born in New York City and grew up in the eastern United States and Canada. He now lives in Toronto where he teaches at the University of Toronto. He has published seven collections of poetry, including *Midland Swimmmer, Mining for Sun, Near Relations*, and *Transformations.*

Monty Reid (1952–) was born in Spalding, Saskatchewan, and lived for many years in Drumheller, Alberta, where he worked at the Royal Tyrrell Museum of Palaeontology. He now lives in Ottawa and is the director of exhibitions at the Canadian Museum of Nature. He has published over fourteen books, most recently *The Luskville Reductions.*

Harold Rhenisch (1958–) was born in Penticton, British Columbia, and was raised in the Similkameen Valley. He studied at the University of Victoria and afterwards worked as an orchardist. He lived for many years at 150 Mile Ranch, British Columbia, and now lives in Campbell River, British Columbia. His most recent collection is *Return to Open Water: Poems New & Selected.*

Charles G. D. Roberts (1860–1943) was born in Douglas, New Brunswick, and grew up near the Tantramar Marshes in New Brunswick. He lived there and in Nova Scotia until 1897 when he moved to New York City, then Europe. In

1925, he returned to Canada and lived in Toronto for the remainder of his life. He was well-known for his animal stories as well as his poetry. His poetry is collected in *The Collected Poems of Sir Charles G. D. Roberts: A Critical Edition*.

Dorothy Roberts (1906–1993), the niece of **Charles G. D. Roberts**, was born and raised in New Brunswick where she also studied and worked as a reporter. In 1940, she moved to New York and then Pennsylvania with her husband. She published seven books between 1927 and 1991. Some of her early works are collected in *The Self of Loss: New and Selected Poems*.

Rachel Rose (1970–) was born in Vancouver and, being a dual Canadian/US citizen, has lived in both countries, as well as Japan. She studied at McGill University and the University of British Columbia. She now lives in Vancouver. Her two books of poetry are *Giving My Body to Science* and *Notes on Arrival and Departure*.

Joe Rosenblatt (1933–) was born and raised in Toronto. He now lives in Qualicum Beach, British Columbia. He is a visual artist, novelist, memoirist, and essayist as well as a poet. His book *Top Soil: Selected Poems (1962–1975)* won the Governor General's Award in 1976. His other works include *Poetry Hotel*, *Bumblebee Dithyramb*, and *Brides of the Stream*.

W. W. E. Ross (1894–1966) was born in Peterborough, Ontario, and grew up in Pembroke, Ontario. He worked as a geophysicist and was director of the Magnetic Observatory at Agincourt, Ontario. His last years were spent in Toronto. In 2003, Exile Editions published a wide selection of his work in *Irrealities, Sonnets & Laconics*.

Armand Garnet Ruffo (1955–) was born in Chapleau in northern Ontario and is a member of the Biscotasing branch of the Sagamok First Nation. He lives in Ottawa and teaches at Carleton University. He is the author of *Opening in the Sky*, *At Geronimo's Grave*, and the creative biography *Grey Owl: The Mystery of Archie Belaney*.

Peter Sanger (1943–) was born in England and moved to Canada in 1953. He studied at the University of Melbourne, the University of Victoria, and Acadia University. He lived in Ontario, British Columbia, and Newfoundland before settling in Nova Scotia in 1970. He is an editor and prose writer, and his books of poetry include *The American Reel*, *Earth Moth*, and *Aiken Drum*.

Charles Sangster (1822–1893) was born in Kingston, Upper Canada (now Ontario), and lived in Ottawa as an employee with the postal service. He wrote most of his poetry when he was a journalist in Kingston in the 1850s. The two volumes published in his lifetime are *The St. Lawrence and the Saguenay and Other Poems* and *Hesperus and Other Poems and Lyrics.*

Robyn Sarah (1949–) was born in New York City. Her parents were Canadian and soon settled in Montreal, where she has since lived. She is the author of several poetry collections, short stories, and a book of essays on poetry. *A Day's Grace* is a selection of her poetry from 1997–2002. *The Touchstone: Poems New and Selected* collects some of her earlier work.

Duncan Campbell Scott (1862–1947) was born in Ottawa where he lived for most of his life. He worked for fifty-three years in the Department of Indian Affairs. A major selection of his work was published in 1926 and, since then, several selected works have been published, including *Powassan's Drum*, which was published in 1985 by Tecumseh Press.

F. R. Scott (1899–1985) was born in Quebec City and studied at Bishop's College, University of Oxford, and McGill University. He practised law briefly and then taught at McGill, eventually becoming dean of Law. Well-known for his social activism, he was also an expert on constitutional law. His *Collected Poems* (1981) won the Governor General's Award.

Frederick G. Scott (1861–1944), father of **F. R. Scott**, was born in Montreal. He was a rector in Quebec City from 1889–1934. He served as senior chaplain for the First Canadian Division during World War I. He wrote numerous works of poetry and a memoir of his war experiences.

Robert W. Service (1874–1958) was born in England and grew up in Glasgow, Scotland. He lived in Victoria and Whitehorse. In 1912, he left the Yukon and settled on the French Riviera where he lived for the rest of his life. His first volume *Songs of a Sourdough* (1907) was followed by nearly two dozen collections of stories and poems.

Anne Simpson (1956–) was born in Toronto and raised in Kingston, Ontario, and Burlington, Ontario. She has lived in Italy, West Africa, and the United Kingdom. She now lives in Antigonish, Nova Scotia, and teaches at St. Francis Xavier University. She is also a visual artist and novelist. Her poetry collection *Loop* (2004) won the Griffin Poetry Prize.

Sue Sinclair (1972–) was raised in St. John's and studied at the University of New Brunswick. She currently lives in Toronto where she studies philosophy. Her books include *Secrets of Weather and Hope* and *Mortal Arguments*. Her next collection of poems, *Breaker*, will be published by Brick Books in 2008.

Robin Skelton (1925–1997) was born in England and moved to Canada in 1963 to teach at the University of Victoria. He lived in Victoria for the rest of his life. He published over eighty books of poetry. His collected works are *Collected Shorter Poems, 1947–1977*, *The Collected Longer Poems, 1947–1977*, and *One Leaf Shaking: Collected Later Poems, 1977–1990*.

A. J. M. Smith (1902–1980) was born in Montreal and studied at McGill University and the University of Edinburgh. He taught at Michigan State University. His book *News of the Phoenix* (1943) won the Governor General's Award. The most recent selection of his work is in *Selected Writings: A. J. M. Smith* published by the Dundurn Group.

John Smith (1927–) was born in Toronto. He attended the University of Toronto, moved to London, England, for a time, and then returned to Toronto before settling in Charlottetown. His works include *Winter in Paradise*, *Sucking Stones*, *Midnight Found You Dancing*, *Fireflies in the Magnolia Grove*, and *Maps of Invariance*.

Karen Solie (1966–) was born in Moose Jaw, Saskatchewan, and grew up on a family farm in southwest Saskatchewan. She has lived in Austin, Texas; Victoria; and Edmonton, and currently lives in Toronto. Her first collection of poems is *Short Haul Engine* and her second is *Modern and Normal*.

Glen Sorestad (1937–) was born in Vancouver but moved to Saskatchewan in 1947 where he still lives, currently in Saskatoon. He co-founded Thistledown Press. He has written over ten books of poetry, including *Blood & Bone, Ice & Stone*.

Raymond Souster (1921–) was born and raised in Toronto and continues to reside in the city. His poetry book *The Colour of the Times* (1964) received the Governor General's Award. His work is collected in the multi-volume *Collected Poems of Raymond Souster* published by Oberon Press.

Heather Spears (1934–) was born in Vancouver, and, although she has lived in Denmark since 1962, she returns frequently to Canada. She is a poet and novelist as well as a visual artist who specializes in drawing children in hospitals and war zones. Her collection of poetry *The Word for Sand* (1989) won the Governor General's Award.

John Steffler (1947–) was born in Toronto and grew up near Thornhill, Ontario. In 1975, he began to teach at Memorial University of Newfoundland. He now divides his time between Montreal and a farm in eastern Ontario. He is a novelist as well as a poet. His books of poetry include *The Grey Islands* and *Helix: New and Selected Poems*.

Andrew Suknaski (1942–) was born in Wood Mountain, Saskatchewan, and now lives in Moose Jaw, Saskatchewan. His books of poetry include *Wood Mountain Poems* and *The Land They Gave Away: New and Selected Poems*.

Anne Szumigalski (1922–1999) was born in England, immigrated to Saskatchewan in 1951, and settled permanently in Saskatoon in 1956. She received the Governor General's Award for *Voice* (1995). She published several other books of poetry, with many poems collected in the volume *On Glassy Wings: Poems New and Selected*.

Bruce Taylor (1960–) was born in Vancouver and now lives in Wakefield, Quebec, where he builds boats and guitars and is raising three children. His books of poetry are *Getting on with the Era, Cold Rubber Feet*, and *Facts*.

John Terpstra (1953–) was born in Brockville, Ontario, and now lives in Hamilton, Ontario. He is a cabinetmaker and has published eight books of poetry, including *Two or Three Guitars: Selected Poems*. He has also written creative non-fiction, including a memoir, *The Boys, or, Waiting for the Electrician's Daughter*.

Sharon Thesen (1946–) was born in Tisdale, Saskatchewan, and grew up in the interior of British Columbia. She lived for many years in Vancouver. She now teaches at the University of British Columbia Okanagan and lives in Lake Country, British Columbia. Many of her early poems are collected in *News & Smoke: Selected Poems*. Her most recent book is *The Good Bacteria*.

Colleen Thibaudeau (1925–) was born in Toronto and raised in St. Thomas, Ontario. She studied at the University of Toronto and, in 1951, married the writer **James Reaney**. She now lives in London, Ontario. Her poetry books include *Ten Letters, My Granddaughters Are Combing Out Their Long Hair, The Martha Landscapes*, and *The Artemesia Book*.

John Thompson (1938–1976) was born in England and studied psychology at Sheffield University and Michigan State University. He then taught at Mount Allison University in Sackville, New Brunswick. The most recent collection of his poetry is *John Thompson: Collected Poems and Translations*, edited by **Peter Sanger**.

Russell Thornton (1959–) was born and currently lives in North Vancouver, British Columbia. For many years, he divided his life between Vancouver and Aberystwyth, Wales, and then between Vancouver and Salonica, Greece. He has published four books of poetry: *The Fifth Window, A Tunisian Notebook, House Built of Rain*, and *The Human Shore*.

Harry Thurston (1950–) was born in Yarmouth, Nova Scotia, and grew up on the family farm. He studied biology at Acadia University. He now lives in Cumberland County, Nova Scotia. He is a journalist, poet, and playwright. His non-fiction books include *A Place Between the Tides: A Naturalist's Reflections on the Salt Marsh*. His most recent book of poetry is *If Men Lived on Earth*.

Peter Trower (1930–) was born in England and immigrated to British Columbia at the age of ten. He worked for twenty-two years as a logger. He now lives in Gibsons, British Columbia. He has published three novels and more than ten books of poetry, including *Haunted Hills and Hanging Valleys: Selected Poems 1969–2004*.

Peter Van Toorn (1944–) was born in Holland and moved to Montreal as a child. He studied at McGill University and taught at John Abbott College for almost thirty years. He now lives in Sainte-Anne-de-Bellevue, Quebec. His only book of poetry is *Mountain Tea and Other Poems*.

Miriam Waddington (1917–2004) was born in Winnipeg and studied at the University of Toronto and the University of Pennsylvania. She moved to Montreal to work as a social worker. In 1962, she began to teach at York University. After her retirement, she moved to Vancouver. She published over a dozen books of poetry. Oxford University Press published her *Collected Poems*.

Fred Wah (1939–) was born in Swift Current, Saskatchewan, and grew up in the West Kootenay region of British Columbia. He currently lives in Vancouver and the Kootenays. His book of poetry *Waiting for Saskatchewan* (1986) received the Governor General's Award. A selection of his early poems can be found in *Loki Is Buried at Smoky Creek: Selected Poems*.

Agnes Walsh (1950–) was born in Placentia, Newfoundland. She now divides her time between St. John's and Patrick's Cove, Newfoundland and Labrador. She is a playwright and artistic director of the Tramore Theatre Troupe in Cuslett, Placentia Bay, Newfoundland and Labrador. Her first collection of poetry is *In the Old Country of My Heart*. Her second collection is *Going Around With Bachelors*.

Wilfred Watson (1911–1998) was born in England and immigrated with his family to Duncan, British Columbia. In 1943, he joined the Canadian navy. He taught for many years at the University of Alberta. After retirement, he lived in Nanaimo, British Columbia. He won the Governor General's Award for his book of poetry *Friday's Child* (1955).

Tom Wayman (1945–) was born in Ontario but has spent most of his life in British Columbia. He currently lives in British Columbia's southern Selkirk Mountains and teaches at the University of Calgary. He has published more than fifteen books, most recently *High Speed Through Shoaling Water*. Many of his earlier poems are published in *Did I Miss Anything? Selected Poems 1973–1993*.

Phyllis Webb (1927–) was born in Victoria. She attended the University of British Columbia and McGill University, and lived in Montreal from 1951 to 1956. In 1969, she moved to Salt Spring Island, British Columbia, where she lives today. Her *The Vision Tree: Selected Poems* (1982), edited by **Sharon Thesen**, won the Governor General's Award.

Zachariah Wells (1976–) is originally from Prince Edward Island. He has lived in Ontario, Quebec, and on all three Canadian coasts, and now calls Halifax home. He is the author of the poetry collection *Unsettled* and the co-author of the children's book *Anything But Hank!*

Ethelwyn Wetherald (1857–1940) was born in Rockwood, Ontario, and lived in New York and the Niagara Peninsula but spent most of her life in the town of Fenwick in Welland County, Ontario. She worked as a journalist, editor, and poet. Many of her poems are collected in *Lyrics and Sonnets*.

Sue Wheeler (1942–) was born and raised in Texas. She immigrated to Canada in 1972. She has lived for some years on a seaside farm on Lasqueti Island, British Columbia. Her three books of poetry are *Solstice on the Anacortes Ferry*, *Slow-Moving Target*, and *Habitat*.

Jon Whyte (1941–1992) was born in Banff, Alberta, and grew up there and in Medicine Hat, Alberta. He was a poet, historian, bookseller, journalist, and conservationist and curator at the Whyte Museum of the Canadian Rockies. His poetry collections include *Homage, Henry Kelsey*, and an unfinished experimental mountain epic, *The Fells of Brightness*.

Anne Wilkinson (1910–1961) was born in Toronto but moved around a great deal as a child. She moved to Toronto with her husband in 1930. She published two collections of poetry in her lifetime, *Counterpoint to Sleep* and *The Hangman Ties the Holly*. Most recently, Véhicule Press published *Heresies: The Complete Poems of Anne Wilkinson*.

Christopher Wiseman (1936–) was born in Hull, England, and grew up in Scarborough, England. He studied at the University of Cambridge and moved to Iowa, Glasgow, and then Calgary, where he still lives and where he taught for many years at the University of Calgary. Many of his poems are collected in *Postcards Home: Poems New and Selected* and *In John Updike's Room*.

J. Michael Yates (1938–) was born in Missouri and studied at the University of Missouri and the University of Michigan. He currently lives in Vancouver. He has published poetry, fiction, drama, translations, and philosophical essays, including *The Great Bear Lake Meditations, Insel: The Queen Charlotte Islands Meditations*, and *Hongyun: New and Collected Shorter Poems, 1955–2005*.

David Zieroth (1946–) was born in Neepawa, Manitoba, and lives in North Vancouver, British Columbia. He teaches at Douglas College in New Westminster, British Columbia. His most recent book of poetry is *The Village of Sliding Time*. He has also published *Crows Do Not Have Retirement, How I Joined Humanity at Last*, and a memoir, *The Education of Mr. Whippoorwill: A Country Boyhood*.

Jan Zwicky (1955–) was born and raised in west central Alberta and now lives in Victoria where she teaches philosophy at the University of Victoria. She has published seven collections of poetry, including *Songs for Relinquishing the Earth* (1999), which won the Governor General's Award.

Copyright
Acknowledgements

485

bill bissett "othr animals toys" reprinted from *Inkorrekt thots* (Talonbooks, 1992) by permission of Talon Books.

E. D. Blodgett "Doma" reprinted from *Apostrophes V: Never Born Except Within the Other* (Buschek Books, 2003) by permission of the author.

Peter Blue Cloud (Aroniawenrate) "For a Dog-Killed Doe" reprinted from *Clans of Many Nations: Selected Poems* (White Pine Press, 1995) by permission of the publisher.

Stephanie Bolster "Many Have Written Poems about Blackberries" reprinted from *Two Bowls of Milk* (McClelland & Stewart, 1999) by permission of the publisher.

Roo Borson "Upset, Unable to Sleep, I Go for a Walk and Stumble Upon Some Geese" and "The Trees" reprinted from *Night Walk: Selected Poems* (Oxford University Press, 1994) by permission of the author. "Snake" from *Water Memory* © 1996, published by McClelland & Stewart, Ltd., used with permission of the publisher.

Tim Bowling "On the Disappearance of Two Million Sockeye Salmon" reprinted from *Low Water Slack* (Nightwood Editions, 1995) by permission of the publisher, "Late August at the Mouth of the Fraser River" reprinted from *The Thin Smoke of the Heart* (McGill-Queen's University Press, 2000) by permission of the publisher.

Diana Brebner Part III from "The Sparrow Drawer" reprinted from *The Ishtar Gate: Last and Selected Poems* (McGill-Queen's University Press, 2005) by permission of the publisher.

Brian Brett "Small Joys on the Farm" and "Blue Heron Moon" reprinted from *The Colour of Bones in a Stream* (Sono Nis Press, 1998) by permission of the author.

Elizabeth Brewster "Starlings," "Blueflag," and "Alchemist" reprinted from *The Collected Poems of Elizabeth Brewster* (Oberon, 2003) by permission of the publisher.

Robert Bringhurst "Anecdote of the Squid" from *The Beauty of the Weapons: Selected 1972–1982* © 1982, published by McClelland & Stewart Ltd. "Rubus Ursinus: A Prayer for the Blackberry Harvest" and "Gloria, Credo, Sanctus et Oreamnos Deorum" reprinted from *The Calling: Selected Poems 1970–1995* © 1995, published by McClelland & Stewart, Ltd. All by permission of the publisher and the author.

Charles Bruce "Fall Grass" and "Orchard in the Woods" reprinted from *The Mulgrave Road: Selected* (Pottersfield Press, 1995) by permission of Harry Bruce.

Julie Bruck "Notice to Cut Tree" reprinted from *The End of Travel* (Brick Books, 1999) by permission of the author.

Alison Calder "The Animals Dream" reprinted from *Wolf Tree* (Coteau Books, 2007) by permission of the publisher.

Mark Callanan "Barn Swallows" reprinted from *Scarecrow* (Killick, 2003) by permission of the publisher.

Peter Christensen "Keeping Fear Away" reprinted from *Rig Talk* (Thistledown, 1981) by permission of the author.

Fred Cogswell "Paleontology Lecture: Birds (Circa 2500 A.D.)" reprinted from *A Long Apprenticeship* (Fiddlehead Poetry, 1980) by permission of the literary trustee of the estate of Fred Cogswell, "A Grey World Lightened by Snow" reprinted from *The Best Notes Merge* (Borealis, 1988) by permission of the publisher.

Eric Cole "Blackpoll Warbler" reprinted from *Man and Beast* (Insomniac Press, 2005) by permission of the author.

Anne Compton "Trees in Summer" and "June Bugs" reprinted from *Processional* (Fitzhenry and Whiteside, 2005) by permission of the publisher.

Karen Connelly "The Moment" reprinted from *The Border Surrounds Us* (McClelland & Stewart, 2000) by permission of the author.

Marlene Cookshaw "Fox" reprinted from *Lunar Drift* (Brick Books, 2005) by permission of the author.

Dennis Cooley "how crow brings spring in" reprinted from *sunfall: new and selected poems* (House of Anansi Press, 1996) by permission of the author.

Allan Cooper "The Seed of the Blue Spruce" reprinted from *Singing the Flowers Open* (Gaspereau Press, 2001) by permission of the publisher.

Stanley Cooperman "The Rivals" reprinted from *Greco's Last Book: Selected Poems* (Intermedia, 1980) by permission of Ed Varney.

Joan Crate "The Year of the Coyote" reprinted from *Foreign Homes* (Brick Books, 2001) by permission of the author.

Lorna Crozier "Carrots" and "A Prophet in His Own Country" reprinted from *The Blue Hour of the Day* © 2007, published by McClelland & Stewart, Ltd., used with permission of the publisher.

Michael Crummey "Cod (1)" and "Cod (2)" reprinted from *Arguments with Gravity* (Quarry Press, 1996) by permission of the author.

Mary Dalton "Pitcher Plant; Bog Pluto" and "Stingers" reprinted from *Merrybegot* (Véhicule Press, 2003) by permission of the author.

Joseph A. Dandurand "Feeding the Hungry" reprinted from *Looking into the Eyes of My Forgotten Dreams* (Kegedonce Press, 1998) by permission of the publisher.

Tom Dawe "Sandpiper" and "Alders" reprinted from *In Hardy Country* (Breakwater Books Ltd., 1992) by permission of the publisher.

Barry Dempster "*Wild*, Wild" reprinted from *The Words Wanting Out: Poems Selected and New* (Nightwood Editions, 2003) by permission of the author.

Christopher Dewdney "August" reprinted from *Fovea Centralis* (Coach House, 1975) by permission of the author. "Out of Control: The Quarry" reprinted from *The Radiant Inventory* (McClelland & Stewart, 1988) by permission of the author.

Adam Dickinson "Great Chain of Being" reprinted from *Kingdom, Phylum* (Brick Books, 2006) by permission of the author.

Don Domanski "Owl" reprinted from *Parish of the Physic Moon* (McClelland & Stewart, 1998), part 1 from "All Our Wonder Unavenged" reprinted from *All Our Wonder Unavenged* (Brick Books, 2007), both by permission of the author.

John Donlan "High Falls" and "Muskrat" reprinted from *Green Man* (Ronsdale, 1999) by permission of the author.

Marilyn Dumont "Liquid Prairie" reprinted from *A Really Good Brown Girl* (Brick Books, 1996) by permission of the author.

Cripsin Elsted "Swan Written" reprinted from *Climate and the Affections* (Sono Nis Press, 1996) by permission of the author.

R. G. Everson "L'Orignal" reprinted from *E: Everson at Eighty* (Oberon Press, 1983) by permission of the publisher.

Robert Finch "Silverthorn Bush" reprinted from *Silverthorn Bush and Other Poems* (Macmillan, 1966) by permission of Danielle Holke.

Joan Finnigan "November on the Orser Farm" reprinted from *The Watershed Collection* (Quarry Press, 1988) by permission of the author's estate.

Len Gasparini "Elegy" reprinted from *The Broken World: Poems 1967–1998* (Guernica Editions, 2005) by permission of the author.

Chief Dan George sequence from "My Heart Soars" reprinted from *The Best of Chief Dan George* (Hancock House, 1990; www.hancockhouse.com) by permission of the publisher.

John Glassco "Catbird" reprinted from *Selected Poems* (Oxford University Press, 1971) by permission of William Toye.

Leona Gom "North of Town" reprinted from *Northbound: Poems Selected and New* (Thistledown, 1984) by permission of Sono Nis Press.

Sue Goyette "Vigil" reprinted from *Undone* (Brick Books, 2004) by permission of the author.

Jim Green "Seismic Line" reprinted from *North Book* (Blackfish Press, 1975) by permission of the author.

Kristjana Gunnars "Thorleifur Joakimsson, Daybook III" reprinted from *Settlement Poems II* (Turnstone, 1980) by permission of the author.

Diana Hartog "The Great Blue Heron" reprinted from *Polite to Bees* (Coach House, 1992) by permission of the author.

Brian Henderson "Theory of the Family" and "Mortals" reprinted from *Light in Dark Objects* (Ekstasis Editions, 2000) by permission of the author.

Cornelia Hoogland "The Orcas, Great Story" reprinted from *You Are Home* (Black Moss, 2001) by permission of the author.

Ken Howe "Notes on the Urban Squirrel" reprinted from *Household Hints for the End of Time* (Brick Books, 2001) by permission of the author.

Paulette Jiles "Blacksnake" and "Life in the Wilderness" © 1984 from *Celestial Navigation* published by McClelland & Stewart Ltd., 1984, used with permission of the publisher and the author.

Rita Joe "The Art of Making Quillboxes" reprinted from *Lnu and Indians We're Called* (Ragweed, 1991) by permission of Breton Books.

S. D. Johnson "Two Magpies" reprinted from *Hymns to Phenomena* (Thistledown Press, 2000) by permission of the publisher.

George Johnston Excerpt from "Under the Tree" and "The Creature's Claim" reprinted from *Endeared by Dark: Collected Poems* (The Porcupine's Quill, 1990) by permission of the author's estate.

D. G. Jones "Snow Buntings" reprinted from *A Throw of Particles: New and Selected* (General Publishing, 1983) by permission of the author.

Lionel Kearns "Trophy" reprinted from *Ignoring the Bomb: New and Selected* (Oolichan Books Books, 1982) by permission of the author.

Barbara Klar "Blue Gramma" reprinted from *Cypress* (Brick Books, 2008) by permission of the author.

A. M. Klein "Beaver" reprinted from *Complete Poems* (University of Toronto Press Inc., 1990) by permission of the publisher.

Joy Kogawa "Rain Day in Beacon Hill" reprinted from *Woman in the Woods* (Mosaic, 1985) by permission of the author.

Robert Kroetsch Part two from "Seed Catalogue" and "How I Joined the Seal Herd" reprinted from *Completed Field Notes: The Long Poems of Robert Kroetsch* (University of Alberta Press, 2000) by permission of the author.

Edward A. Lacey "Mossbacks" reprinted from *The Collected Poems and Translations of Edward A. Lacey* (Colombo & Co, 2000) by permission of Fraser Sutherland.

M. Travis Lane "Field" reprinted from *Solid Things: New and Selected* (Cormorant Books, 1989), "Trout Lily" reprinted from *Touch Earth* (Guernica Editions, 2006), both by permission of the author.

Patrick Lane "Buffalo Stones," "Winter 13," and "Cougar Men" reprinted from *Selected Poems 1977–1997* (Harbour Publishing, 1997) by permission of the author.

Irving Layton "The Predator" from *A Wild Peculiar Joy: Selected 1945–1989* © 2004, published by McClelland & Stewart Ltd. "Lake Selby" from *The Collected Poems of Irving Layton* © 1971, published by McClelland & Stewart Ltd. Both printed in Canada with permission of the publisher and printed outside Canada with permission of the estate of Irving Layton.

Ross Leckie "The Natural Moose" reprinted from *The Authority of the Roses* (Brick Books, 1997) by permission of the author.

Dennis Lee "Civil Elegy 3" reprinted from *Civil Elegies and Other Poems* (House of Anansi Press, 1972), "if" and "holdon" reprinted from *Yesno* (House of Anansi Press, 2007), both by permission of House of Anansi Press.

John B. Lee "The Day I Found Four Score of Starlings Dead in the Franklin" reprinted from *The Half-Way Tree: Poems New and Selected* (Black Moss, 2001) by permission of the author.

Douglas LePan "The Green Man" and "Black Bear" reprinted from *Weathering It: Complete Poems 1948–1987* (McClelland & Stewart, 1987) by permission of Don LePan.

Kenneth Leslie "Tasseled Thought" reprinted from *Windward Rock* (Macmillan, 1934) and "Day slipped out of the web…" reprinted from *By Stubborn Stars and Other Poems* (Ryerson, 1938), both by permission of Rosaleen Dickson.

Tim Lilburn "Ghost Song" reprinted from *Tourist to Ecstasy* (Exile Editions, 1989) by permission of the publisher; "Contemplation Is Mourning" reprinted from *Moosewood Sandhills* (McClelland & Stewart, 1994) by permission of the author; "13" from *To the River* © 1999, published by McClelland & Stewart, Ltd., used with permission of the publisher.

Charles Lillard "Little Pass Lake" reprinted from *Drunk on Wood* (Sono Nis Press, 1973) by permission of the publisher.

Dorothy Livesay "Pioneer" and "'Haunted House'" reprinted from *Collected Poems: Two Seasons* (McGraw-Hill/Ryerson, 1972) by permission of Jay Stewart, literary executrix of the estate of Dorothy Livesay.

Douglas Lochhead "Open wide a wilderness" reprinted from *The Full Furnace: Collected Poems* (McGraw-Hill/Ryerson, 1975) by permission of the author.

Pat Lowther "Anemones" and "Elegy for the South Valley" reprinted from *Time Capsule: New and Selected Poems* (Polestar, 1996) by permission of the author's estate.

Randy Lundy "The Great Sand Hills" reprinted from *The Gift of the Hawk* (Coteau, 2004) by permission of the publisher.

Laura Lush "Winter" reprinted from *The First Day of Winter* (Ronsdale, 2002) by permission of the author.

Gwendolyn MacEwen "Dark Pines Under Water" reprinted from *Gwendolyn MacEwen: The Early Years* (Exile Editions, 1993) by permission of Carol Wilson.

L. A. Mackay "Snow Story" reprinted from *Marked by the Wild* (McClelland& Stewart, 1973) by permission of Pierre Mackay.

Eli Mandel "From the North Saskatchewan" reprinted from *The Other Harmony: Collected Poetry of Eli Mandel* (Canadian Plains Research Center, 2000) by permission of the author's estate.

Daphne Marlatt "retrieving madrone" reprinted from *This Tremour Love Is* (Talonbooks, 2001) by permission of the publisher.

Anne Marriott "Sandstone" reprinted from *Sandstone and Other Poems* (The Ryerson Press, 1945), "Self-Guided Nature Trail" reprinted from *The Circular Coast: Poems New and Selected* (Mosaic, 1981), both by permission of Marya McLellan.

Sid Marty "Three Bears" reprinted from *Headwaters* (McClelland & Stewart, 1973), "Big Game" reprinted from *Nobody Danced with Miss Rodeo* (McClelland & Stewart, 1981), both by permission of the author.

David W. McFadden "My Grandmother Learns to Drive" reprinted from *Gypsy Guitar* (Talonbooks, 1987), "Dead Belugas" reprinted from *There'll Be Another* (Talonbooks, 1995), both by permission of the author.

Don McKay "Field Marks" from *Birding, or Desire* © 1983, published by McClelland & Stewart, Ltd.; "Song for the Song of the Varied Thrush" from *Apparatus* © 1997, published by McClelland & Stewart, Ltd.; "Load" from *Another Gravity* © 2000, published by McClelland & Stewart, Ltd.; "Precambrian Shield" from *Strike/Slip* © 2006, published by McClelland & Stewart, Ltd., all used with permission of the publisher.

Kenneth McRobbie "Something Wild for Our Room" reprinted from *First Ghost to Canada* (Turnstone Press, 1979) by permission of the author.

Eric Miller "Song of the Vulgar Starling" reprinted from *Song of the Vulgar Starling* (Broken Jaw Press, 1999) by permission of the publisher.

A. F. Moritz "The Ravine" reprinted from *Early Poems* (Insomniac Press, 2002) by permission of the author.

Daniel David Moses "A Spider Song" reprinted from *Delicate Bodies* (Nightwood Editions, 1992) by permission of the publisher.

Erin Mouré "Vision of a Woman Hit by a Bird" and "Tropic Line" reprinted from *Domestic Fuel* (House of Anansi Press, 1985) by permission of the publisher.

Jane Munro "Salmonberries" from *Point No Point* © 2006, published by McClelland & Stewart Ltd., used with permission of the publisher.

George Murray "Memories of the Snake" from *The Cottage Builder's Letter* © 2001, published by McClelland & Stewart Ltd., used by permission of the publisher.

Rona Murray "The Death of the Bear" reprinted from *Journey* (Sono Nis Press, 1981) by permission of the publisher.

Susan Musgrave "I Took a Wire Cage into the Woods" reprinted from *What the Small Day Cannot Hold* (Beach Holme Publishing, 2000) by permission of the author.

John Newlove "The Well-Travelled Roadway" and "In the Forest" reprinted from *Apology for Absence: Selected Poems* (Porcupine's Quill, 1993) by permission of Chaudiere Books.

Barbara Nickel "Athabasca Falls, 8:40 a.m." reprinted from *Domain* (House of Anansi Press, 2007) by permission of the publisher.

Alden Nowlan "St. John River" and "The Bull Moose" reprinted from *An Exchange of Gifts: Poems New and Selected* (Irwin, 1985) by permission of House of Anansi Press.

Michael Ondaatje "Breaking Green" and "Beaver" reprinted from *Rat Jelly* (Coach House, 1973) by permission of the author.

Eric Ormsby "Wood Fungus" reprinted from *For a Modest God: New and Selected Poems* (Grove Press, 1997) by permission of the author.

Martha Ostenso "Lexicon" and "The Return" reprinted from *A Far Land* (Thomas Selzer, 1924). Rights holder not found.

Richard Outram "Turtle" reprinted from *Promise of Light* (Anson-Cartwright Editions, 1979) by permission of the Literary Estate of Richard Outram.

P. K. Page "Personal Landscape," "Summer," and "Planet Earth" reprinted from *The Hidden Room: Collected Poems* (The Porcupine's Quill, 1997) by permission of the publisher.

Elise Partridge "Plague" reprinted from *Chameleon Hours* (University of Chicago Press, 2008) by permission of University of Chicago Press and Véhicule Press.

John Pass "Kleanza Creek" reprinted from *Water Stair* (Oolichan Books, 2000) by permission of the publisher.

Philip Kevin Paul "ĆIAÁĆU" reprinted from *Taking the Names Down from the Hill* (Nightwood Editions, 2003) by permission of the publisher.

Elizabeth Philips "Tales from the Green Revolution" reprinted from *Time in a Green Country* (Coteau, 1990) by permission of the author.

Gregory J. Power "Bogwood" reprinted from *The Power of the Pen: Writngs of Gregory J. Power*. (Harry Cuff Publications, 1989) by permission Power's son, Gregory Power.

E. J. Pratt "The Ice-Floes," "Sea-Gulls, "The Good Earth," and excerpt from *Towards the Last Spike* reprinted from *E. J. Pratt Complete Poems, Parts 1 & 2* (University of Toronto Press Inc., 1989) by permission of the publisher.

Al Purdy "Trees at the Arctic Circle," "The Winemaker's Beat-Étude," and "Red Leaves" reprinted from *Beyond Remembering: Collected Poems* (Harbour, 2000) by permission of the publisher.

James Reaney "The Crow" and "The Morning Dew" reprinted from *Poems* (New Press, 1972) by permission of James Stewart Reaney.

Michael Redhill "True Story" reprinted from *Lake Nora Arms* (Coach House, 1993) by permission of the author.

John Reibetanz "The Call" reprinted from *Midland Swimmer* (Brick Books, 1996), "Hummingbird" reprinted from *Mining for Sun* (Brick Books, 2000), both by permission of the author.

Monty Reid "83H 2 9 78" and "84F 8 11 78" reprinted from *The Alternate Guide* (Red Deer College Press, 1985), both by permission of the author.

Harold Rhenisch "Hymn for Herbicide" reprinted from *Iodine* (Wolsak and Wynn, 1994) by permission of the author, "The Hidden One" reprinted from *The Blue Mouth of Morning* (Oolichan Books, 1998) by permission of the publisher.

Dorothy Roberts "Private" reprinted from *The Self of Loss: New and Selected* (Fiddlehead Poetry Books, 1976) by permission of John Leisner.

Rachel Rose "Raccoons in Garbage" from *Notes on Arrival and Departure* © 2005, published by McClelland & Stewart Ltd., used by permission of the publisher.

Joe Rosenblatt "Mansions" and "Caterpillar Disarmed" reprinted from *Brides of the Stream* (Oolichan Books, 1983) by permission of the author.

W. W. E. Ross "Fish" and "The Snake Trying" reprinted from *Irrealities, Sonnets and Laconics* (Exile Editions, 2003) by permission of the publisher.

Armand Garnet Ruffo "Bear Death" and "Kebsquasheshing" reprinted from *Opening in the Sky* (Theytus Books, 1994) by permission of the author.

Peter Sanger "Silver Poplar" reprinted from *Earth Moth* (Goose Lane Editions, 1991) by permission of the publisher.

Robyn Sarah "Nature Walk" reprinted from *The Touchstone: Poems New and Selected* (House of Anansi Press, 1992) by permission of the author.

F. R. Scott "Laurentian Shield" and "Flying to Fort Smith" reprinted from *F. R. Scott Selected Poems* (Oxford University Press, 1966) by permission of William Toye.

Anne Simpson "Deer on a Beach" from *Light Falls Through You* © 2000, published by McClelland & Stewart Ltd., used by permission of the publisher.

Sue Sinclair "The Least Terns" reprinted from *Secrets of Weather and Hope* (Brick Books, 2001) by permission of the author.

Robin Skelton "Stone-Talk" reprinted from *One Leaf Shaking: Collected Later Poems* (Porcepic Book/Beach Holme Publishing, 1996) by permission of The Dundurn Group.

A. J. M. Smith "The Lonely Land" reprinted from *Poems: New and Collected* (Oxford University Press, 1967) by permission of William Toye.

John Smith "The Birds Returned" reprinted from *Strands the Length of the Wind* (Ragweed, 1993) by permission of the author.

Karen Solie "Sturgeon" reprinted from *Short Haul Engine* (Brick Books, 2001), "Pastoral" reprinted from *Modern and Normal* (Brick Books 2005), both by permission of the author.

Glen Sorestad "Shitepoke" reprinted from *Leaving Holds Me Here: Selected Poems* (Thistledown Press, 2001) by permission of the author.

Raymond Souster "Weeping Willow" and "Queen Anne's Lace" reprinted from *Collected Poems of Raymond Souster* (Oberon Press, 1982, 1984) by permission of the publisher.

Heather Spears "How Animals See" reprinted from *Poems Selected and New* (Wolsak and Wynn, 1998) by permission of the author.

John Steffler Excerpts from *The Grey Islands* (Brick Books, 2000) by permission of the author, "The Green Insect" from *That Night We Were Raveneous* © 1998, 2007, published by McClelland & Stewart Ltd., used with permission of the publisher.

Andrew Suknaski "Soongeedawn" reprinted from *Wood Mountain Poems* (Hagios Press, 2006) by permission of the author.

Anne Szumigalski "On Conquest" reprinted from *Journey/Journée* with Terrence Heath (Red Deer College Press, 1988) by permission of the author's estate.

Bruce Taylor "Stovewood" reprinted from *Cold Rubber Feet* (Cormorant Books, 1989) by permission of the author.

John Terpstra "Varieties: *Acer negundo*" reprinted from *Two or Three Guitars: Selected Poems* (Gaspereau Press, 2006) by permission of the publisher.

Sharon Thesen "Axe Murderer" reprinted from *News & Smoke: Selected Poems* (Talon Books, 1999) by permission of the author. "Scenes from the Missing Picture" reprinted from *The Good Bacteria* (House of Anansi Press, 2006) by permission of the publisher.

Colleen Thibaudeau "Getting the High Bush Cranberries" reprinted from *My Granddaughters Are Combing Out Their Long Hair* (Coach House, 1977) by permission of the author.

John Thompson "Poem of Absence" reprinted from *John Thompson: Collected Poems and Translations* (Goose Lane Editions, 1995) by permission of Goose Lane Editions, "Ghazal V" reprinted from *I Dream Myself into Being: Collected Poems* (House of Anansi Press, 1991) by permission of House of Anansi Press.

Russell Thornton "Creek Trout" reprinted from *The Fifth Window* (Thistledown Press, 2000) by permission of the publisher, "Heron" reprinted from *House Built of Rain* (Harbour Publishing, 2003) by permission of the publisher.

Harry Thurston "Dragging Bottom" reprinted from *If Men Lived on Earth* (Gaspereau Press, 2000) by permission of the publisher.

Peter Trower "Goliath Country" and "The Alders" reprinted from *Between the Sky and Splinters* (Harbour Publishing, 1974) by permission of the author.

Peter van Toorn "Mountain Maple" from *Mountain Tea* by permission of Signal Editions, Véhicule Press.

Miriam Waddington "Understanding Snow" and "Dead Lakes" reprinted from *Collected Poems* (Oxford University Press, 1986) by permission of Jonathan Waddington.

Fred Wah "Don't Cut Me Down" reprinted from *Selected Poems: Loki is Buried at Smoky Creek* (Talonbooks, 1980) by permission of the author.

Agnes Walsh "Angel's Cove" reprinted from *In the Old Country of My Heart* (Killick, 1996) by permission of the author.

Wilfred Watson "Sermon on Bears" reprinted from *Poems Collected, Unpublished and New* (Longspoon/NeWest, 1986) by permission of Shirley Neuman.

Tom Wayman "The Ecology of Place" reprinted from *Waiting for Wayman* (McClelland & Stewart, 1973), "The Man Who Logged the West Ridge" reprinted from *The Astonishing Weight of the Dead* (Polestar, 1994), both by permission of the author.

Phyllis Webb "A Long Line of Baby Caterpillars" and extract from "A Question of Questions" reprinted from *The Vision Tree: Selected Poems* (Talon Books, 1982) by permission of Talon Books.

Zachariah Wells "Duck, Duck, Goose" reprinted from *Unsettled* (Insomniac, 2004) by permission of the author.

Sue Wheeler "Sing a Song of Blackbirds" reprinted from *Habitat* (Brick Books, 2005) by permission of the author.

Jon Whyte "Larix Lyallii" reprinted from *Gallimaufry* (Longspoon Press, 1981) by permission of Harold Whyte.

Anne Wilkinson "A Poet's-Eye View" and "Nature Be Damned," reprinted from *Heresies: The Complete Poems of Anne Wilkinson 1924–1961*, edited by Dean Irvine, are used by permission of Signal Editions, Véhicule Press.

Christopher Wiseman "Snaring Valley" reprinted from *An Ocean of Whispers* (Sono Nis Press, 1982) by permission of the author.

J. Michael Yates from *The Great Bear Lake Meditations* reprinted from *The Great Bear Lake Meditations* (Oberon Press, 1970) by permission of the author.

David Zieroth "Coyote Pup Meets the Crazy People in Kootenay National Park" reprinted from *Mid-River* (House of Anansi Press, 1981) by permission of the author.

Jan Zwicky "Lancey Meadows" reprinted from *Songs for Relinquishing the Earth* (Brick Books, 1998), "Bee Music" and "Aspen in the Wind" reprinted from *Robinson's Crossing* (Brick Books, 2004), all by permission of the author.

Author and Title Index

Subject Index, or
The Alternate Guide

Hawk
Raymond Knister, "The Hawk," 125
Randy Lundy, "The Great Sand Hills," 438
Heron
Brian Brett, "Blue Heron Moon," 363
Diana Hartog, "The Great Blue Heron," 291
Brian Henderson, "Mortals," 354
Russell Thornton, "Heron," 415
Hummingbird
Adam Kidd, from *The Huron Chief*, 46
John Reibetanz, "Hummingbird," 317
Magpie
S. D. Johnson, "Two Magpies," 453
Robert Kroetsch, from *Seed Catalogue*, 216
Migration
Eric Cole, "Blackpoll Warbler," 416
Adam Dickinson, "Great Chain of Being,"
454
D. G. Jones, "Snow Buntings," 221
Raven
Peter Christensen, "Keeping Fear Away," 374
Harold Rhenisch, "The Hidden One," 410
Seagull
Malcolm Lowry, "The Glaucous Winged
Gull," 147
E. J. Pratt, "Sea-Gulls," 111
Sparrow
Margaret Avison, "Sparrows," 188
Diana Brebner, from "The Sparrow Drawer,"
405
Don Domanski, from "All Our Wonder
Unavenged," 366
Don McKay, "Load," 294
Starling
Elizabeth Brewster, "Starlings," 197
John B. Lee, "The Day I Found Four Score
of Starlings Dead in the Franklin," 373
Eric Miller, "Song of the Vulgar Starling," 421
Swallow
Mark Callanan, "Barn Swallows," 457
Adam Dickinson, "Great Chain of Being,"
454
Other
Brian Bartlett, from "Talking to the Birds"
[gannet], 385
Fred Cogswell, "A Grey World Lightened by
Snow" [pine grosbeak], 180
Eric Cole, "Blackpoll Warbler," 416
Tom Dawe, "Sandpiper," 282

Don Domanski, "Owl," 365
Crispin Elsted, "Swan Written," 349
John Glassco, "Catbird," 145
D. G. Jones, "Snow Buntings," 221
Lionel Kearns, "Trophy" [blue jay], 248
Patrick Lane, "Winter 13" [ptarmigan], 265
Don McKay, "Song for the Song of the Var-
ied Thrush," 293
Monty Reid, "83H 2 9 78 (two rock doves)"
[pigeon], 383
Sue Sinclair, "The Least Terns," 452
Glen Sorestad, "Shitepoke" [yellow bittern],
249
Phyllis Webb, from "A Question of Ques-
tions" [woodpecker], 213
Ethelwyn Wetherald, "The Hornèd Larks in
Winter," 68
Sue Wheeler, "Sing a Song of Blackbirds,"
298

CANOE
Margaret Atwood, "Sundew," 275
Isabella V. Crawford, "The Lily Bed," 63
Cornelia Hoogland, "The Orcas, Great
Story," 381

CATALOGUE
Thomas Cary, from *Abram's Plain*, 35
Susan Frances Harrison (Seranus), "A Cana-
dian Anthology," 70
Elise Partridge, "Plague," 411

CHILDHOOD
Diana Brebner, from "The Sparrow Drawer,"
405
Elizabeth Brewster, "Blueflag," 198
Christopher Dewdney, from "Out of Con-
trol: The Quarry," 371
Leona Gom, "North of Town," 337
Brian Henderson, "Theory of the Family,"
353
Lionel Kearns, "Trophy," 248
Edward A. Lacey, "Mossbacks," 251
Patrick Lane, "Cougar Men," 266
David McFadden, "Dead Belugas," 280
Erin Mouré, "Tropic Line," 395
George Murray, "Memories of the Snake,"
450
Rona Murray, "The Death of the Bear," 204

A. F. Moritz, "The Ravine," 340
Philip Kevin Paul, "ĆIAAĆU," 448
Peter Sanger, "Silver Poplar," 305
Frederick G. Scott, "The Unnamed Lake," 92
John Smith, "The Birds Returned," 215
Glen Sorestad, "Shitepoke," 249
Jan Zwicky, "Lancey Meadows," 397

NATURAL PHENOMENA
Forest (*see also* Nature as Resource: Logging;
   Trees)
Ross Leckie, "The Natural Moose," 388
Kenneth Leslie, from "By Stubborn Stars," 119
Douglas Lochhead, "Open wide a wilder-
   ness," 192
Gwendolyn MacEwan, "Dark Pines Under
   Water," 284
Alexander McLachlan, "The Hall of Shad-
   ows," 50
Susan Musgrave, "I Took a Wire Cage into
   the Woods," 372
John Newlove, "In the Forest," 258
Duncan Campbell Scott, "The Wood by the
   Sea," 99
Lake
E. D. Blodgett, "Doma," 245
Wilfred Campbell, "How One Winter Came
   to the Lake Country," 74
Charles Lillard, "Little Pass Lake," 319
Gwendolyn MacEwen, "Dark Pines Under
   Water," 284
Frederick G. Scott, "The Unnamed Lake," 92
A. J. M. Smith, "The Lonely Land," 132
Miriam Waddington, "Dead Lakes," 177
Mountain
Earle Birney, "David," 135
Charles Lillard, "Little Pass Lake," 319
Ocean (*see also* Aquatic Life; Birds; Fish)
Brian Bartlett, from "Talking to the Birds,"
   385
Cornelia Hoogland, "The Orcas, Great
   Story," 381
Anne Marriott, "Sandstone," 163
E. J. Pratt, "The Ice-Floes," 107
Anne Simpson, "Deer on a Beach," 403
Sue Sinclair, "The Least Terns," 452
Prairie
Marilyn Dumont, "Liquid Prairie," 402
Barbara Klar, "Blue Gramma," 434

Tim Lilburn, "Ghost Song," 356
Eli Mandel, "From the North Saskatchewan,"
   191
Elizabeth Philips, "Tales from the Green Rev-
   olution," 424
River
Sue Goyette, "Vigil," 427
Susan Frances Harrison (Seranus), "Rhap-
   sodie II," 69
Archibald Lampman, "To the Ottawa River,"
   90
Tim Lilburn, from *To the River*, 359
Alden Nowlan, "St. John River," 232
Armand Garnet Ruffo, "Kebsquasheshing,"
   401
Charles Sangster, from *The St. Lawrence and
   the Saguenay*, 53
Storm
John Donlan, "Muskrat," 314
E. J. Pratt, "The Ice-Floes," 107
Tundra (*see also* Arctic/The North)
Jim Green, "Seismic Line," 302
J. Michael Yates, from *The Great Bear Lake
   Meditations*, 260
Waterfall
Adam Allan, "A Description of the Great
   Falls, of the River Saint John, in the
   Province of New Brunswick," 38
John Donlan, "High Falls," 313
William Kirby, from *The U.E.*, "Niagara," 48
Barbara Nickel, "Athabasca Falls, 8:40 a.m.,"
   435
Wetlands
Margaret Atwood, "Sundew," 275
Mary Dalton, "Pitcher Plant; Bog Pluto," 367
Brian Henderson, "Mortals," 354
Gregory Power, "Bogwood," 150
Charles G. D. Roberts, from "Ave!," 76
John Steffler, "black spongy paths," from *The
   Grey Islands*, 341

NATURE AS RESOURCE
Fishing
Margaret Atwood, "Fishing for Eel Totems,"
   277
Tim Bowling, "On the Disappearance of Two
   Million Salmon," 429
Stanley Cooperman, "The Rivals," 225
Michael Crummey, "Cod (1)," 431

Duncan Campbell Scott, "The Height of Land," 94

Ethelwyn Wetherald, "Unheard Niagaras," 67

Nature as perceiver

Karen Connelly, "The Moment," 439

Patrick Lane, "Couger Men," 266

Al Purdy, "The Winemaker's Beat-Étude," 184

Harold Rhenisch, "The Hidden One," 410

Perception itself

Margaret Avison, "Snow," 187

Anne Wilkinson, "Poet's Eye View," 151

Stewardship (*see also* Earth)

Patrick Anderson, "Landscape," 169

Roo Borson, "The Trees," 277

PIONEERS

Adam Hood Burwell, from *Talbot Road*, 41

Isabella V. Crawford, from *Malcolm's Katie*, 65

Kristjana Gunnars, "Thorleifur Joakimsson, Daybook III," 352

Adam Kidd, from *The Huron Chief*, 46

Dorothy Livesay, "Pioneer," 148

Eli Mandel, "From the North Saskatchewan," 191

Standish O'Grady, from *The Emigrant*, 44

PLANTS

See also Fungi; Lichen; Nature as Resource: Harvesting/Gathering; Nature as Resource: Logging; Trees

General

Elise Partridge, "Plague," 411

Julie Berry, "daisy cole's woods," 379

Susan Frances Harrison (Seranus), "A Canadian Anthology," 70

Berries

Stephanie Bolster, "Many Have Written Poems about Blackberries," 443

Robert Bringhurst, "Rubus Ursinus: A Prayer for the Blackberry Harvest," 329

Dorothy Livesay, "Haunted House," 149

Jane Munro, "Salmonberries," 306

Colleen Thibaudeau, "Getting the High Bush Cranberries," 207

Grass

Milton Acorn, "Crabgrass," 203

Charles Bruce, "Fall Grass," 143

Barbara Klar, "Blue Gramma," 434

Kenneth Leslie, "Tasseled Thought," 118

Martha Ostenso, "Lexicon," 129

Seeds

Allan Cooper, "The Seed of the Blue Spruce," 392

Adam Dickinson, "Great Chain of Being," 454

Weeds

Milton Acorn, "Crabgrass," 203

Harold Rhenisch, "Hymn for Herbicide," 408

Other

Milton Acorn, "The Goldenrods Are Coming Up," 202

Margaret Atwood, "Sundew," 275

Elizabeth Brewster, "Blueflag," 198

Isabella V. Crawford, "The Lily Bed" [water lily], 63

Lorna Crozier, "Carrots," 350

Mary Dalton, "Pitcher Plant; Bog Pluto," 367

Mary Dalton, "Stingers" [nettles], 368

Adam Dickinson, "Great Chain of Being" [corpse flowers], 454

Brian Henderson, "Mortals" [cardinal flower], 354

Adam Kidd, from *The Huron Chief* [lily], 46

Archibald Lampman, "In November" [mullein], 88

M. Travis Lane, "Trout Lily," 239

Al Purdy, "Trees at the Arctic Circle" [ground willow], 182

Al Purdy, "The Winemaker's Beat-Étude" [wild grape], 184

Raymond Souster, "Queen Anne's Lace," 190

POLLUTION

John Donlan, "High Falls," 313

Irving Layton, "Lake Selby," 159

Alden Nowlan, "St. John River," 232

Harold Rhenisch, "Hymn for Herbicide," 408

Armand Garnet Ruffo, "Kebsquasheshing," 401

Karen Solie, "Sturgeon," 436

Miriam Waddington, "Dead Lakes," 177

POST-APOCALYPSE

Fred Cogswell, "Paleontology Lecture: Birds (Circa 2500 AD)," 179

Environmental Humanities Series

Environmental thought pursues with renewed urgency the grand concerns of the humanities: who we think we are, how we relate to others, and how we live in the world. Scholarship in the environmental humanities explores these questions by crossing the lines that separate human from animal, social from material, and objects and bodies from techno-ecological networks. Humanistic accounts of political representation and ethical recognition are re-examined in consideration of other species. Social identities are studied in relation to conceptions of the natural, the animal, the bodily, place, space, landscape, risk, and technology, and in relation to the material distribution and contestation of environmental hazards and pleasures.

The Environmental Humanities Series features research that adopts and adapts the methods of the humanities to clarify the cultural meanings associated with environmental debate. The scope of the series is broad. Film, literature, television, Web-based media, visual art, and physical landscape—all are crucial sites for exploring how ecological relationships and identities are lived and imagined. The Environmental Humanities Series publishes scholarly monographs and essay collections in environmental cultural studies, including popular culture, film, media, and visual cultures; environmental literary criticism; cultural geography; environmental philosophy, ethics, and religious studies; and other cross-disciplinary research that probes what it means to be human, animal, and technological in an ecological world.

Gathering research and writing in environmental philosophy, ethics, cultural studies, and literature under a single umbrella, the series aims to make visible the contributions of humanities research to environmental studies, and to foster discussion that challenges and reconceptualizes the humanities.

SERIES EDITOR
Cheryl Lousley, English and Film Studies, Wilfrid Laurier University

EDITORIAL COMMITTEE
Adrian J. Ivakhiv, Environmental Studies, University of Vermont
Catriona Mortimer-Sandilands, Tier 1 CRC in Sustainability and Culture, Environmental Studies, York University
Susie O'Brien, English and Cultural Studies, McMaster University
Laurie Ricou, English, University of British Columbia
Rob Shields, Henry Marshall Tory Chair and Professor, Department of Sociology, University of Alberta

FOR MORE INFORMATION, CONTACT
Lisa Quinn
Acquisitions Editor
Wilfrid Laurier University Press
75 University Avenue West
Waterloo, ON N2L 3C5
(519) 884-0710 ext. 2843
Email: quinn@press.wlu.ca

**Titles in the Environmental Humanities Series
from Wilfrid Laurier University Press**

Animal Subjects: An Ethical Reader in a Posthuman World, edited by Jodey Castricano / 2008 / x + 314 pp. / ISBN 978-88920-512-3

Open Wide a Wilderness: Canadian Nature Poems, edited by Nancy Holmes / Introduction by Don McKay / 2009 / xviii + 516 pp. / ISBN 978-1-55458-033-0